# THE HONG KONG READER

# THE HONG KONG READER

## Passage to Chinese Sovereignty

### An Interdisciplinary Reader

Ming K. Chan and
Gerard A. Postiglione, Editors

Foreword by Ezra F. Vogel

An East Gate Book

M.E. Sharpe
Armonk, New York
London, England

**An East Gate Book**



**Library of Congress Cataloging-in-Publication Data**

The Hong Kong reader : passage to Chinese sovereignty /
Ming K. Chan and Gerard A. Postiglione, edtiors.
p. cm.
"An East gate book."
Includes bibliographical references and index.
ISBN 1-56324-870-0 (pbk. : alk. paper)
1. Hong Kong—Politics and government.
2. Hong Kong—Economic conditions.
3. Education—Hong Kong.
4. Hong Kong—Relations—China.
5. China—Relations—Hong Kong.
I. Chan, Ming K.
II. Postiglione, Gerard A., 1951– .
DS796.H757H658 1996
951.25—dc20
96-10816
CIP

Printed in the United States of America

The paper used in this publication meets the minimum requirements of the American National Standard for Information Sciences—Permanence of Paper for Printed Library Materials, ANSI Z 39.48-1984.

∞

BM (p) 10 9 8 7 6 5 4 3 2 1

# Contents

# Foreword

Rarely has the return of a colony to its motherland received such careful attention. Since 1982, Beijing and London officials have carried on almost continuous negotiations about Hong Kong's future. Hong Kong businessmen have shuttled to Beijing and back, cultivating the good will of high Chinese officials and learning how to operate under Communist rule, while looking after their own business interests. For fifteen years the people of Hong Kong have avidly followed a daily fare of newspaper and TV reporting and speculation about events in China that will shape their future.

To Beijing, the return of Hong Kong is the penultimate great step in ending the century and a half of humiliation of bending to the might of Japanese and Westerners. After 1997 only Taiwan will remain outside Beijing's jurisdiction. Beijing leaders have made it clear they want to maintain Hong Kong's vitality, but they have also shown that they will not hesitate to take a tough line when they feel that Hong Kong might be a haven for critics mobilizing opposition to Beijing.

To London, the return of Hong Kong is a last final step in ending the British Empire. London officials are trying to assure an honorable exit, providing for the continued welfare of civil servants and loyal subjects, while walking a delicate tightrope between a hard line in Beijing and demanding voices in Hong Kong.

Hong Kong citizens are resourceful in trying every possible way of enhancing their viability after 1997. Lawyers and business people, now protected by laws and predictable government, are trying to ensure the vitality of the legal system. Rich families have already diversified their holdings and family members to North America, Europe, and Australia. Professionals remaining in Hong Kong are busily strengthening their ties with counterparts abroad. Business people have long since learned how to do business on the other side of the border. Some businessmen, confident that competitive cost structures will determine their future, are busily building modern roads and railroads to Wuhan, the critical gateway to inner China. They believe that if transport costs from Wuhan to Hong

Kong can become lower than those from Wuhan to Shanghai, goods will flow from inner China to Hong Kong, enabling them to stay a step ahead of Shanghai.

This collection of writings by academics, mostly living in Hong Kong, looks at some of the basic issues governing Hong Kong's future: politics, judicial practice, education, migration, economics. Hong Kong scholars have been prolific in writing about Hong Kong's future. This volume is one of the last to be published before reversion of Hong Kong to mainland rule. Perhaps there will be no better indicator of Hong Kong's freedoms and independence than whether books like this will continue to appear after June 1997.

Ezra F. Vogel
Cambridge, Massachusetts
March 7, 1996

# Acknowledgements

We are grateful to Doug Merwin and Tom Bacher of M. E. Sharpe for suggesting the idea which led to the present volume. As the chapters are based on amended and revised selections from the six already-published volumes in our series *Hong Kong Becoming China: the Transition to 1997*, we wish to extend our appreciation to the contributors to these volumes. Our assistant, Roy Chi-Kwong Man, has made the preparation of the present volume a much more manageable task under tight time constraints and we owe him a debt of gratitude. Last but definitely not least, the editorial/production staff at M. E. Sharpe have rendered great assistance in the production of all the volumes in our series and the present *Reader*, and they deserve our heartfelt thanks time and again.

Ming K. Chan
Gerard A. Postiglione
January 1, 1996

# The Contributors

**Ming K. Chan** is a member of the History Department, University of Hong Kong, and Executive Coordinator of the Hong Kong Documentary Archives, Hoover Institution, Stanford University. His recent books include *The Hong Kong Basic Law: Blueprint for "Stability and Prosperity" Under Chinese Sovereignty?* (1991), *Schools into Fields and Factories: The Anarchists, the Guomindang, and the National Labor University in Shanghai, 1927–32* (1991), and *Precarious Balance: Hong Kong Between China and Britain, 1842–1992* (1994).

**Gerard A. Postiglione** is a member of the Department of Education, University of Hong Kong, and Director of Advanced Studies in Education and National Development Program. His books include *Education and Society in Hong Kong: Toward One Country and Two Systems* (1992), *Social Change and Educational Development: Mainland China, Taiwan, and Hong Kong* (1995), and *Hong Kong in the World Community: Internationalization at Risk?* (forthcoming).

**Frank Ching** is an editor with the *Far Eastern Economic Review*. He is the author of *Hong Kong and China: For Better or for Worse* (New York, 1985) and *Ancestors: Nine Hundred Years in the Life of a Chinese Family* (New York, 1988).

**Berry Hsu** is a member of the Surveying Department, University of Hong Kong. His books include *The Common Law System in Chinese Context* (1992), *Economic Analysis of Canadian Tax Cases* (1993), and *A Guide to Hong Kong Taxation* (1996).

**Reginald Yin-Wang Kwok** is a Professor of Asian Studies and Urban and Regional Planning, University of Hawaii. He was the founding Director of the Centre of Urban Studies and Urban Planning, University of Hong Kong. His books include *The Shek Kip Mei Syndrome: Economic Development and Public Housing in Hong Kong and Singapore* (1990), and *The Hong Kong–Guangdong Link: Partnership in Flux* (1995).

**Peter Kwong** is Director of Asian-American Studies at Hunter College, City University of New York. He is the author of *The New Chinatown* (1987).

**Julian Y.M. Leung** is a member of the Department of Curriculum Studies, University of Hong Kong. He is Assistant Director of Education in the Hong Kong Government. His publications include *Education and Society in Hong Kong: Toward One Country and Two Systems* (1992).

**Ronald Skeldon** is a member of the Department of Geography, University of Hong Kong. His recent books include *Reluctant Exiles: Migration from Hong Kong and the New Overseas Chinese* (1994), and *Emigration From Hong Kong: Tendencies and Impacts* (1995).

**Alvin Y. So** is a Professor of Sociology, University of Hawaii. His books include *The South China Silk District: Local Historical Transformation and World System Theory* (1986), *East Asia and the World Economy* (1995), and *The Hong Kong–Guangdong Link: Partnership in Flux* (1995).

**Yun-Wing Sung** is a member of the Department of Economics, Chinese University of Hong Kong. His books include *The China–Hong Kong Connection: The Key to China's Open Door Policy* (1991) and *The Fifth Dragon: The Emergence of the Pearl River Delta* (1995).

**James T.H. Tang** is a member of the Political Science Department, University of Hong Kong. His books include *Britain's Encounter with Revolutionary China, 1949–54* (1992), *Human Rights and International Relations in the Asian Pacific Region* (1995), and *Hong Kong in the World Community: Internationalization at Risk?* (forthcoming).

# THE HONG KONG READER

# 1

# Introduction: Hong Kong's Uneasy Passage to Chinese Sovereignty

*Ming K. Chan and Gerard A. Postiglione*

Hong Kong's success is legendary. After a meager start as a British crown colony established on fishing villages of nearly barren rock in 1842—part of the spoils of victory from the Opium War—Hong Kong has become a cosmopolitan city-state of global significance. Though it ranks nintieth in terms of population, it is the world's eighth largest trading economy, with a per capita income higher than some developed countries including Britain, its colonial master. With eighty-five of the world's top one hundred banks, it is one of the five international financial centers. Hong Kong's miracle economy has made it one of the Four Little Dragons of East Asia, a title shared with Singapore, South Korea, and Taiwan. Finally, Hong Kong is the undisputed gateway to China, which is Hong Kong's largest trading partner (Hong Kong is China's second largest trading partner after Japan). Hong Kong serves as a powerful catalyst for the economic development of South China, where Hong Kong companies employ over three million workers in neighboring Guangdong Province alone. Thus, it is natural that most Hong Kong people see their future as inextricably linked to China's economic growth and political modernization.

Hong Kong's developmental experience is worth emulating. Yet, its free trade, market economy and open society have been in stark contrast to its lack of a full-scale, genuinely democratic form of government. In this sense, its prosperity and stability within the context of freedom without democracy have been the hallmarks of British colonialism—indeed, the colony is a remarkable case of borrowed place, on borrowed time, and with borrowed people.

In late 1984, Hong Kong was compelled to embark on its most dramatic historical change. The Sino-British Joint Declaration mandated the end of British rule and the resumption of sovereignty by China on July 1, 1997. The policy toward Hong Kong's sovereignty retrocession is based on the'' One Country, Two Systems'' formula and has two principal objectives: China's national reunification with Hong Kong, which would set the example for Macau and Taiwan, and the maintenance of Hong Kong's stability and prosperity so that it would continue to contribute significantly to China's economic reform and modernization.

The 1984 Sino-British Joint Declaration promises to preserve Hong Kong's existing legal, economic, and social systems and lifestyle for fifty years from July 1, 1997, when the colony is to become a Special Administration Region (SAR) of the People's Republic of China (PRC). Furthermore, this promise became enshrined in the SAR Basic Law which codified the constitutional framework that is to give effect to the promised ''high degree of autonomy'' with ''Hong Kong people ruling Hong Kong,'' as well as to regulate central government-SAR relations. The Joint Declaration explicitly calls for the Hong Kong SAR legislature to be fully elected—a major departure from the (until 1985) totally appointed colonial legislature. As such, preparation for the future SAR political system necessitated the most drastic and fundamental change in Hong Kong's colonial polity. These constitutional and electoral reforms triggered controversies and confrontations within the local community and between Britain and China. The resulting tensions and conflicts that have characterized the transformation of Hong Kong since the mid-1980s, unfolded under the ever looming "China factor."

The China factor has become an overwhelming influence on life in Hong Kong. It is the single most dominant force shaping Hong Kong public affairs, government decision-making, and policy implementation as well as Hong Kong's external links and global interactions. This situation gave impetus to the further development of Hong Kong's new political culture. A growing civic awareness, political activism, and articulation of social value orientations began to have a decisive effect on the rising expectations and future perspectives of the Hong Kong people. Meanwhile, the increasingly close relationship between Hong Kong and the Chinese mainland in trade, manufacturing, investment, transportation, finance, skills and technology transfer created an intimate economic interdependence, even integration, between the two. In this respect, the China factor remains the principal force underwriting much of Hong Kong's economic prosperity.

The China factor has also been the accelerator, stimulant, and even midwife to the processes of decolonization, localization, internationalization, and democratization which are still unfolding in the current transition. This has given rise to an identity awareness among the local populace, who have come to see themselves as Chinese nationals with aspirations for a more modern, post-colonial, Chinese community that is self-conscious of its heritage. In this sense, the China factor has promoted a fundamental change in Hong Kong's polity and socio-cultural mentality. This could yield great opportunities and new dynamics for a challenging future for Hong Kong and China well into the next century.

This same China factor has also displayed its potential as a destabilizing force, as it periodically precipitates a crisis of confidence and highlights the imperfect nature of the transition. The core problem revolves around Sino-British discord and the transfer of power in the sunset years of British rule. Beijing's intolerance of the rapid pace of local democratization has deepened mutual distrust between itself and a large segment of Hong Kong society. Thus, prospects for a smooth reintegration toward 1997 and beyond have begun to diminish. Furthermore, as the "One Country, Two Systems" formula will be be used to further the reunification with Taiwan, the challenge of Hong Kong's sovereignty retrocession can have a major affect on prospects for cross-strait rapprochement. Finally, the China-Hong Kong integration experience will come to shape China's relations with Hong Kong's many global partners, including the U.S. and other industrial democracies.

As 1997 approaches, Hong Kong is facing many questions: Can the common law legal system remain anchored in Chinese culture given its alien roots? Can the education system be transformed from one kind of colonial socializing agency to another? Will Hong Kong's complex relations with Beijing and London cease to be so precarious after 1997? By then, will more Hong Kong people still opt to migrate overseas, or will many of its reluctant exiles return from overseas out of economic need or due to newly gained confidence? Finally, will Hong Kong's influence, through its economic links with Guangdong, further extend from the Pearl River Delta through Shanghai and right up to the outskirts of Beijing? Any meaningful answer hinges on one thing—Hong Kong's autonomy as a PRC SAR until the mid-twenty-first century.

The central issue for Hong Kong's future is autonomy. As a British colony Hong Kong has enjoyed a high degree of autonomy in its internal affairs. The Sino-British Joint Declaration and the Basic Law of the post-1997 SAR promise greater autonomy than was legally provided under the present British administration. The common anxiety among the people of Hong Kong has less to do with the future polity of Hong Kong, than with the turbulent politics, abuse of power, and suppression of civil liberties in China, where a one party dictatorship and totalitarian regime continue to rule with little reform in sight.

Although Hong Kong presents the PRC with an exciting challenge for the extension of its sovereignty toward the twenty-first century, it is not an entirely new challenge. The PRC has shown its ability to permit and contain various levels of regional autonomy since its establishment in 1949. It has almost half a century of experience with five autonomous provinces, including Xinjiang and Tibet. While major difficulties still exist, China has been able to maintain national unity in the face of strong separatist movements in a world that has seen the disintegration of many major countries, including the former Yugoslavia and the former Soviet Union. China is committed to maintain national sovereignty in a world where division of states is not uncommon, yet, it has chosen to extend considerable autonomy to its Special Economic Zones and the other "open cities." While this autonomy is largely economic and not political, the result has, at times, strained center-regional relations within China, with implications for the reunification with Hong Kong, Macau, and Taiwan.

The present collection of essays delineates many of the key dimensions of Hong Kong's transition to Chinese sovereignty, with its profound global implications. In-depth analysis and insightful discussion are provided by the individual essays, each focusing on a specific area or addressing issues of basic concern from an interdisciplinary perspective.

The first three essays focus on political development and constitutional change. The essay by Ming K. Chan highlights the drafting process of the Hong Kong Basic Law that strained Beijing-Hong Kong relations. The undemocratic personnel and procedures adopted by Beijing in this very crucial united front operation not only derailed Hong Kong's democratization but also delegitimized the PRC, especially after the 1989 Tiananmen crisis. The essay by James Tang and Frank Ching reviews the shaping of the Beijing-London-Hong Kong "Three Legged Stool" since the 1970s and the Sino-British negotiations mandating the 1997 retrocession. Many of the difficulties being experienced by the people of Hong Kong in the transition stem from this uneasy and unbalanced tripartite relationship with little weight given to Hong Kong's own voice. Berry Hsu's essay affords an expert discourse on the Basic Law's impact on the common law legal culture and notions in Hong Kong. He pinpoints specific areas of concern that might eventually undermine the present independent judiciary and public trust in the entire legal system.

On the social front, there are four essays highlighting changes in both education and system as well as in overseas migration and settlement. The essay by Gerard Postiglione looks at the various aspects of the decolonization of education, and suggests three possible scenarios regarding the direction of future educational policy. He specifically emphasizes the role of education in the democratization and the nurturing of future political leaders for autonomy. In his essay Y.M. Leung sketches the convergent and divergent themes between the Hong Kong and the PRC education systems. He questions China's tolerance of the future internationalization of the local school system. Ronald Skeldon's essay offers a sweeping portrayal of the roots of Hong Kong emigration and its contemporary manifestations. He constructs an extensive statistical reference to illustrate the patterns of migratory traffic and its impact on Hong Kong society and its external links. Peter Kwong's case study examines the metamorphosis of New York's Chinese community under the influx of Hong Kong human and economic resources. The problems of "Dickensian" labor practices, organized crime, and new cultural style have characterized the new "Hong Kong town" phenomenon.

Finally, the last two essays chart the economic achievements of Hong Kong's integration with China and the problems that lie ahead. The essay by Yun-wing Sung documents the very fruitful economic symbiosis between Hong Kong and neighboring Guangdong Province, creating the economic miracle of South China. However, the future prosperity of "Greater Hong Kong" is far from assured owing to volatile international factors and external economic forces. Such a sense of uncertainty is affirmed by the future scenarios in the chapter by Alvin Y. So and Reginald Yin-Wang Kwok.

As a whole, this volume of scholarly essays offers a wide-ranging vista illuminating the Sino-British politicking, constitution-making, legal and educational reforms as well as economic outreach and migratory patterns in transitional Hong Kong as shaped by the China factor. Such an in-depth understanding of the key dimensions of Hong Kong's transformation will provide an informed baseline for the articulation and appreciation of the great complexity of China's reintegration efforts toward the twenty-first century.

2

# Democracy Derailed: Realpolitik in the Making of the Hong Kong Basic Law, 1985–1990

*Ming K. Chan*

## I. Introduction

After some 140 years of political stasis as a British colony, Hong Kong found itself in 1982 on the verge of the most drastic political change in its history. In that year the Sino-British negotiations on the future of Hong Kong commenced. After a period of conflict, the parties signed an agreement on December 19, 1984, that restores China's sovereignty over Hong Kong on July 1, 1997.[1]

China's policy toward Hong Kong is based on the concept of "One Country, Two Systems," and is intended to achieve two objectives: the reunification of the country and economic modernization.[2] The slogan was launched in 1978 and was also intended to apply to Taiwan and Macao. The agreement with Britain promised the preservation of the existing legal, economic, and social systems of Hong Kong for fifty years from July 1, 1997. The promises made in the Sino-British Joint Declaration were to be enshrined in a Basic Law for the Hong Kong Special Administrative Region (SAR), and included the promise of a "high degree of autonomy" for the SAR and "Hong Kong people ruling Hong Kong."[3] In fact, the Joint Declaration explicitly called for the Hong Kong legislature to be fully elected after 1997. To most local people, this meant the Western-style democratic system of one-man–one-vote

The original version of this chapter appeared in *The Hong Kong Basic Law: Blueprint for "Stability and Prosperity" Under Chinese Sovereignty*, ed. Ming K. Chan and David J. Clark (Armonk, NY: M.E. Sharpe, 1991).

universal franchise leading to a directly elected legislature. However, to the Chinese authorities and local conservatives and pro-Beijing elements, it meant many types of electoral arrangements, not just universal franchise direct elections. This crucial difference between the two schools of thought eventually divided the local political scene and contributed much to the deterioration of the Beijing–Hong Kong–London relationship.

Less than a year after the conclusion of the agreement, the Chinese government announced in June 1985 the formation of the Basic Law Drafting Committee (BLDC) and the Basic Law Consultative Committee (BLCC).[4] In December 1985, at the inaugural meeting of the BLCC, the Chinese announced a timetable for the drafting process. Under this timetable, there would be two rounds of drafting before the final document would be enacted and promulgated by the National People's Congress (NPC) in 1990.[5] This process would involve what was called "two ups and two downs," that is, the draft would twice be handed down by the BLDC for consultation, and then it would go up to the NPC Standing Committee (NPC-SC) for discussion and decision. As the draft has developed, certain issues that proved to be the most contentious were dealt with in the last stages: that is, the protection of human rights, the high degree of autonomy to be enjoyed by the SAR, the election or appointment of the chief executive, the composition of the elected legislature, and the question of amendment and interpretation.

In April 1988, a first draft of the Basic Law was issued for public discussion. The second draft was released in February 1989, and the period for consultation, originally scheduled to conclude on July 31, 1989, was extended for three more months until the end of October 1989 because of the tumultuous events of May–June 1989 in Beijing.[6]

During the first round of the drafting process, which ended in January 1989, there had been an impressive and fairly widespread outpouring of commentaries and public debates on the first draft.[7] However, public enthusiasm in Hong Kong for the second and final round of the drafting process was much less even before the May–June events broke out in Beijing. Despite all these developments, the People's Republic of China (PRC) authorities insisted on adhering to the original timetable for the completion of the entire drafting process of the Basic Law in 1990. On April 4, 1990, the PRC formally promulgated the Basic Law of the Hong Kong Special Administrative Region.

In view of the paramount importance of the Basic Law in determining Hong Kong's future model of government and the fate of its nearly six million people, this chapter, by analyzing the dramas and conflicts that arose during the drafting process, has the following purposes:

(1) To delineate briefly the larger political implications of the Hong Kong Basic Law and its drafting process for the Chinese people (on the mainland, Taiwan, and Hong Kong) and the outside world.[8]

(2) To highlight some of the basic problems in the Basic Law drafting process, especially institutional, procedural, and personnel practices, that have

caused serious concerns among the Hong Kong people in their uneasy passage to Chinese sovereignty.

(3) To illustrate, with a few selected cases, the impact of the Basic Law drafting process upon the domestic democratization efforts within Hong Kong society.

(4) And, to provide a preliminary assessment of the fallout effects of the Tiananmen events on the democratic movement in Hong Kong in relation to the Basic Law drafting process.

It is hoped that this chapter will bring into closer focus some of the crucial dimensions of the Realpolitik of the Basic Law drafting process and local democratization trends, thus enhancing academic analysis of the complex forces shaping the future of Hong Kong at this critical juncture of transition. Furthermore, the essay will illustrate the changing relationship of the actors in this process—between the PRC government, the British colonial regime, and the Hong Kong people. In the case of the latter, this chapter will show that they were left powerless and unable to decide their own future in view of the political maneuvering between Britain and China.

## II. Political Implications of the Basic Law and Its Drafting Process

It perhaps will be useful as background to delineate briefly here some of the significant aspects and political implications of the Hong Kong Basic Law and the drafting process:

(1) The Basic Law (as a basic statute of the PRC under Article 31 of the Chinese Constitution of 1982) provides the constitutional basis for the establishment of Hong Kong as a Special Administrative Region (SAR) of China from July 1, 1997, through June 30, 2047. It will set out in legal form the principles, policies, and premises enshrined in the Sino-British Joint Declaration of 1984. As such, it will shape the future development of Hong Kong well into the middle of the twenty-first century.

(2) The PRC adopted the official "One Country, Two Systems" formula as the guiding principle for the Hong Kong settlement. The Basic Law provisions define in institutional and constitutional terms the future relationship between the central authorities in China and the Hong Kong SAR, which is to enjoy "a high degree of autonomy." The central-local arrangement was expected to have strong domestic impact on Beijing's approach to other supposedly "autonomous" areas within the PRC, such as Tibet.

(3) As the reunification with Taiwan remains a fundamental and high priority national policy objective of the PRC, the Hong Kong Basic Law as the embodiment of the "One Country, Two Systems" formula will become a crucial component in Beijing's approach to Taipei. While Taipei still harbors very deep mistrust of the PRC's intentions and actions, Beijing is keenly aware of, and repeatedly stresses, the Basic Law's positive demonstration effects on Taiwan.[9] The April 1987 settlement of Macao's future status, currently under Portuguese administration until December 20, 1999, when Chinese sovereignty will be re-

stored, is a direct application of the "Hong Kong model" to Beijing's credit.[10]

(4) Even more reflective than the actual provisions of the Basic Law itself, the rather complicated and prolonged drafting process from 1985 to 1990 reveals much about the PRC leadership's real understanding of and official stance on such fundamental principles as constitutionality, jurisprudence, administrative control, elections, autonomy, public accountability, human rights, and, above all, representative democracy. If China's current drive toward the Four Modernizations necessitates extensive change in its institutional framework and bureaucratic mentality, the Basic Law drafting exercise is highly indicative of the extent of any such changes in recent years. Likewise, the post–June 4, 1989, policy and leadership realignment in Beijing also found expression in the final stages of the Basic Law drafting process.

(5) The much publicized "two ups and two downs" (up to Beijing for revision and down to Hong Kong for public discussion) procedure and mechanism for Basic Law drafting and consultation is a vivid and important example of Chinese Communist united front strategies and tactics in practice. In the case of the Hong Kong Basic Law, the external and international nature and implications of such united front efforts on the part of the PRC and its organs and supporters in Hong Kong had added much to the significance of this case.

(6) The Basic Law as the constitutional framework for the absorption by the world's most populous Communist state of a thriving, free, open, cosmopolitan, and capitalist city of nearly six million under British colonial rule warrants serious international attention. It is a total departure from the traditional Western mode of decolonization in the Third World. The gradual, conditional, and regulated process of Hong Kong's full reintegration into the PRC polity over fifty years, in addition to twelve years (1985–97) of transition to Chinese sovereignty, adds an interesting temporal dimension to this novel experiment. This prolonged process also provides ample opportunities to examine the inherent contradictions and dilemmas in the PRC policy of maintaining Hong Kong's "stability and prosperity" on the one hand, and the full realization of Chinese "sovereignty" on the other.

(7) Beijing's demands before 1990 that any post-1984 change must "converge" with the Basic Law means that the then yet to be promulgated Basic Law has also exerted direct, dominant, and preemptive influences on British attempts at political changes in Hong Kong during the transition era to 1997. As such, the yet to be constitutionally effective Basic Law is the PRC's not so invisible hand that has already restricted domestic developments in Hong Kong more than a decade ahead of its effective date of jurisdiction, despite the Joint Declaration's promise that the British alone would be responsible for the administration of Hong Kong until June 30, 1997.

It is against such a complex and sensitive political situation that the Hong Kong public has interacted with the PRC establishment over the Basic Law drafting process during the past five years. It is also in the face of these political realities that the local populace responded in an unprecedented manner to the events in China of May–June 1989 that directly and seriously affected the drafting process. In this sense, the formal promulgation of the Basic Law on April 4, 1990, signaled the end of the beginning phase of Hong Kong's transition to Chinese sovereignty. Yet it is by no means the beginning of the end of the current crisis of confidence in Hong Kong under the 1997 China syndrome.

## III. Institutional, Procedural, and Personnel Problems of the Drafting Process and Mechanism

Almost from the very beginning, the whole range of institutions, procedures, and personnel of the PRC's Basic Law drafting mechanism have been the subject of grave public concern, strong criticism, and even heated controversies in Hong Kong. There is no doubt that the Basic Law drafting process was a very important operation of the PRC State Council's Hong Kong and Macao Affairs Office. Thus, Beijing exercised tight and direct control over the proceedings of the BLDC through a combination of institutional, procedural, and personnel measures. As for the actual functioning of the BLCC, the "local public opinion sounding board" of the BLDC, Beijing also exerted considerable influence through the BLCC Executive Committee and Secretariat personnel appointment.

The BLDC had a majority of mainland members (thirty-six from China and twenty-three from Hong Kong), and neither it nor the 180-member BLCC committee (which was wholly composed of Hong Kong residents from many walks of life) was elected. The Hong Kong members on both committees were overwhelmingly drawn from professional and business sectors of the economy, with only one representative of a leftist trade union included in the BLDC.[11]

In fact, the very formation of the BLCC Executive Committee in late 1985 sparked off the first of many major clashes between the PRC's local establishment, the New China News Agency (NCNA) Hong Kong Branch, and pro-democratic elements in Hong Kong. It stemmed from the nonadherence to the charter of the BLCC, which stipulated that its 180 members would "elect" among themselves nine members to form the BLCC Executive Committee, which would set the agendas for deliberation, lay down policy guidelines, and oversee the daily operation of the BLCC Secretariat. Instead of a genuine, open "election" with the participation of its full membership of 180, the Beijing regime, through its NCNA arm in Hong Kong, handpicked and installed nine particular members to form the BLCC Executive Committee. The local NCNA's explanation for this "nonvoting" form of "election" in which only secret "nomination" and private "consultation" took place was that it was the sufficient and adequate "equivalent" of an open "election." This attempt failed to win popular acceptance in Hong Kong.

A week later, under mounting public criticism, the BLCC was forced to hold another session and go through the motion of an elective process in which a single (and only) slate of the same nine "candidates" was "nominated" for election into the Executive Committee. With the strong guiding hand of the local NCNA behind the scenes, these nine BLCC members were duly "elected" without opposition.[12] This was not an auspicious start to the confidence and consensus-building "consultative" aspects of the Basic Law drafting process. This incident unmasked beyond any doubt the PRC establishment's understanding and interpretation of the key concept of "election" within the Hong Kong context.

While the composition of the 180-member BLCC is not as lopsided as the BLDC (PRC members form the majority, and most of its Hong Kong members are business tycoons and professionals serving big business interests), its public image of fairness, integrity, and credibility has also been seriously tarnished by the personnel appointments to its Secretariat. Unlike the BLDC, which is an organ directly under the jurisdiction of the PRC's Hong Kong and Macao Affairs Office, the BLCC is supposedly a genuine local Hong Kong–based organization to "collect and consult" public opinions on the Basic Law drafts. Yet, the head of the BLCC Secretariat, the secretary general, was far from a politically neutral, impartial nonpartisan functionary. The first occupant of this key post was one of the deputy directors of the local NCNA branch and a card-carrying member of the Chinese Communist party. The second and last secretary general was a professional land surveyor who has been the principal spokesman for the influential "Group of 89," a coalition of conservative BLDC and BLCC members (mainly from big business) who bitterly oppose the adoption of a more democratic approach of "direct election" with universal franchise for the local legislature, both for the transition period and for the post-1997 Hong Kong SAR.[13] By selecting a conservative, anti-direct election spokesman for this influential and sensitive post, the PRC establishment not only created the appearance of a serious case of conflict of interest, but also showed very clearly its strong bias against the local prodemocracy movement. Such prejudice was not confined to the actual contents of the Basic Law drafts, but, more alarming to the people of Hong Kong, it also extended to the entire drafting process.[14]

If the rule of law and the formation of a representative government for local autonomy were, above all, a matter of fair and open procedure in governance and public policy making, then from start to finish the BLCC's entire setup has been counterproductive. Indeed, rather than promoting much-needed local confidence through genuine consultation and collection of public opinions as the basis for the Basic Law drafts, its flawed procedures and tainted personnel have contributed much to the now endemic crisis of confidence in the future of Hong Kong.

In this regard, the BLDC's operational mode has been an even more fatal cause for the well-justified political anxieties of the majority of Hong Kong people coming under the shadow of China. A good case in point is the so-called mainstream archconservative model adopted by the BLDC in December 1988 for the formation of the SAR legislature and executive after 1997. The details and significance of this case can be better understood within the larger context of the Hong Kong pro- and antidemocratic campaigns during the last six years.

## IV. Campaigns for and against Democracy in Hong Kong, 1984–88

Concurrent with the Basic Law drafting process, both influencing and being influenced by it, had been a rapid politicization of the Hong Kong people.[15] The official British policy before 1984 was not to permit any constitutional change at all in the colony.[16] On July 18, 1984, before the Sino-British agreement on the future of Hong Kong was finalized, but after its main outlines had been leaked to the public, the Hong Kong government issued a consultation Green Paper, *The Future Development of Representative Government in Hong Kong*, inviting public comment on the government's proposals for constitutional reform. The stated aims of these proposals were: "(a) to develop progressively a system of government the authority for which is firmly rooted in Hong Kong, which is able to represent authoritatively the views of the people of Hong Kong, and which is more directly accountable to the people of Hong Kong; (b) to build this system on our existing institutions, which have served Hong Kong well, and, as far as possible, to preserve their best features, including the maintenance of the well-established practice of government by consensus; and (c) to allow for further development if that should be the wish of the community."[17]

On November 21, 1984 (after the Sino-British Joint Declaration was initiated but yet to be formally signed by the Chinese and British prime ministers), the Hong Kong government announced its policy decision on limited democratization in the form of a White Paper on *The Future Development of Representative Government in Hong Kong*. While no member of the Legislative Council (Legco) was to be directly elected, it provided for twenty-four indirectly elected members for the election in 1985, with a further increase in elected (perhaps even directly elected) elements for the election to be held in 1988. The whole tenor of the 1984 White Paper was optimistic and clearly contemplated a substantial reduction in the extent of the executive branch's control of the legislature through the appointments of members by the governor. The legislature and the executive were to be partially separated, with the majority of the members of the legislature elected either directly or indirectly. It called for another review of the whole system of representative government and constitutional reform in 1987.[18] This 1984 British commitment to decolonialization reform and the first ever election of twenty-four seats to the local legislature held in September 1985 were regarded by many (perhaps even by PRC leaders) as a necessary and vital inducement behind the Hong Kong people's grudging acceptance of the 1984 Sino-British Joint Declaration which was formally ratified and came into effect in June 1985.[19]

On May 27, 1987, the Hong Kong government published the long-awaited

Green Paper entitled *The 1987 Review of Developments in Representative Government* for public consultation which was to last through the end of September 1987. In contrast to the 1984 White Paper, this Green Paper did not advocate any specific political or electoral reform. Instead, it invited public comment on a number of options. Direct election of some members to the Legco in 1988 was listed as an option. Besides the issue of direct election, the Hong Kong government has all but jettisoned its aim as stated in the 1984 White Paper of trying to develop a system of representative government firmly rooted in Hong Kong "which is more directly accountable to the people of Hong Kong." Indeed, the Green Paper failed to include important constitutional issues raised in 1984, and this caused widespread local criticism that the British authorities (in London and in Hong Kong) were not sincere in their claims to consult the Hong Kong people and in their commitment to advance the democratization process.

On the other side of the border, the PRC authorities lost no time to express their opposition to direct elections and to castigate the British attempt to develop representative government in Hong Kong before 1997 as a violation of the 1984 Sino-British Joint Declaration. The first major PRC offensive against the attempts in Hong Kong to introduce direct elections took the form of an orchestrated press release from Beijing which was echoed by pro-PRC elements in Hong Kong. On June 18, 1987, the News Department of the NCNA Hong Kong Branch distributed an advanced summary of an interview with Li Hou which would appear in the forthcoming (June 22, 1987) issue of *Liaowang*, overseas edition. Li Hou, deputy director of the PRC State Council's Hong Kong and Macao Affairs Office and secretary general of the BLDC, was originally quoted in this interview as claiming that the Hong Kong direct elections in 1988 would fail to "converge" with the Basic Law being drafted by China for promulgation in 1990 and were contrary to the "spirit" of the Sino-British Joint Declaration. Li further said that direct elections in 1988 would only sharpen the contradictions among the different classes and segments of Hong Kong society, leading to political, economic, and social instability, and this would also be harmful to a smooth transfer of sovereignty in 1997.[20]

Li's statement, widely reported in the local media, delivered an immediate and powerful shock to the Hong Kong public. Advocates of direct elections in 1988 reacted swiftly. They condemned Li's blatant attempt at derailing the whole democratization process and preempting reforms working toward popular one-man–one-vote direct election. These political activists, as well as pressure groups and local academic critics, pointed out in public that Li's statement represented both an act of official PRC intimidation against the Hong Kong people and direct interference with the internal administration of Hong Kong. They charged that in making such a statement, it was Li himself, rather than the Hong Kong government, who violated the "letter" (not just the "spirit") of the 1984 Sino-British Joint Declaration which stipulated that: (1) the British shall be responsible for the administration of Hong Kong until 1997; and (2) the post-1997

Hong Kong SAR legislature should be constituted by elections.

They also criticized the lack of factual and legal foundation in Li's statement as an attempt at freezing constitutional reform in Hong Kong prior to 1997. The Joint Declaration never prohibited change before 1997, it only called for no change for fifty years in the autonomous Hong Kong SAR after 1997. They also pointed out the unfairness in demanding local developments at the present stage must "converge" with an unknown, yet to be finalized Basic Law (the first draft of which would not be ready for public consultation until 1988 and the promulgation of the final version of which must wait until 1990). Further, they rejected Li's statement as it dangerously undermined public confidence in the future of Hong Kong and created harmful effects against its "stability and prosperity."[21]

To counteract these barrages of strong public criticism, pro-PRC public figures (including two elected members of the Legco from the functional constituencies of (a) the pro-PRC Chinese General Chamber of Commerce, and (b) the leftist Hong Kong Federation of Trade Unions, the sole labor element in the BLDC) soon issued statements supporting Li Hou's view. Leftist organizations also were mobilized to mount a counterattack. On the other hand, although Li Hou in his statement indirectly challenged the right of the Hong Kong government to run the territory as it saw fit until 1997, the colonial authorities publicly reacted in a firm but restrained, low-profile manner. The Hong Kong government refused to comment directly on the "press reports" and only stated that the various possibilities for the future development of the Legco as outlined in the Green Paper were all genuine options fully in accordance with the Joint Declaration. It also insisted this review exercise was simply part of an evolutionary process of constitutional reform which began with the publication of the 1984 White Paper before the signing of the Sino-British agreement. However, it was widely believed that the Hong Kong governor took up the matter in his private meeting on June 20 with Chinese Foreign Minister Wu Xueqian, who happened to be passing through Hong Kong on his return to China from a trip abroad.[22]

Almost simultaneous with Wu's "courtesy call" on Governor Wilson in Hong Kong was an even stronger criticism of the Hong Kong government's electoral reform by an "anonymous" senior Chinese official in an "off-the-record talk" with Hong Kong journalists in Shenzhen, the PRC Special Economic Zone bordering Hong Kong. This senior Chinese official was widely identified in the Hong Kong press and media as none other than Xu Jiatun, director of the local NCNA. Xu's "off-the-record" remark was that the promise of an elected legislature in the Joint Declaration was Beijing's concession for the sake of maintaining good relations with London. This implied that either the provisions for elections were a promise not to be taken literally or that Britain had tacitly indicated it would be satisfied with indirect elections. However, when TVB, Hong Kong's leading television station, referred to this remark in its evening news on June 21, the local NCNA spokesman issued an immediate rebuttal labeling the TVB news report as "inaccurate."[23]

This NCNA denial was soon followed by a surprising about-face retraction from Beijing. On June 23, 1987, the China News Service (CNS) (Zhongguo Xinwen She) issued a release from Beijing carrying Li Hou's latest "clarification." In this June 23 statement, Li explained that in his interview with the reporter from *Liaowang,* which took place at a BLDC meeting in Guangzhou, he did express his concern that Hong Kong's proposed direct election in 1988 may pose a problem of convergence with the Basic Law, but Li insisted that he never said "this does not conform to the spirit of the Sino-British Joint Declaration."[24]

On the surface, Li's denial seemed to end the public controversy and prevent a possible crisis of direct Sino-British confrontation over the pre-1997 democratization attempts. Li's hasty retraction was interpreted by many only as a tactical retreat by PRC officialdom but not a strategic surrender on the direct election issue. Some observers suggested that Li had been put in his place by the more diplomatic and much senior Wu Xueqian, and an uneasy equilibrium was restored. Others thought that the PRC leadership ordered Li to retract in order to preserve some "face" for the British authorities in Hong Kong, who were already suffering from an inevitable and increasingly serious "lame duck" image.

Nonetheless, retraction, denial, or whatever, the PRC authorities did not end their opposition to the introduction of direct elections in 1988. Local leftist leaders and pro-PRC organizations and conservative business elites joined forces and actively rejected this option in the Green Paper public consultation. The British side, even with Li's rhetorical retreat, was only too aware of Beijing's true intentions and ultimately backed down from its earlier democratization commitment under PRC pressure. In February 1988, the Hong Kong government issued another White Paper, *The Development of Representative Government: The Way Forward*, which stressed "prudent and gradual change." The official line was that there was a strong public desire for further development of a representative system of government, but there was no clear consensus on the timing or the extent of the introduction of direct elections. The White Paper promised that in 1991 (the year after the Basic Law was promulgated), at least ten out of fifty-six members of the Legco would be directly elected. And it even acknowledged the need (as demanded by Beijing) for a "convergence" between Hong Kong internal developments before 1997 and the future Basic Law.[25]

Indeed, Hong Kong government spokesmen, taking up a theme introduced by the chairman of the BLDC and the head of the PRC's Hong Kong and Macao Affairs Office, Ji Pengfei, argued for a "convergence" between internal developments and the future Basic Law, while the Chinese used the as yet unfinished Basic Law as a means to slow down Hong Kong's political and constitutional reform before 1997. Throughout these debates, the Hong Kong government refused to offer the Hong Kong people a simple choice through a referendum, but preferred to obfuscate the issues by a barrage of complex and not easily understandable options. The results of the colonial government's own assessment, not surprisingly, were indecisive, and this enabled the government to claim that no clear preference for direct election had emerged.[26]

So, it seemed that despite retractions and denials, the Chinese side had scored a great victory. The Li Hou incident and the British retreat in many senses only confirmed the worst fears of many people in Hong Kong about the future and added to the worsening crisis of confidence both for the countdown era to 1997 and for their fate under Chinese sovereignty after 1997.

To many local social activists and democratic advocates, these setbacks were bitter pills of defeat and betrayal. Some felt that they were encircled by a hostile, unholy political alliance of the PRC regime, the local leftist organs and the conservative business elites (who had in the past enjoyed the prerogatives and patronage of the British colonial government and now were turning toward Beijing), with an unsympathetic and unprincipled colonial sunset regime acting out the role of an appeasing accomplice toward the derailment of local democracy. It was against such Sino-British crossfire, realignment of political allegiance, crisis of confidence, and "brain drain" overseas that the BLDC, in adopting the so-called mainstream model of constitutional development in December 1988, dealt a near fatal blow to the democratic aspirations of many Hong Kong Chinese.

## V. From Consultation to Confrontation: Rancor over the "Mainstream" Model, 1988–89

After the Basic Law first draft was released for public comment in 1988, the most controversial and heated debates focused on the constitutional structure for the post-1997 SAR—the formation of the legislature through election and the election or appointment of the chief executive of the SAR government. The five-month-long (from April to September 1988) public consultation did not yield any consensus on this vital area of the Basic Law.

Taking advantage of this vacuum due to the "lack of a clear and genuine consensus" (not unlike the pretext used by the colonial regime in the 1987 Green Paper–1988 White Paper fiasco), Louis Cha, an influential Hong Kong member of the BLDC and publisher of a local Chinese daily, *Ming Pao*, promoted his so-called mainstream model which was against the early introduction of direct elections for both the SAR legislature and its chief executive. Using his institutional status as the Hong Kong co-convener of the BLDC panel on constitutional structure (the other convener is a PRC-based legal expert), Cha advanced his highly restrictive model at the BLDC panel meeting in Guangzhou in late November 1988. Claiming to have incorporated all the major common features of the various competing alternatives (as advocated by the liberal, democratic "Lobby of the 190,"[27] the conservative "Group of 81,"[28] and pro-Beijing organs), Cha, with the full blessing of the PRC establishment, labeled his last-minute proposed version the "mainstream" model.

In essence, the "mainstream" model postponed the introduction of a fully directly elected legislature for at least the first fifteen years of the SAR, that is, not until 2012. It further stipulated that even then, the decision for a fully directly elected legislature would depend on the outcome of a referendum to be held once every ten years. Only if more than 67 percent of voters favored this, then direct election would be introduced. Furthermore, the "mainstream" model suggested that only 27 percent of the sixty legislative seats be directly elected in 1997. Directly elected seats would increase to 38 percent in 2003 of a legislature of sixty-five seats, then to 50 percent in the 2017 election of an expanded eighty-member legislature in its fourth term. The rest of the legislature would be indirectly elected via the functional constituencies. The SAR officials in the first three terms are not publicly elected. Furthermore, one-man–one-vote direct election for the entire SAR legislature and the chief executive will be decided by a referendum in 2011. That means Hong Kong people will have to wait fifteen years after 1997 to have the opportunity to decide whether direct election will be introduced for the legislative and executive branches of the SAR government. In effect, this would postpone, if not completely derail, the possibility of a directly elected legislature and executive, perhaps until 2047.[29] (Also see Table 2.1.)

However, this model had never been listed as one of the alternatives in the BLCC's five-volume consultation report and collection of public opinions on the first draft issued in October–November 1988. Even most of the BLDC Hong Kong members were caught by surprise when Cha hurriedly produced his "mainstream" model just one day before the BLDC panel meeting. The Hong Kong public was enraged by this highly unusual twist and improper, preemptive procedural strike by Cha as BLDC panel co-convener. Some regarded Cha's maneuver as a conspiracy and front for the antidirect election coalition of Beijing, the Hong Kong tycoons, and the Hong Kong leftist organs.[30]

Cha himself and his "mainstream" model became the targets of verbal assaults from the prodemocratic lobby and fair-minded intellectual and progressive academics. The public was particularly disturbed by Cha's "improper" use of his daily paper to present deliberately misleading editorials and feature articles grossly distorting descriptions of the elective process and institutions in the Western democracies as justification and historical precedents in defense of his antidemocratic "mainstream" model. The Hong Kong Journalists' Association even demanded Cha resign from the BLDC in order to avoid a conflict of interest.[31] Local undergraduates even publically burned Cha's *Ming Pao* outside its editorial premises. Perhaps foretelling the Beijing students' hunger strike by half a year, in early December 1988 local democratic advocates staged a month-long relay-style marathon hunger strike in downtown Hong Kong to protest against the BLDC's high-handed, procedurally improper, and politically unjustified adoption of the so-called mainstream model.[32] Despite such a display of "confrontational politics" (as Li Hou labeled the hunger strike), the BLDC in its full session in January 1989 adopted this model, and this formed the basis for the

Table 2.1

**Competing Models for Political Structure in the Basic Law**

| Louis Cha's "mainstream" model | The "T.S. Lo" model | The "4:4:2" compromise model | The "Omelco Consensus" model |
|---|---|---|---|
| **Composition of the Legislative Council:** | | | |
| 1. Direct election | | | |
| 1997: 27%<br>2003: 38%<br>2007: 50%<br>2012: 100%(?) | 1997: 25%<br>2003: to be decided by the SAR government | 1997: 40%<br>2001: 60%<br>2005: to be decided by the SAR government | 1995: not less than 50%<br>1997: not less than 50%<br>1999: 67%<br>2003: 100% |
| 2. Functional constituency election | | | |
| 1997: 73%<br>2003: 62%<br>2007: 50% | 1997: 50%<br>2003: to be decided by the SAR government | 1997: 40%<br>2001: 40%<br>2005: to be decided by the SAR government | 1995: 50%<br>1997: 50%<br>1999: 33%<br>2003: 0% |
| 3. Grand electoral college election | | | |
| | 1997: 25%<br>2003: to be decided by the SAR government | 1997: 20%<br>2001: 0% | |
| **Selection of the chief executive:** | | | |
| Universal suffrage in 2012(?) | Universal suffrage in 2003 | Universal suffrage in 2005 | Universal suffrage in 2003 |

constitutional section of the second draft of the Basic Law released in February 1989.

By then, it had become clear to more informed observers that the PRC establishment, in its determination to preempt any local push toward a more democratic form of SAR government (with a directly elected chief executive accountable to a popularly and directly elected legislature), destroyed any pretense of a fair, open, and proper drafting procedure. Beijing, it seemed, wanted so much to assert "Chinese sovereignty" over Hong Kong vis-à-vis the lingering influence of the British colonialists and the growing voice of the local democratic elements that it was willing to incur almost any political cost, by risking open confrontation with the local populace and worsening their already serious crisis of confidence toward the post-1997 era. In a sense, this particular exercise in adopting the so-called mainstream model for the Basic Law only confirmed the worst suspicions of many Hong Kong people, that is, if the PRC is not willing to abide by the rules and play a fair game now, nearly a decade before 1997, with Hong Kong still under the British flag as buttressed by the 1984 Joint Declaration, then how could anyone take China at its word and trust its guarantees as codified in the Basic Law for the half-century after 1997?

Indeed, one significant result of this public disillusionment and the pro-democratic lobby's disappointments has been the emergence of a serious legitimacy crisis for both the British Hong Kong and PRC governments in the eyes of many Hong Kong people. Not only did the Joint Declaration sharply reduce the authority of the Hong Kong colonial regime in the countdown to China's resumption of sovereignty in 1997, but the British inability to resist the PRC's interference in the pre-1997 political developments in Hong Kong further diminished their effective capacity to rule Hong Kong until 1997. Furthermore, failing to fulfill its earliest promise of democratic reform, the Hong Kong government in effect was presiding over the transition from one form of colonialism to another, one with even less popular legitimacy, as displayed in the Basic Law drafting process.[33] The local activists' experience with the Realpolitik of the Basic Law drafting exercise from 1985 to 1988 can be summarized as follows:

The Basic Law drafting process inevitably called forth various political groups in Hong Kong, and the liberal lobby has striven, unsuccessfully, to ensure that both the future SAR chief executive and the legislature are directly elected and thus are fully accountable and responsive to Hong Kong concerns. At the same time, the liberals argued for direct elections to the legislature beginning in 1988. As mentioned above, this was defeated. One consequence of this was the growing feeling that neither the Hong Kong, British, nor Chinese government is responsive to the Hong Kong people's wishes. In particular, none of these governments wishes to allow the public to choose directly, through the ballot box, the options for their future. Neither the Joint Declaration nor the Basic Law was subject to ratification by the Hong Kong people. Similarly, the Basic Law is, in the PRC view, an internal matter for China and an expression of national sovereignty and therefore cannot be subject to a Hong Kong veto. Both the British and the Chinese authorities have ruled out any referendum or plebiscite, but instead preferred to invite submission of opinions, which they then chose to evaluate according to their criteria before announcing the results and making their decisions on constitutional development. At no time were the Hong Kong people given a direct and decisive voice in the process or the result.

Hence, by winning a blatantly unfair and politically costly battle in the first round of the Basic Law drafting process over the trampled aspirations of the local democratic elements, the PRC unintentionally, but irrevocably, lost the hearts and minds of the great majority of the Hong Kong people. The PRC's avowed objective of maintaining the "stability and prosperity" of Hong Kong has also been jeopardized since huge numbers of professionals began leaving the territory because of lack of confidence in the future. From the pre–Sino-British negotiations figure of 18,300 in 1981 to 45,800 in 1988, the total number of Hong Kong people migrating overseas has drastically increased in the course of the Basic Law drafting, and probably will reach an all-time record of 62,000 in 1990.[34]

## VI. "Today Beijing, Tomorrow Hong Kong": The Basic Law Drafting Process under the Shadow of Tiananmen, May–June 1989

The PRC's all-out efforts to suppress the drive for democracy in Hong Kong during the 1988–89 period soon found an even more brutal expression on the mainland. However, in the full twist of historical irony, the PRC establishment only managed to delegitimize itself further and provoke massive and unprecedented patriotic, prodemocratic outbursts among the Hong Kong Chinese that almost derailed the entire Basic Law drafting process. The events of May–June 1989 and the unfolding drama of Beijing–Hong Kong discord in the aftermath of the June 4 Incident bear witness to this very uneasy and seriously strained relationship.

From the very beginning of the Chinese student democratic movement in April 1989, the Hong Kong public had been more than attentive to developments on the mainland. Not only did the local newspapers (including the left-wing press such as *Wen Wei Po* and *Ta Kung Pao*) provide detailed and up-to-date coverage, but they adopted a clearly sympathetic editorial orientation toward the Beijing students. The democratic lobby and the student organizations in Hong Kong were strongly supportive of their counterparts on the mainland as they saw the Beijing demonstrators acting in ways similar to their own efforts in demanding constitutional rights from the same PRC establishment.[35]

The sentiments of the prodemocratic movement in Hong Kong reached their climactic eruption following the imposition of martial law in Beijing on May 20, 1989. The very sharp, swift, and massive echoes to the Beijing events in Hong Kong reflected more than the genuine patriotic concern of the local Chinese populace. These were unmistakably clear signals that after suffering some seven years under the 1997 China syndrome, the people of Hong Kong fully realized that their own fate had been inevitably linked to the mainland and that they must now stand up and show their true colors. To many of them, the plight of the Beijing masses in pursuit of democratic reform vis-à-vis the CCP/PRC party/state was too close a real-life parallel to their own uphill battle in the still ongoing Basic Law drafting process and the abortive attempts for constitutional reforms in 1987–88.

Indeed, events in Beijing galvanized the people of Hong Kong into full-scale collective action. They were transformed almost overnight from apolitical and apathetic residents of a colony to citizens of a threatened community committed to preserve their freedom and fight for their rights. It was this fully awakened and mobilized Hong Kong citizenry that filled the ranks of the May 21 one million and May 28 one and one-half million people mass protest marches on the island. These were so unprecedented in size, scale, magnitude, and intensity that they were powerful signs for the PRC and the rest of the world to appreciate.

The following aspects of the Hong Kong mass protest movement against the PRC's suppression of prodemocracy demonstrations in the summer of 1989 deserve greater emphasis in the context of the Basic Law drafting process:

(1) The protest movement in Hong Kong was without doubt an unexpected but much needed morale-boosting political windfall opportunity for the local democratic lobby to re-enter the central political arena and even seize the high ground in the last round of the Basic Law drafting consultation and in the realignment of political forces in the countdown to 1997. The massive outpouring of sympathy and strong support for the Beijing students on the part of the Hong Kong public, especially among the grass roots, meant, in a very real and immediate sense, that the moral and practical support for a similar democratic cause long championed by the local activists was reinforced. The leading figures of the local democratic lobby were the true leaders of the Hong Kong protest movement. Both in fact and symbolically, they marched at the head of the million people parades in late May and took the podium as keynote speakers in numerous other rallies and public commemorations during the summer of 1989.

(2) These leading figures in the local democratic camp took full advantage of the Beijing crisis to form a new, large-scale umbrella coalition, the Alliance in Support of the Patriotic Democratic Movement in China, linking many of the prodemocratic organizations and civic groups into a coordinated, if not centralized, and unified network. This new alliance had at its disposal some HK$30 million (U.S.$3.8 million) in its war chest as a result of highly successful fund-raising concerts and public donations received from all walks of life in less than one month. These democratic advocates are still the controlling elements of this alliance which has been condemned by the CCP/PRC leadership as a ''counter-revolutionary, subversive'' organization aimed at overthrowing the Communist state in China.[36] Hence, the personal and institutional input from the democratic lobby into the protest movement had earned the wrath of Beijing in the post–June 4 purge. Yet, during the summer of 1989, not unlike the student leaders in Beijing, Hong Kong's democratic figures also became popular heroes to the local population. In one sense, Beijing's name calling only further enhanced their local appeal and international prestige as champions for the democratic cause which could be translated into valuable political assets for future battles.

(3) The real political casualties in Hong Kong from the fallout of the Tiananmen Incident were the PRC establishment and its local organs and personnel.

The once-influential local mouthpiece of the PRC, *Wen Wei Po*, openly sided with the students and severely condemned the Beijing leadership, while the other leftist dailies turned ambiguous. They, in effect, nearly ruined the PRC's local propaganda and united front mechanism, as journalists working for the leftist papers came out and joined the protest marches with great fanfare. Even in the purge of mid-July, which saw the forced removal from office of *Wen Wei Po*'s executive director and the resignation en bloc of many of its editors and reporters, enough damage had been done before the NCNA finally regained control of the paper and turned around its editorial direction in autumn 1989. Press freedom after 1997 became a moot point if it could not be respected before 1997.[37]

(4) Other previously pro-PRC mass organizations also took to the streets and joined hands with the democratic elements in condemning the brutal suppression of the Beijing student demonstrators. For instance, the president (a BLCC member) and vice-president (a BLDC member) of the Hong Kong Federation of Trade Unions (HKFTU), the umbrella organ of all local leftist unions with a combined membership of over 170,000, were in the front row of the May 21 and May 28 protest marches. Members of many leftist organizations and staff in PRC-owned business concerns (such as the Bank of China) took out full-page, signed advertisements in the local dailies in support of the Beijing students.[38] The PRC's "patriotic" front in fact had collapsed after May 20 and current efforts at reorganizing it have yet to yield concrete, reliable results. For the immediate future, they have been so compromised and neutralized that their actual effectiveness as an acceptable and legitimate counterbalance to the democratic elements in the direct elections to the Legco in September 1991 is highly questionable. (In this regard, former NCNA Hong Kong Branch Director Xu Jiatun's unauthorized departure through Hong Kong to the United States in May 1990 for "visit and relaxation" further undermined the solidarity and prestige of the PRC front in Hong Kong.)

(5) Of even greater direct negative impact and to the great embarrassment of the Basic Law drafting mechanism was the resignation of two Hong Kong members from the BLDC; the boycott by another two members (both leading pro-democracy figures) of the BLDC proceedings; as well as the temporary suspension of work of the BLCC and the extension of the second draft consultation period by three months, from July 31 to October 31, 1989. Of greater irony and perhaps even historic justice is the fact that one of the two BLDC members who resigned was none other than Louis Cha, mastermind of the infamous "mainstream" model only a half-year earlier.[39] Some ten members of the BLCC also resigned during the summer and autumn of 1987.

(6) The shocks of Tiananmen forced the once-conservative, antidirect election big business lobby to lay low and seek cover from the political fallout from Beijing. The delegitimization of the Beijing leadership also undermined any claim by the PRC for local support and public acceptance of their previous die-hard stance against popular democracy through genuine representative gov-

ernment for the transition era and the post-1997 SAR. It also contributed to the eventual split within the big business circles on the political structure model for the future SAR and retarded their efforts for the formation of a political party in preparation for the 1991 Legco election.

(7) The British authorities lost no time in capitalizing on the Beijing events. London unilaterally suspended scheduled meetings of the Joint Liaison Group for the summer.[40] Departing from its previous (i.e., up to June 4, 1989) stance (that the people of Hong Kong should have faith in their future as guaranteed by the Joint Declaration and the Basic Law which was still being drafted), the British government was quick to acknowledge the existence of a serious crisis of confidence in Hong Kong. Hence, it decided to introduce three measures to restore local confidence during the transition era:

(i) to speed up the pace of democratization before 1997;
(ii) to enact a Hong Kong Bill of Rights; and
(iii) to offer U.K. citizenship with a full right of abode package to a very limited number of the 3.25 million local holders of British Dependent Territories citizen passports (among Hong Kong's 5.8 million residents) as an insurance option to encourage those deemed vital for the territory's functioning to remain.

In early July 1989, British Foreign Secretary Geoffrey Howe made a three-day visit to Hong Kong where he firmly ruled out giving all Hong Kong people the right of abode in Britain in the event that "things did go catastrophically wrong." At the same time, the British Parliament House of Commons Foreign Affairs Committee released a report on its earlier inquiry on Hong Kong. It called for a much faster pace of democracy by having half of Hong Kong's Legco directly elected by 1991 and the entire council to be directly elected by 1997.[41] This was by far the most progressive model put forward, and naturally the local democratic lobby supported this recommendation warmly.

Even the Hong Kong colonial establishment tried to make amends for its 1988 decision (made under threats from Beijing and pressure from the local conservative big business lobby) that only ten out of sixty seats in the Legco would be directly elected by universal suffrage in 1991. On May 24, 1989, members of the Executive and Legislative Councils (Omelco) expressed their "strong desire" to speed up pre-1997 constitutional reform. Labeled the "Omelco Consensus" model, it aimed at having one-third of the Legco directly elected in 1991 and then increasing it to 50 percent by 1995, the last such election to be held while Hong Kong remained under British rule. It also suggested that the entire Legco should be directly elected by 2003.[42] In the summer and early fall of 1989, both the British and Hong Kong governments repeatedly emphasized the negative effects of Tiananmen on Hong Kong people's confidence and urged more careful efforts to examine the provisions of the Basic Law draft.[43]

## VII. The Tightening of the Screw, Summer–Fall 1989

The most controversial issue in the Basic Law drafting process is the introduction of direct elections which will specify the creation of the SAR's executive and legislative arms. According to a poll conducted before the Tiananmen Incident, 70 percent of the people surveyed believed the SAR's chief executive and principal officials should be elected by universal suffrage. A total of 60 percent wanted direct elections and only 16 percent favored the electoral college approach. More importantly, more than 55 percent of the Hong Kong people polled did not believe China would keep its "One Country, Two Systems" pledge. There is every indication that such statistics are much higher after the Tiananmen Incident. For instance, a public poll in October 1989 revealed that some 70 percent of the local people did not trust that "China will honor the Basic Law in guaranteeing individual rights and a separate economic system."[44]

Because of widespread distrust toward China, present long before May–June 1989, many Hong Kong people want to leave the territory before 1997. Even in better times, Hong Kong–PRC political relations had been uneasy and distrustful. It is, therefore, not surprising to find that results of a poll conducted by local scholars in 1985 (still in the relatively euphoric atmosphere of the immediate post–Joint Declaration Sino-British "honeymoon" period, but before the actual Basic Law drafting began), showed that only 22.3 percent of the Hong Kong people believed the PRC would truly let "Hong Kong people rule Hong Kong."[45] As a matter of fact, the pre–June 4, 1989, Basic Law drafting process had already added much to the tension. In May 1989, when the students were demonstrating in Beijing, a poll conducted in Hong Kong indicated that one out of every four Hong Kong persons wished to leave Hong Kong, including almost half of those with a college education.[46]

To many Hong Kong people, the Basic Law draft's contents and the drafting process had already violated many key provisions of the 1984 Joint Declaration. For instance, a very crucial stipulation stated that "The chief executive shall abide by the law and shall be accountable to the legislature." But the Basic Law second draft specified that the chief executive is accountable to Beijing (see Article 43 of the Basic Law first and second drafts), so it is clear that a case of divided loyalty would be the result as the chief executive of the SAR would not be solely accountable to Hong Kong. Furthermore, under the Basic Law draft, the SAR legislature will have little power. In fact, the chief executive can exempt officials from testifying or can dissolve the legislature. Yet, the chief executive can only nominate senior officials; only Beijing can appoint them. (See Article 48 of the second draft.) Moreover, the legislature supposedly will have the power to impeach the chief executive, but the final decision rests with Beijing and the legislature has no role in choosing or dismissing officials. Other issues showing Beijing's intention to control tightly Hong Kong affairs after 1997 through the Basic Law are abundant. For example, the SAR budget will be presented to the legislature on a "take-it-or-leave-it" basis. Revenue and expenditure bills and government policy cannot be introduced without the chief executive's approval. (See Articles 48 and 73 of the second draft.)

Following the shock of the Tiananmen Incident, there have been some notable shifts in favor of direct elections in Hong Kong. The "Omelco Consensus" model was an early example, even though it was still rather conservative when compared with the U.K. parliamentary report which recommended an even faster formula. However, the Chinese government dismissed the Omelco model as part of a British "conspiracy" involving local Hong Kong pro-British interests at the expense of Chinese sovereignty. All along, Beijing has insisted that the drafting of the Basic Law was entirely a domestic Chinese matter with input from Hong Kong residents. As such, British official views regarding the Basic Law's full compliance with the Sino-British Joint Declaration could only be transmitted to Beijing through proper diplomatic channels. And this included the views of the Hong Kong Executive and Legislative Councils which were considered by Beijing as part and parcel of the British administration, not representative of the true interests of the local Chinese populace. Thus, the *Comments on the Basic Law (Draft)* issued by Omelco in October 1989 had to be sent via British diplomatic channels to the Chinese authorities who regarded this a British-"tinted" reflection of local views.[47]

While the conservative big business elites, particularly the "Group of 89" BLCC/BLDC members, by the summer of 1989 had relaxed somewhat their once very firm opposition to introduce directly elected components into both the pre- and post-1997 legislature as "too much, too soon," they still did not fully endorse the "Omelco Consensus" model. Instead, they took the lead in October 1989 in reaching an eleventh-hour compromise "4:4:2" model between the "Group of 89," the so-called moderates, and some elements of the prodemocratic lobby. This "4:4:2" model referred to the proportional distribution of directly elected (40 percent), functional constituencies (40 percent), and electoral college-originated seats (20 percent) for the legislature from 1995 to 2001. (Also see Table 1.) Even though two-thirds of the surveyed local public opinions in fall–winter 1989 found this "4:4:2" model acceptable, it did not receive popular endorsement as a genuinely democratic blueprint for the future constitutional structure.[48] Many prodemocracy activists and some leftist elements also had reservations about this compromise model.

To counter both the "Omelco Consensus" and the "4:4:2" models, as well as to regain lost momentum and initiative in the Basic Law drafting process, Beijing put forward its own preferred design through a local "front." In September 1989 a BLCC vice-chairman, T.S. Lo (a former British-appointed Exco and Legco member), entered the arena with an ultraconservative political model advocated by his New Hong Kong Alliance. It proposed a bicameral legislature with only 25 percent of the seats directly elected by universal suffrage, the rest to be returned by functional constituencies (50 percent) and an electoral college (25 percent). Lo's proposed model not only would split the legislature into two tiers, but it was designed to enable an indirectly elected upper house to exercise veto power over the decision of a partially (or even later on fully) elected lower house. (Also see Table 1.) This ''T.S. Lo'' model provoked an immediate and angry retort from liberal, democratic circles, as well as strong disapproval from the general public. According to a November 1989 public opinion survey on SAR political models conducted by the conservative Hong Kong General Chamber of Commerce, the ''T.S. Lo'' model of a bicameral legislature obtained the least support (2.9 percent) among the four major proposed models. The ''4:4:2'' model gained the greatest support (47 percent), followed by the ''Omelco Consensus'' model (45 percent). The ''Louis Cha" model, which was written into the Basic Law second draft, received very low (4.1 percent) support.[49] Even many of the business elites were reluctant to support T.S. Lo's model, which was a totally new (as it had never been listed in the Basic Law's two drafts for public consultation) introduction of a bicameral legislature with obvious ''divide-and-rule'' implications. In fact, some prominent members (including another BLCC vice-chairman) of the New Hong Kong Alliance later resigned from that organization in order to dissociate themselves from Lo and his model.[50]

Notwithstanding the extreme unpopularity and widespread questioning of both the practical effects of this model and Lo's motives for his advocacy at that particular juncture of what was a very late stage of the drafting process, the PRC was not prepared to yield any ground. Despite the fact that the extended period for the second round of the supposedly open local ''public consultation'' on the Basic Law draft was still ongoing until the end of the month, Beijing rushed to endorse publicly this ''T.S. Lo" model in October 1989. Under heavy pressure from Beijing, various once-protesting but now redisciplined leftist organizations, including the HKFTU, began to rally around this ''T.S. Lo'' model in an attempt to project a facade of mass support. However, the events of May–June had left too deep a scar on the hearts and minds of the grass roots for them to remain docile. Some members of individual labor unions affiliated with the HKFTU publicly repudiated claims of popular support by the umbrella federation. They pointed out the fact that the rank-and-file union membership had never even been consulted by their own union nor by the HKFTU on their response to this model, and if they had been asked, they said that they definitely would oppose this unacceptable model for political structure.[51] This only further tarnished the already diminished public image of the BLDC/BLCC. But by then the post–June 4 Beijing leadership with its siege mentality was obsessed with regaining control of the situation even at the expense of its relationship with Hong Kong.

Indeed, the atmosphere in Hong Kong during the autumn of 1989 was clouded by the most blatant forms of threats, intimidation, and even outright condemnation by the PRC of key actors in the political scene. This only added fuel to a burning fire. The PRC press, both on the mainland and in Hong Kong, singled out the two preeminent democratic advocates, Szeto Wah and Martin

Lee, for engaging in activities aimed at "subverting the PRC government."[52] Szeto and Lee, BLDC members who boycotted the BLDC's work after June 4, were the president and vice-president respectively of the Alliance in Support of the Patriotic Democratic Movement in China—the umbrella organization that staged most of the mass protests and fund-raising campaigns. On the one hand, the PRC establishment rejected these two BLDC members' expressed desire in October 1989 to resume full participation in the BLDC.[53] The NPC Standing Committee, in its late October 1989 meeting, announced that Szeto and Lee must "explain, repent and account for their past activities which are subversive, anti-PRC state and destructive of the Joint Declaration, otherwise they should not be permitted to return to the BLDC to resume active participation."[54] Furthermore, Beijing had exerted pressure to have the alliance dissolve itself and even attempted to force the British colonial regime to outlaw the alliance which was registered as a limited company in Hong Kong.

It should be clear then that the Basic Law drafting process was of only secondary concern to Beijing in its attempt to reassert control by silencing critics and rebuking challenges from outside the PRC. Under these circumstances, the Basic Law which is supposed to function as a guarantee for the future stability and prosperity of Hong Kong can enjoy little practical appeal even before 1997. And by attacking the local BLDC members at this critical juncture of Hong Kong–PRC relations, the entire Basic Law drafting process in itself became a most serious destabilizing force undermining the situation of Hong Kong. This seems to be the direct opposite of the original intent of the Basic Law and contrary to the desired effect of the drafting process as a major instrument for Beijing's united front efforts toward the Hong Kong people.

From the above analysis, it is clear that the once faltering democratization process in Hong Kong rebounded most remarkably in the immediate aftermath of the Beijing crisis. This seemed to reflect the old cliché that "Hong Kong has always benefited from the misfortunes of China." In fact, the unfolding drama of a repressive purge of prodemocratic elements on the mainland, and the continuous PRC condemnation of prodemocracy figures and organizations in Hong Kong as "subversive and counterrevolutionary" did not bode well for a smooth and easy process in completing the final version of the Basic Law. The events of May–June 1989 had rendered almost meaningless Beijing's earlier pledge of "a high degree of autonomy" for Hong Kong under the "One Country, Two Systems" formula. However, of even greater destructive impact has been Beijing's post–June 4 damage control and crisis management measures in the Hong Kong political scene. The post-Tiananmen PRC approach vis-à-vis Hong Kong has almost wrecked beyond repair the once very close and mutually beneficial bilateral relationship built upon economic interactions as well as social-cultural human linkages between the two societies.

The damage done was so severe that the Hong Kong governor, Sir David Wilson, felt it necessary to point out in very clear terms the importance of political self-discipline of the Hong Kong people as necessary for their survival after 1997. In his annual address to the Legco on October 11, 1989, Sir David pointed out:

> Hong Kong is linked to China but, in another important sense, separate from it. That will continue to be the case in the future under the concept of "One Country, Two Systems." We have our own laws and freedoms which we cherish. They must not be eroded. Equally, we should use them with a sense of responsibility and self-restraint. For many years our community has recognized the importance of not becoming directly involved in China's often complicated domestic politics. At the same time, given both the economic and political realities, there is every reason to expand our already close economic links with the mainland. We can strengthen the basis of our special future political status by the contribution that we make to the modernization of the Chinese economy and by the access to world markets, advanced technology and expertise that we can provide for China.
>
> We for our part have made it clear to the Chinese government that action is needed to restore confidence in the arrangements of Hong Kong's future. We need to restore mutual trust as the necessary cornerstone for the unprecedented political experiment that will begin in 1997, the foundations for which must be laid securely in the next eight years.[55]

## VIII. The Finalization Stage, January–April 1990

The first two months of the new 1990s decade turned out to be the most crucial period in the entire Basic Law drafting process. January 1990 was punctuated by a secret trip to Beijing by Sir Percy Cradock (personal adviser to Prime Minister Thatcher and former British ambassador to the PRC), then an official visit to Beijing by Governor Wilson, and right after that, a visit to Hong Kong by the new British Foreign Secretary Douglas Hurd, as well as BLDC panel meetings in Guangzhou to amend the Basic Law second draft contents after the final round of "public consultation."[56]

Wilson's mission was basically that of a salesman trying to convince Beijing to be "reasonable" and accept a faster pace of democratization than envisaged in the latest Basic Law draft, preferably with the "Omelco Consensus" model's stipulation for a one-half directly elected legislature in 1995 as the baseline for the post-1997 political structure. He also tried to calm down PRC opposition to the granting of U.K. right of abode to selected Hong Kong residents as a necessary insurance policy to maintain local confidence. Only after Wilson had obtained the PRC's consent, and the Basic Law's relevant contents had been finalized, could the Hong Kong government make good its long-promised announcement of constitutional development for the 1991–95 period. Unfortunately, Wilson's fence-mending trip was not much of a success on both issues, and he returned emptyhanded.[57] Hurd's four-day visit to Hong Kong had done little to boost local morale on the uncertain future under Chinese rule with the yet to be finalized Basic Law. Hurd in fact adhered to the 1987-established bilateral Sino-British understanding on "convergence" between pre-1997 developments and the Basic Law provisions. He left Hong Kong people in no doubt that with regard to the pre-1997 democratization process, Beijing's wishes outweighed local aspirations even in the aftermath of June 4 events.[58]

In response to the overtures from Wilson and Hurd, PRC officials remained firm in their opposition to any rapid introduction of universal suffrage direct elections. They set a maximum quota of only eighteen out of sixty seats in the 1997 legislature to be directly elected and this 30 percent limit on a directly elected component would be frozen for a decade until 2007.[59] PRC officials, however, did not really make it their final stand on this crucial aspect of the Basic Law as if they were bolting the door to a watertight compartment on their leaking ship of state. Rather, they deliberately left the door slightly open with the possibility for further bilateral negotiations to shape the final arrangements on the political structure in the Basic Law. It was in the midst of the final plenum meetings of the BLDC held in Beijing during mid-February 1990 that an ultimate "compromise" on this area of the Basic Law was hammered out at the last minute, in behind-the-scenes, closed-door diplomatic bargaining between London and Beijing. On February 16, the BLDC plenum voted to accept all final amendments, more or less unanimously among the fifty members present.[60] By then, the Basic Law final version was, for all practical intents and purposes, set in stone and thus concluded the entire drafting process of five years.

The Hong Kong people were completely excluded from this final and crucial stage of the drafting process. Despite the PRC's repeated assertion of sovereign rights over a purely "domestic" law-making exercise that would bode no "foreign interference," this was in fact a bilateral Sino-British secret deal. Neither the expressed views of the local populace as "collected" in the final round of the BLCC consultation nor as "reflected" (definitely not represented in any sense) by local BLDC members were genuinely taken into consideration by the PRC authorities. By then, most of the BLDC Hong Kong members, for the sake of posterity and public image, had openly adopted at the January 1990 panel meetings a stronger stance favoring a slightly faster pace and larger scope of SAR legislature democratization.[61]

Indeed, people in Hong Kong literally woke up on February 15 to the shock of reading news headlines that Britain and China had reached a secret deal on their future. Not only were they denied the opportunity to participate in making this decision on their own future, but the British government did not even tell them the terms of the deal. Instead, they only learned about it through press reports of official PRC statements regarding the final draft.

As a matter of fact, the final draft of the Basic Law depressed public confidence in Hong Kong to a level even lower than that immediately after the June 4 Incident according to a poll in late February 1990. This public opinion poll indicated that the majority of local people either did not care any more or were disappointed with the Basic Law final draft.[62] Following public knowledge of the contents of the Basic Law final version on constitutional structure, the Hong Kong colonial regime on March 21, 1990, unveiled its own constitutional reform for its remaining sunset years. Under this "triumph of convergence," the 1991 Legco election will witness a major realignment of the sixty seats: eighteen will be directly elected from nine geographic constituencies, with each returning two members; civil servant official seats will be reduced from the current ten to three (only the chief secretary, the financial secretary, and the attorney-general will remain); appointed members will also be reduced from twenty to eighteen; while functional constituency seats will increase from fourteen to twenty-one. The last British-conducted election in 1995 for the sixty-seat Legco will have two more directly (i.e., a total twenty seats, or 33.3 percent) elected seats; the three official members' seats and all the eighteen appointed seats will be abolished; the rest of the Legco will be a combination of thirty functional seats (i.e., 50 percent) and ten seats (16.7 percent) returned by an electoral college whose exact composition and procedure are yet to be determined.[63]

Under the Basic Law this 1995 formula will remain in effect until 1999. Then, the SAR political system will evolve at a snail's pace over the next decade. The number of directly elected legislators will rise to twenty-four in the second term (1999–2003) and to thirty (i.e., 50 percent) in the third term (2003–2007). Indirectly elected legislators from the functional constituencies will occupy half of the sixty seats in the legislature from 1995 to 2007. The legislature will have ten members returned by the electoral college in the first term (1995–99), but it will drop to six in the second term and disappear altogether after 2003. The balance between directly and indirectly elected SAR legislators may shift after 2007, probably in favor of the latter. (See Basic Law, Annex II.)

As evident in the Legco debate on "the future political system in Hong Kong" on February 28–March 1, 1990, the commonly felt relief in Hong Kong that the Basic Law's actual drafting was finally over was coupled with general and deep disappointment that the "Omelco Consensus" model was not adopted. Some Legco members, in vividly conveying the prevailing sentiments of broad cross sections of the Hong Kong community, openly denounced the Sino-British bilateral secret deal on the "convergence compromise" as nothing but a "British sellout," "London's betrayal," and a "shameful act of surrender" of Hong Kong interests.[64]

Of course, by then, nothing more could be done to the Basic Law. The British and Hong Kong governments began to redirect public attention to look forward and focus on the 1991 Legco election. The Hong Kong government has hoped that this would be a real success so as to demonstrate to the PRC that Hong Kong is well prepared for electoral democracy and that the democratization process could be further developed, for 1995 and beyond. However, Beijing has been firm in its position that absolutely no change in the Basic Law would be allowed before 1997.[65]

It was against such a background of a strained trilateral relationship between London, Hong Kong, and Beijing, of deep suspicion and mutual distrust, as well as bitter disappointment felt by a majority of Hong Kong people that the promulgation of the final draft of the Basic Law became something of an anticlimax in Hong Kong. On April 4, 1990, the National People's Congress in Beijing formally enacted and promulgated the Basic Law of the Hong Kong Special Administrative Region of the People's Republic of China. This final version was either greeted with indifference or by bitter denunciations from the local population. However, on the Chinese side, the final version was seen as a victory for China, and Deng Xiaoping personally hailed it as a "creative masterpiece" with historical and international significance "for the whole of mankind."[66]

Indeed, the Basic Law ensures that all of the crucial levers of power are left in China's hands. The chief executive is to be appointed by China and, as Article 48 shows, is given great power. China also has the power to appoint all senior officials (Articles 15 and 61). The legislature will remain weak and, while the ultimate objective is to have a fully directly elected legislature (Article 68), there is no guarantee that this will ever occur. While the elected element will steadily increase until it reaches 50 percent in 2007, a fully directly elected legislature requires the endorsement of two-thirds of the members and the approval of the chief executive (Annex II(III)). There is, in short, no guarantee that the legislature will ever be fully elected by direct universal suffrage.

While the judiciary is independent of the executive, China has introduced a distinction between adjudication and interpretation, unknown to Hong Kong's existing common law legal system. Thus while the Hong Kong Final Court of Appeal may have the power of final adjudication (Article 82), the final power of interpreting the Basic Law lies with the Standing Committee of the National People's Congress in Beijing (Article 158). In addition, Article 17 gives the Standing Committee the power to return (i.e., reject) laws enacted by the SAR that the Standing Committee considers are not in conformity with the Basic Law. The Standing Committee also has the power to return laws enacted before 1997 on the same grounds (Article 18).

The current PRC leadership's tightening reign over political behavior on the mainland also led to additional limitations on Hong Kong's autonomy, especially the modifications to Article 23, which was strengthened after June 1989, to ban "subversion" against the Central People's Government. Yet it fails to define the term. Subversion, of course, has no place in the common law, and conjures up the worst aspects of China's current insecurity and paranoia. Article 18 states that Beijing may declare an "emergency" in times of turmoil and apply martial law to the SAR. The same law in force on June 4, 1989, in Beijing could be implemented in Hong Kong. In addition, political groups that do set up in Hong Kong after 1997 will be isolated from the international community since they may not have ties with foreign political organizations or bodies. This will not, however, preclude ties with political bodies in China itself. Taken together, none of these late changes to the Basic Law bodes well for the future of Hong Kong, since even the PRC feels that it has the right to impose upon the promised "high degree of autonomy" (Article 2) and, in effect, interfere in the internal political affairs of the SAR.

## IX. Epilogue: Decolonization without Democracy

As a matter of fact, the general mood of the Hong Kong Legco debate on the Basic Law held on April 4, the same day as its official promulgation in Beijing, is clearly one of disappointment. Recent pronouncements by political figures in Hong Kong indicate a continuing sense of pessimism about the future under Chinese sovereignty.[67] British policy continues to insist that the 1984 Sino-British Joint Declaration on the future of Hong Kong was a good arrangement, the best possible under the circumstances. As revealed in House of Commons debates on Hong Kong matters, the British have been fairly critical of some parts of the Basic Law, but are also anxious not to overemphasize this since they neither wish to antagonize China, nor do they wish to deepen the already very strong and pervasive sense of despair in Hong Kong. British strategy in Hong Kong remains the maintenance of economic growth and political stability in the transition period to 1997.

Some of the earlier measures that were introduced by the British in order to bolster confidence in Hong Kong have also begun to take shape. The publication of a proposed Bill of Rights for Hong Kong the same week as the Basic Law was promulgated was clearly intended to reassure the local population, though China has made threatening noises against it. In December 1989, the British government, over the opposition of its own back bench in the House of Commons, announced a scheme to issue full British citizenship passports with the right of abode in the U.K. to 50,000 selected Hong Kong families (approximately 225,000 persons) without first requiring them to leave the territory to qualify. This measure passed the British Parliament as the British Nationality (Hong Kong) Act in late July 1990, and the first group of qualified Hong Kong residents are expected to receive their U.K. passports in 1992.[68] However, Beijing still objects strongly to the U.K. passport package as violating the Joint Declaration's "Chinese Memorandum" on nationality issues.

In October 1989, the Hong Kong government also announced ambitious plans for the expansion of tertiary education enrollment and a massive public-works program calling for the construction of a new international airport and container-port facilities to stimulate the economy in the 1990s.[69] Recently, official efforts were also taken to transmit more detailed plans for these massive infrastructural developments to Beijing in an attempt to gain PRC endorsement and even participation. Nonetheless, PRC authorities remain lukewarm toward the proposed airport and port projects with sharply expressed reservations on both their basic design and high cost (at HK $127 billion according to Hong Kong government estimates) and the possible financial burden on the future SAR.[70]

The effectiveness of all these British measures to contain if not fully mitigate the local crisis of confidence remains questionable as China is the master of Hong Kong's future fate and the very cause of this political crisis. Perhaps one can address the crux of the situation by reviewing the following factors underlining or undermining Hong Kong's stability and prosperity:

(1) The confidence of the people of Hong Kong toward both the British and the PRC governments has been fully shattered and needs to be rebuilt drastically. Studies and survey results have shown that the political expectations and confidence of Hong Kong people has been declining since the signing of the Sino-British Joint Declaration.[71] Since then, many people in Hong Kong feel that both the British and the Chinese leaders cannot be trusted. On the one hand, the British government has shied away from its moral responsibility of providing right of abode to some three and one-quarter million Hong Kong British-passport holders and has taken a weak stance toward the PRC's interference in Hong Kong affairs.[72] On the other hand, the Chinese leaders are not sincere in granting autonomy to Hong Kong people, and they showed their willingness to resort to brutal force when they suppressed the demonstrations in Tiananmen Square. A very clear indicator of the sharp decline in public enthusiasm in Hong Kong toward the entire Basic Law drafting exercise during the 1985–90 period is the markedly different response to the two rounds of the BLCC "public consultation." For the Basic Law first draft, some 74,000 submissions of views were received by the BLCC during the five-month consultation period, May–September 1988. In contrast, less than 7,000 submissions on the Basic Law second draft were received by the BLCC during the extended period of final consultation during March–October 1989.[73] Public interest to participate in Basic Law discussions had waned considerably even before the June 4 Incident as most local people regarded any such efforts as futile and even counterproductive given China's high-handed approach. Indeed, as shown in the controversies of late 1988 and late 1989 on political structure, the PRC adopted the models by lack of thorough deliberation, hasty introduction, and acute absence of public support. Taken as a whole, the Basic Law drafting process utterly failed to generate confidence in China's credibility and/or enhance its legitimacy among the Hong Kong public.

(2) Related to the current twin confidence crisis (i.e., a serious lack of confidence both in the British colonial regime's effective capacity to rule and maintain "stability and prosperity" in Hong Kong during the transition to 1997, as well as in the PRC's sincerity to implement the Basic Law faithfully according to the letter and spirit of the Joint Declaration) is the massive "brain drain" and the exodus of Hong Kong professional talent to other countries. It is common knowledge that nearly every other person in Hong Kong is contemplating migration overseas. This "exodus fever" reached a new peak following the Tiananmen events, with Singapore joining Canada, the United States, Australia, and the U.K. as the popular emigration destinations of Hong Kong's "best and brightest who

vote with their feet.'' In this regard, the political twists and turns in the Basic Law drafting process only served to reinforce the local populace's urge to seek security overseas ahead of 1997.[74]

(3) Politically speaking, many sectors in the Hong Kong community are becoming highly politicized and more inclined toward collective action and popular mobilization over public affairs. The democratization process and the parallel Basic Law drafting process only serve to provide the necessary opportunities for public discourse and participation in the political arena. In a sense, the 1982–84 Sino-British negotiations unlocked a Pandora's box, and the Basic Law drafting process accelerated the tempo of their political maturity, with the formation of political groups or parties the natural and necessary outcome. However, the Basic Law provisions are devoid of any reference to political parties, leaving the status of a democratic parliamentary-type system uncertain. It is definitely not Beijing's intention to allow the Basic Law and its drafting process to serve as the midwife to the birth of Hong Kong's democratic system.[75] Despite uncertain prospects, the prodemocracy circle's two new political ''parties,'' the United Democrats of Hong Kong and the Hong Kong Democratic Foundation, were formally established on April 23 and June 24, 1990, respectively.

(4) The actions and attitude of the PRC, combined with the continuous retreat of the moral and actual responsibilities of the British colonial regime in this transition era, had induced a very pervasive political cynicism among the Hong Kong public. In this regard, the widespread ''spiraling of political silence'' is a powerful indictment against the discredited and delegitimized Basic Law drafting process by a despised regime in Beijing. Under this politically depressed atmosphere of ''induced public silence,'' those who can emigrate overseas are now trying their best to accumulate wealth and liquid assets and/or enhance personal skills and professional qualifications before their departure from Hong Kong. Hence, they do not wish to rock the boat any further while they are still in Hong Kong. On the other hand, a large majority of the local populace who for one reason or another cannot go overseas also prefer to advance themselves and improve their own lot in Hong Kong before 1997, and since they will eventually live under Chinese rule, they prefer to keep a low political profile and maintain their silence in order to avoid any post-1997 reprisal. The postures of the PRC authorities since 1985 in fact only further discourage their active participation in public affairs. Therefore, the recently discernible lowering of the level of political activism and critical voices does not signal genuine acceptance by the Hong Kong populace of their imposed fate. This is no more than a false facade masking the great anxiety and deep frustration of a troubled community facing an uncertain destiny.

Taken together, all these are significant indicators that the Basic Law drafting process has contributed directly and seriously to the crisis of confidence in the future of Hong Kong—a future that is fast becoming unsalvageable without an effective democratization process. Indeed, the crisis of Hong Kong's future is a genuine case of democracy in crisis. The Basic Law drafting exercise in a sense provides a vivid, real-life illustration of the historic tragedy of a derailed democratization process resulting in "decolonization without democracy" for the nearly six million people of Hong Kong. If the post-1997 developments in Hong Kong after the demise of British colonialism could indeed be comparable to the unknown prospect of a "life after death," then the Basic Law might perhaps be regarded as the "birth certificate" to Hong Kong's "life after death" under Chinese sovereignty.

## Notes

1. The formal instruments of ratification were exchanged on May 28, 1985. The full text of the Joint Declaration is included as Appendix A in Ming K. Chan and David J. Clark, eds., *The Hong Kong Basic Law: Blueprint for "Stability and Prosperity" under Chinese Sovereignty?* (Armonk, N.Y.: M. E. Sharpe, 1991).

2. See Deng Xiaoping, *Fundamental Issues in Present-Day China* (Beijing: Foreign Languages Press, 1987), 48–52, 59–60, 64–66, 93–96; his "Current Policies and Prospects for Hong Kong," *Beijing Review* (January 4–10, 1988): 14–17; and Wen Wei Po, ed., *The Birth of Basic Law* (Hong Kong: Wen Wei Po, 1990), 180–86.

3. The slogan "Hong Kong people ruling Hong Kong" was once popular but is now almost never referred to by PRC officials.

4. For the history of the period to August 1988, see Emily Lau, "The Early History of the Drafting Process," in *The Basic Law and Hong Kong's Future,* ed. Peter Wesley-Smith and Albert Y.H. Chen (Singapore: Butterworths, 1988), 90–106.

5. Speech by Ji Pengfei, *Xin Wan Bao* (New Evening Post), December 18, 1985.

6. *People's Daily,* July 13, 18, and 21, 1989, overseas edition.

7. Hong Kong Government Information Service, *Hong Kong 1989: A Review of 1988* (Hong Kong: Government Printer, 1989), 52. According to the BLCC's official report, *Reference Papers for the Basic Law of the Hong Kong Special Administrative Region of the People's Republic of China (Draft)* (Hong Kong: February 1989), 2, some 74,000 opinions on the first draft of the Basic Law were collected and compiled into a five-volume report by October 1988.

8. See John P. Burns, "The Process of Assimilation of Hong Kong (1997) and Implications for Taiwan," *AEI Foreign Policy and Defense Review* 6, no. 3 (1988): 19–26; and Andrew Scobell, "Hong Kong's Influence on China: The Tail That Wags the Dog," *Asian Survey* 28 (June 1988): 599–612.

9. See Burns, "The Process of Assimilation."

10. See *Asia 1988 Yearbook* (Hong Kong: Far Eastern Economic Review, 1988), 173–74. The Sino-Portuguese negotiations were relatively smooth and lasted only nine months. The Macao Basic Law is still in the drafting process with its own BLDC and BLCC.

11. Mr. Tam Yiu-chung represents the pro-Beijing Hong Kong Federation of Trade Unions. Independent trade unionists were effectively excluded when one of their leaders, Lau Chin-shek, was kept out of the BLCC in December 1985. Some leaders representing independent unions then withdrew from the BLCC.

12. *Asia 1986 Yearbook* (Hong Kong: Far Eastern Economic Review, 1986), 125.

13. *Asia 1988 Yearbook,* 128. See also Ming K. Chan, *The British Sunset in Hong Kong* (Hong Kong: Hong Kong Economic Journal Press, 1989), 26–30.

14. Item no. 6 in Part II (page 162) in Ming K. Chan and David J. Clark, eds., *The Hong Kong Basic Law*, offers a comparative listing of the key areas of difference between the first and second drafts.

15. For an overall analysis of Hong Kong's political change, see Lau Siu-kai, *Hong Kong's Political Structure Reform and Political Development* (Hong Kong: Wide Angle Publications, 1988), and particularly, the chapter on "The Basic Law and Hong Kong's New Political Order," 97–148.

16. For the earlier abortive attempts at constitutional reform, see Steve Tsang, *Democracy Shelved: Great Britain, China, and Attempts at Constitutional Reform in Hong Kong, 1945–1952* (Hong Kong: Oxford University Press, 1988) and the review by Ming K. Chan in *Hong Kong Law Journal* 21, pt. I (January 1991).

17. See Hong Kong Government Information Service, *Hong Kong 1985: A Review of 1984* (Hong Kong: Government Printer, 1988), 42.

18. The full text of this White Paper can be found in ibid., 42–51. In Hong Kong government practice, a White Paper is an official policy position and is usually preceded by a Green Paper, which is issued for the solicitation of public comments, a hallmark of the colonial-style "consultation and consensus."

19. The official Hong Kong government report on the public acceptability of the Joint Declaration including views from the local press, opinion survey findings, mass organizations, professional bodies, and members of the Exco/Legco can be found in ibid., 31–41.

20. The full text of this interview, "The Future Development of Hong Kong's Political System," by Tan Hua appeared in the "Taiwan, Hong Kong and Macao Special Column" (in Chinese) of *Liaowang* (overseas edition), no. 45 (June 22, 1987): 20.

21. The criticism of Li's statement was reported in the following Hong Kong newspapers: *South China Morning Post, Hong Kong Standard, Ming Pao, Sing Tao Jih Pao, Wah Kiu Yat Po, The Express,* and *Oriental Daily News* during June 19–25, 1987.

22. "Directing the Elections," *Far Eastern Economic Review (FEER),* July 2, 1987, 30–31.

23. The NCNA rebuttal was carried in most of the local papers. See, for example, *Wah Kiu Yat Po,* June 22, 1987, 2.

24. The full text of Li Hou's retraction was reported in both *Ta Kung Pao* and *Wen Wei Po,* June 24, 1987, as headline stories.

25. The public criticisms against the Hong Kong government for its blatant retreat from its rather firm 1984 commitment to democratization forced the colonial regime to adopt a very low profile on this 1987/88 Green Paper/White Paper exercise. For instance, the official yearbooks, *Hong Kong 1988: A Review of 1987* and *Hong Kong 1989: A Review of 1988,* devote only a brief paragraph each to the exercise (p. 17 and p. 23 respectively), while *Hong Kong 1985: A Review of 1984* contains the full text of the 1984 White Paper.

26. A survey commissioned by one of Hong Kong's leading newspapers found that in May 1987, 75 percent of those polled favored direct elections to the legislature in 1988. *South China Morning Post (SCMP),* May 31, 1987, 1–2. A second poll conducted in July 1987 found that 54 percent of the respondents favored direct elections; 62 percent professed to being baffled by the forty options presented in the government's Green Paper. *SCMP,* July 24, 1987.

27. This liberal group suggested that at least half of the seats in the SAR legislature *should* be directly elected, and the chief executive should be elected by universal suffrage.

28. This conservative group advocated a mixed election system, that is, a combination of direct election and electoral colleges.

29. Louis Cha's proposed model was strongly supported by another local BLDC member, industrialist Chi-min Cha, who had made some modifications to Louis Cha's original scheme which were accepted by Louis Cha and the BLDC panel. As such, the Louis Cha "mainstream" model was also known as the "Cha-Cha" model. On the details of this "mainstream" model, see *South China Morning Post Hong Kong Review 1989* (Hong Kong: South China Morning Post, 1989), 11; Miron Mushkat, *Basic Law*

*Therapy* (Hong Kong: Baring Securities Ltd., 1990), 3; and *SCMP*, October 2, 1989, which compares it with the other three models that emerged later in summer–fall 1989.

30. On the highly unpopular political play by Cha in the Basic Law drafting process as a whole, see *FEER*, June 29, 1989, 32; *SCMP*, October 2, 1989, and November 5, 1989.

31. For the Hong Kong academics' criticism of Cha's misrepresentation and distortion of the Western elective process, see *Hong Kong Economic Journal (HKEJ)*, December 6, 1988, 17; *SCMP*, December 2, 1988, and also *South China Morning Post Hong Kong Review 1989*, 11.

32. See John D. Young, "Words of a Hunger Striker" (in Chinese), *Jiushi Niandai*, January 1989, 36–37, for a report of the hunger strikers. Young was one of the first two hunger strikers who started this protest action on December 8, 1988.

33. Ian Scott, *Political Change and the Crisis of Legitimacy in Hong Kong* (Hong Kong: Oxford University Press, 1989) provides an in-depth analysis of this situation.

34. *Wah Kiu Yat Po*, September 9, 1989, which also reports a Hong Kong government projection (made in 1989) of 50,000 emigrants in 1990. However, in the "Governor's Annual Address to the Legislative Council, October 10, 1990," the official estimate was revised upward to 62,000 emigres for 1990 (para. 21). See Ho Lap, "BLDC: The Political Structure Is More Conservative" (in Chinese), *Jiushi Niandai*, February 1989, 36–38.

35. The following accounts of Hong Kong's reportage of and local response to the Beijing events during April–June 1989 are based mainly on the following major newspapers: *Hong Kong Economic Journal, Ming Pao, Wen Wei Po, Ta Kung Pao, Wah Kiu Yat Po, Sing Tao Jih Pao,* and *South China Morning Post.* An analysis of the Hong Kong journalistic front's response to the Beijing events is Ming K. Chan and Tuen-yu Lau, "Dilemma of the Communist Press in a Pluralistic Society: Hong Kong in the Transition to Chinese Sovereignty, 1988–1989," *Asian Survey* 30 (August 1990).

36. See *Renmin ribao* (People's Daily), July 8, 1989. *HKEJ*, July 7, 1989 carried a rebuttal interview with those leaders named in *Renmin ribao.* See also Emily Lau, "A 'Subversive' Alliance: China Attacks Territory's Democrats," *FEER*, August 3, 1989, 29.

37. See Chan and Lau, "Dilemma of the Communist Press"; also see *FEER*, June 29, 1989, 32.

38. See, for example, the report in *HKEJ*, June 7, 1989.

39. Also resigned was the Anglican Bishop of Hong Kong who had been criticized by some as too willing to go along with Beijing's antidemocratic stance.

40. The meetings were resumed in late September 1989.

41. House of Commons Debates, July 5, 1990. See item no. 11 in Part II of this volume.

42. See Executive and Legislative Councils (Omelco), *Comments on the Basic Law (Draft)* (Hong Kong: October 1989).

43. See *FEER*, August 31, 1989, 29, for the shouting match across the border between Beijing and Hong Kong officials on the Basic Law draft and other issues underlining Sino-British tension.

44. The figures from the pre–June 4 poll are reported in Joseph Y.S. Cheng, "The Post-1987 Government in Hong Kong," *Asian Survey* 29 (August, 1989): 733. Findings of the October 1989 poll conducted by Inrasia are reported in *SCMP*, October 31, 1989, 1.

45. Hsiu Chi Kuan and Siu Kai Lau, "The Civil Self in a Changing Polity: The Case of Hong Kong," *The Asian Journal of Public Administration*, forthcoming, cited in Cheng, "The Post-1987 Government in Hong Kong," 733, 745.

46. Cheng, "The Post-1987 Government in Hong Kong."

47. *FEER*, August 31, 1989, 17.

48. *HKEJ*, November 1, 1989; *SCMP*, October 2, 1989; and *Hong Kong Standard*, October 31, 1989, for details of this model and public reaction which was generally favorable.

49. On the "T.S. Lo model," see Mushkat, *Basic Law Therapy*, 3–4. Also see *South*

*China Morning Post Hong Kong Review 1990* (Hong Kong: South China Morning Post, 1990), 13, on this poll and the power play among local political activists on these models.

50. *Asia 1990 Yearbook* (Hong Kong: Far Eastern Economic Review, 1990), 122–23 and *South China Morning Post Hong Kong Review 1990,* 12–13.

51. *Asia 1990 Yearbook,* 123; *SCMP,* October 2, 1989, reveals the fact that the "4:4:2" model rather than the "T.S. Lo" model was closer to the HKFTU's own preference. Also see Hong Kong Federation of Trade Unions, *Federation of Trade Union Press* (October 1989). *Ming Pao,* October 30, 1989, reports the complaints from members of the HKFTU's affiliated unions.

52. See Lau, "A 'Subversive' Alliance," 29.

53. The two had originally stated that they would not participate in the BLDC working group if the Deng-Li-Yang clique, who were believed to have ordered the massacre of students, remained in power.

54. *HKEJ,* November 1, 1989.

55. "Governor's Annual Address to the Legislative Council, October 11, 1989," para. 7 and 8. The full text is also included in Hong Kong Information Service, *Hong Kong 1990: A Review of 1989* (Hong Kong: Government Printer, 1990), chap. 1, 4–22.

56. *FEER,* January 18, 1990, 19.

57. Ibid., 10.

58. *FEER,* January 25, 1990, 17.

59. Ibid.

60. *SCMP,* February 17, 1990, 19.

61. *HKEJ,* January 22, 1990, "Hong Kong Pulse" column.

62. *SCMP,* February 23, 1990. This poll was conducted by Survey Research Hong Kong in conjunction with Radio Television Hong Kong.

63. *SCMP*, March 22, 1990, 7.

64. Hong Kong Legislative Council Debate, February 28–March 1, 1990 (especially the speeches by Martin Lee, Hui Yin-fat, and Ronald Chow). See item no. 8 in Part II of this volume.

65. *FEER*, March 1, 1990, 14–15.

66. *Beijing Review* (February 26–March 4, 1990): 5; *SCMP,* February 18, 1990; and *Ta Kung Pao,* February 18, 1990. Also see Wen Wei Po, ed., *The Birth of Basic Law,* for pro-PRC positive views on the Basic Law.

67. Hong Kong Legislative Council Debate, April 4, 1990 (especially the speeches by Martin Lee and James McGregor). See item no. 9 in Part II of this volume.

68. See *SCMP*, October 15, 1990, for details of the selection criteria of this scheme which is highly restrictive.

69. "Governor's Annual Address, 1989" in Government Information Service, *Hong Kong 1990: A Review of 1989,* 12–20.

70. "Governor's Annual Address, 1990," para. 65–76. On the PRC's strong reservations, see *SCMP* and *Wen Wei Po,* October 13 and 22, 1990.

71. See Joseph Y.S. Cheng, "Hong Kong: The Decline of Political Expectations and Confidence," *The Australian Journal of Chinese Affairs,* nos. 19, 20 (January and July 1988): 241–67.

72. Emily Lau, "Lobbying London: Britain Rejects Colony's Plea for Right of Abode," *FEER,* July 6, 1989, 30.

73. *HKEJ,* November 1, 1989.

74. *South China Morning Post Hong Kong Review 1990,* 11–12; *FEER,* March 15, 1990, 17–18.

75. See Lo Shiu-hing, "Citizen Participation: Decolonization and Political Development in Hong Kong," *Asian Survey* 28 (June 1988): 613–28.

# 3

# Balancing the Beijing–London–Hong Kong "Three-Legged Stool," 1971–1986

*James T.H. Tang and Frank Ching*

### The Concept of the "Three-Legged Stool"

The triangular relationship of Britain, China, and Hong Kong entered a new and very different phase during the governorships of Sir Murray MacLehose (1971–82) and Sir Edward Youde (1982–86). The fifteen years between 1971 and 1986 saw the normalization of Sino-British diplomatic relations and witnessed the Sino-British negotiations for Hong Kong's future. The balance of Britain's and China's relations with Hong Kong was critically changed during this period.

Prior to the MacLehose and Youde years, Britain had recognized the central government of the People's Republic of China as the legal government of China, but the two countries' diplomatic relations had only been maintained at the chargé d'affaires level. Although Beijing made no attempt to challenge British rule in Hong Kong, and the British and Hong Kong governments did not tolerate communist subversion in the colony, the need to develop a working relationship with Beijing was well recognized by London and the Hong Kong authorities. Unlike in other British colonial territories, however, Britain refrained from introducing democratic reforms in the colony on the grounds that the colony would not be able to attain political independence because of the China factor. Hong Kong is a case of "decolonization without independence."[1]

Although the 1970s was a period of stability and rapid economic expansion,

The original version of this chapter appeared in *Precarious Balance: Hong Kong Between China and Britain, 1842–1992*, ed. Ming K. Chan (Armonk, NY: M.E. Sharpe, 1994).

questions about Hong Kong's uncertain political status became a serious concern toward the end of MacLehose's terms of office. The early 1980s proved to be a far more troublesome period for the colony, as Britain and China engaged in two years of difficult negotiations on the future of Hong Kong. The Sino-British Joint Declaration in 1984 cleared the uncertainty about Hong Kong's political status, but the colony has since witnessed rapid political changes. Incorporating Hong Kong into China as a special administrative region under the "one country two systems" formula with "a high degree of autonomy" in 1997 is proving to be a highly complex process.

Writing in 1971, the year Maclehose's governorship began, John Rear concluded that Hong Kong was not a democracy. He noted: "Power, both administrative and executive, is in the hands of civil servants who are in law primarily responsible, through the Governor, to the United Kingdom."[2] The colonial administration, however, managed to maintain its political control and succeeded to a surprising degree in avoiding challenges to its legitimacy. Hong Kong's population has been seen as largely apolitical. Observing the stable and nonparticipatory nature of the colonial polity, political sociologist Lau Siu-kai conceptualized Hong Kong as a "minimally integrated social-political system" with the coexistence of a bureaucratic polity and a Chinese society.[3]

The colonial administration succeeded in maintaining its political position also through what Ambrose Yeo-chi King called "administrative absorption of politics," as emerging socioeconomic elites were being coopted into an administration-dominated polity.[4] In short, the political stability in the colony had been maintained by a tacit, if not always harmonious, understanding between the British and Chinese governments to allow the continuation of the existing arrangements; an apolitical population, many of whom fled to Hong Kong from the mainland as refugees; and an effective colonial administration, supported by powerful business groups, incorporating local elites into the system.

Rapid economic growth and attendant social changes during the MacLehose years, however, helped to stimulate aspiration for wider and more public involvement in the political process. By the time MacLehose's governorship approached its end, the growing middle class, led by groups such as the Hong Kong Observers, had become far more vocal and critical of many government policies and the administration's reluctance to widen public participation in the political process.[5] The Sino-British negotiations over Hong Kong's political future further created a new political situation and more pressure for political reform and democratization in Hong Kong during Youde's governorship in the 1980s.

During the Sino-British negotiations on the colony's future, Lord Belstead, British minister of state with special responsibility for Hong Kong, used the term *three-legged stool.* During a visit to the colony in December 1982, he said that any agreement reached had to be acceptable to China, to the British Parliament, and to the people of Hong Kong.[6] The Chinese government rejected this formulation, apparently because it implied a basic equality among the three "legs."

From China's viewpoint, Hong Kong was part of its territory, and Britain was a foreign power temporarily occupying this Chinese territory. Neither could be put on a par with the Chinese government.

Yet the three-legged stool can be a useful practical concept on the understanding that it is not a legal term and is not meant to introduce concepts anathema to China such as the political independence of Hong Kong or joint rule by Britain and China. Stripped of these politically loaded implications, the term *three-legged stool* is merely a figure of speech, a convenient shorthand way of understanding Hong Kong. Basically, the three-legged stool concept means that, in Hong Kong, things go smoothly when all three parties—Britain, China, and Hong Kong—are in agreement. It does not mean that all three parties must act in concert; it does mean that each of the three has a voice and can give or withhold its support. When all parties consent, openly or tacitly, the stool is steady. When any party is in opposition, the stool wobbles and a crisis results.

Analyzing Hong Kong's political development by looking at the interaction among Britain, China, and Hong Kong is of course not a new perspective. Speaking in November 1971, Denis Bray, a former senior Hong Kong civil servant, suggested that Hong Kong's stability rested on a tripod of consents. He maintained that the continuation of the colony's way of life required "the consent of the Hong Kong people, the consent of China and the consent of Britain." Political scientist Norman Miners applied a modified version of this concept in his standard text on Hong Kong politics, calling the book an extended commentary on Bray's remarks. He argued that the colony's political institutions must operate within the parameters set by four factors: the policies of China and Britain, the attitudes of the local population, and the state of the economy.7 In many ways, Hong Kong's development from a quiet fishing village to an international metropolis and a major trader in the world (the tenth largest in 1991) has been the result of all three parties' efforts. The British have provided the administrators, the legal framework, and the necessary infrastructure; the Chinese have provided tacit approval of the British arrangements and supplied such necessities as food and water at low cost; while Hong Kong itself has provided the manpower, skills, and capital. All three parties have proven indispensable. Each has had to cooperate with the other two.

The Britain–China–Hong Kong relationship, however, has always been asymmetrical—the tripod's three legs are uneven. Maintaining the balance of the three-legged stool became rather more delicate during the MacLehose and Youde years, when Britain and China sought to reach an agreement for settling the colony's political future, with the people of Hong Kong excluded from participating directly in the process.

## Sino-British Relations and Hong Kong's Future: 1971–81

MacLehose served as governor for more than ten years, an extraordinarily long time. When his tour as governor began, Britain still had a consulate in Taiwan and was represented in Beijing only by a chargé d'affaires. The MacLehose years saw Britain–China as well as Hong Kong–China relations develop to such an extent that MacLehose in 1979 became the first Hong Kong governor to be invited to China on an official visit.

In the larger picture, the dawn of the MacLehose era saw a rapprochement between China and the West. Henry Kissinger, that master in geopolitics, commenting on the new international situation created by the dramatic breakthrough in Sino-American relations, had this to say in his memoirs, *The White House Years*: "Our relations to possible opponents should be such that our options toward both of them were always greater than their options toward each other." Kissinger went on to say that having the Soviet Union and China compete for good relations with the United States "was the essence of triangular strategy." The hostility between China and the Soviet Union, Kissinger said, served American purposes best if the United States maintained closer relations with each side than the two other sides did with each other.[8]

While Sino-American rapprochement may well have arisen out of a complex set of strategic calculations in both Washington and Beijing, the overall improvement of China's relationship with the West had direct implications for Sino-British relations as well as for Hong Kong. Chinese political leaders clearly accepted that their country had more to gain by developing better relations with the capitalist West. British leaders in London had long recognized the need to maintain diplomatic links with the People's Republic; Britain on January 6, 1950, became the first major Western country to recognize the Beijing government—and the two countries established diplomatic relations at the chargé d'affaires level in 1954.[9] But past British imperial involvement in China and cold war politics had prevented the normalization of Sino-British relations for more than two decades after the establishment of the People's Republic of China.

By 1971 Britain had ceased to be an imperial power. It had declined as a major world power and no longer sought to maintain its former position in East Asia. Using Fred Northedge's phrase, the British "descent from power" was completed when the London government announced in 1968 its decision to withdraw British troops from east of Suez by the end of 1971.[10] The end of Sino-American estrangement removed the last major obstacle in Sino-British relations. For Chinese leaders, better Sino-British relations would serve China's interests. Apprehensive of a Soviet security threat and seeking to improve China's economic situation after the destructive years of the Cultural Revolution, the People's Republic was keen to improve relations with the Western world. Britain's role in the European Community was particularly important as China attempted to broaden its international links yet remained wary of its newfound friendship with the Americans. Formal talks on upgrading Sino-British diplomatic relations to full ambassadorial level began in Beijing at the beginning of 1971.[11]

Thus, MacLehose took over as the governor of Hong Kong at an auspicious moment; the Sino-British relationship had just entered a new and friendlier phase. The turbulent years of the Cultural Revolution were over, and China was seeking to break its diplomatic isolation. One of Beijing's first moves after gaining entry into the world community, however, caused widespread concern in the British colony of Hong Kong. The Chinese government raised the question of Hong Kong's future in the United Nations a few months after claiming the China seat at the United Nations. In March 1972, the Chinese ambassador, Huang Hua, formally placed on record at the United Nations Special Committee on Colonization China's position on Hong Kong and Macau in a letter:

> The questions of Hong Kong and Macau belong to the category of questions resulting from the series of unequal treaties which the imperialists imposed on China. Hong Kong and Macau are part of Chinese territory occupied by the British and Portuguese authorities. The settlement of the questions of Hong Kong and Macau is entirely within China's sovereign right and do not at all fall under the ordinary category of colonial territories. Consequently they should not be included in the list of colonial territories covered by the declaration on the granting of independence to colonial countries and people. With regard to the questions of Hong Kong and Macau, the Chinese government has consistently held that they should be settled in an appropriate way when conditions are ripe.[12]

The Huang Hua statement reflected the state of Britain–China–Hong Kong triangular relations at the time. As far as London was concerned, Hong Kong was its colony; as far as Beijing was concerned, Hong Kong was its territory. Despite this basic difference in outlook, however, both Britain and China preferred not to directly challenge the other's position vis-à-vis Hong Kong. China's statement to the United Nations was seen as a reassertion of an old posture. By removing Hong Kong from the list of colonies expected to become independent, China in effect allowed the status quo to continue in Hong Kong. The Huang Hua statement can be seen as a manifestation of the three-legged stool in practice. China, while asserting its sovereignty over Hong Kong, was willing to allow the British to continue administering the territory; Britain, on its part, was willing to continue as the administrator; and there was every indication that the people of Hong Kong acquiesced to the arrangement. So all three parties were in agreement. The legs of the stool were firmly planted.

However, Huang's letter had another important implication: by placing on record China's position on Hong Kong's status as part of Chinese territory, the letter claimed that the political future of the territory should be determined by the Chinese government, through diplomatic negotiations if necessary, but not by the people of Hong Kong themselves. The British government, on the other hand, by refraining from challenging Huang's statement directly, acquiesced to the Chinese assertion. On November 2, the United Nations General Assembly accepted the Special Committee on Colonialism's recommended exclusion of Hong Kong and Macau from the United Nations' list of colonial territories. Britain swiftly stopped a twenty-six-year-old practice of transmitting information on Hong Kong's conditions annually to the secretary-general of the United Nations after Hong Kong was removed from the list.[13] Huang Hua's statement was seen as "nothing new," and British officials in London insisted that it would not present new obstacles to Britain's relations with China. The significance of Beijing's affirmation of its position and London's connivance was perhaps overlooked at that time.

Beijing's position toward Hong Kong, therefore, did not pose any obstacle in the improvement of relations between Britain and China. In early 1971, the negotiations for the normalization of Sino-British relations centered on the British consulate in Taiwan and the legal status of the Nationalist government on Taiwan. Only a few days after Huang Hua's statement on Hong Kong, the British and Chinese governments reached an agreement to normalize their diplomatic relations. Acknowledging the Chinese position that Taiwan is a province of the People's Republic of China, the British government, in a joint communiqué, agreed to remove the British official representation in Taiwan. Official exchanges soon followed. In October 1972, the British foreign secretary, Alec Douglas-Home, visited China. Both London and Beijing emphasized the two countries' trade relations and cultural exchanges, with hardly any reference to Hong Kong throughout the early 1970s. One exception was in 1973, when, as a gesture of goodwill to Beijing, London put pressure on the Hong Kong government for the release from prison of the last of the pro-Beijing rioters who had taken part in the 1967 civil disturbance in the colony.[14]

On the whole, both London and Beijing appeared to have deliberately kept the Hong Kong question out of formal discussions and off the agenda of their bilateral relations, preferring to allow the continuation of Hong Kong's status quo. The relative closeness of the Britain–Hong Kong and Britain–China relationships during the early and mid-1970s and the tacit understanding of the colony's special position were illustrated by the visit to the colony of Queen Elizabeth II in 1975. At the time, China would not officially acknowledge the British role in Hong Kong, so a royal visit to Beijing was out of the question.

Formal Sino-British discussions about Hong Kong's future actually took place for the first time toward the end of the MacLehose years, but the discussions were kept behind closed doors. In 1979, for the first time, China invited Hong Kong's governor to pay an official visit. At the time, people in Hong Kong were worried about the approaching deadline of 1997, when Britain's lease over the New Territories would expire. This meant that the Hong Kong government could not authorize leases of New Territories land beyond June 1997. The legal problem created a difficult issue in Hong Kong's economic development, with important implications for business confidence. The Hong Kong government thus faced pressure from the business community for seeking clarification from the Beijing government about Hong Kong's status after 1997. As early as 1976, the director of the Hong Kong General Chamber of Commerce, Jimmy McGregor, suggested that large-scale investors would need some indications from the Chinese government about Hong Kong's status before making a commitment to the colony.[15]

Partly in response to such pressure, the British and Hong Kong governments devised a plan by which the Legislative Council in Hong Kong would unilaterally adopt legislation setting aside the 1997 deadline, without Britain laying formal and permanent claim to the land. A rough precedent was the unilateral declaration by the Hong Kong government in 1899 that the Kowloon Walled City was to be administered in the same manner as the rest of the colony, even though the Beijing Convention of 1898 had stipulated that the Walled City remain under Chinese jurisdiction.[16]

The British intention was to remove the obstacle posed by the 1997 deadline. Chinese consent had to be obtained first, however. This was the primary goal of MacLehose's eleven-day visit to Beijing in March–April 1979. The inside story of that visit, which is not widely known, is an illustration of the three-legged stool theory in action.

During the meeting with the Chinese leader, Deng Xiaoping, the governor broached the subject. He said that investors were concerned about the future and informed the Chinese leader of the British plan for setting aside the 1997 deadline by acting "unilaterally" on the surface, but actually with China's blessing. To his disappointment, Deng refused to go along with the plan. Acquiescing to it would have meant that China would allow the status quo to extend beyond 1997. Withholding acquiescence meant that, for the time being at least, China retained all her options. After listening to MacLehose, the Chinese leader made clear that, in principle, China would take back Hong Kong but did not specify a date. He said that there were only two possibilities: one was that China would take back Hong Kong; the other was that the status quo would remain. In either event, the Chinese leader said, investors had nothing to worry about: they should "put their hearts at ease."[17]

According to the official account of the meeting provided by the Chinese, Deng Xiaoping insisted that the People's Republic of China had sovereignty over Hong Kong. He suggested that "a negotiated settlement of the Hong Kong question in future should be based on the premise that the territory is part of China. However, we will treat Hong Kong as a special region. For a considerable length of time, Hong Kong may continue to practise its capitalist system while we practise our socialist system."[18]

When the governor returned to Hong Kong, he announced in a press conference that Deng had asked investors to set their hearts at ease. The governor told the people of Hong Kong that Deng's remark suggested "a complete understanding of Hong Kong's economic importance to China." Referring to Deng's assurance, MacLehose also said, "it was a most realistic and helpful comment for the record." Responding to the governor's optimistic remarks, the share market's Hang Seng Index—often regarded as the barometer of the colony's business confidence—went up immediately. The mood in Hong Kong was almost euphoric.[19] However, MacLehose kept to himself China's refusal to cooperate in the plan to remove the 1997 deadline.

The general improvement in China's relations with the West and, in particular, Sino-British relations contributed to a more relaxed international atmosphere and growing confidence about political stability in Hong Kong. Another encouraging sign toward the end of the 1970s was China's new economic policies. Under Deng Xiaoping's leadership, Beijing began to adopt the policy of opening to the outside world. In September 1978, the Hong Kong branch of the Xinhua News Agency's number two man repudiated the 1967 riots as a mistake and suggested that China would learn from the economic success of Hong Kong and other newly industrializing countries. In December the Third Plenum of the Eleventh Central Committee declared that China would "actively expand cooperation in terms of equality and mutual benefits with other countries."[20] Hong Kong's political status after 1997 remained uncertain, however, and people in Hong Kong continued to be nervous about their future.

There were reasons for that apprehension. The passage of the British Nationality Act of 1981, for example, downgraded British nationals in Hong Kong by turning them into "British dependent territory citizens" and had the effect of double-locking Britain's doors against potential immigrants from Hong Kong. The bill was widely seen in Hong Kong as a distinct shift by Britain, a move toward ultimately relinquishing British responsibilities to Hong Kong. While the British government maintained that the new bill would not affect Britain's links with Hong Kong, it was widely seen as an attempt by Britain "to shed its obligations and commitments toward Hong Kong."[21]

During the final stage of the debate on the nationality bill, the Unofficial Members of the Executive and Legislative Councils UMELCO wanted to send a delegation to London to lobby members of both houses of Parliament and persuade them to vote against the bill. However, Governor MacLehose gave the Unofficial members a tongue-lashing and told them to cancel the trip. The members, all of whom were appointed by the governor, meekly complied. As a result, the bill was passed by a razor-thin majority in the House of Lords. A last-minute move by Lord Elystan-Morgan to introduce an amendment to give a common status of British nationality under the bill in the House of Lords on October 14, 1981, was defeated 105–102, a government majority of only three. If UMELCO had launched its lobbying effort and changed only one or two minds, the bill would have been defeated.[22]

It is clear that British, Chinese, and Hong Kong interests have not always been identical. The events surrounding the 1981 Nationality Act highlighted one crucial problem: Who would speak for Hong Kong? In most cases, of course, it would be the Hong Kong government, just as the British government would speak for Britain and the Chinese government would speak for China. But, as the events of 1981 made clear, in the absence of a representative political system, where the interests of Britain and Hong Kong diverge, the Hong Kong government, headed by the governor, would not always speak for Hong Kong. Similarly, the Legislative Council, dominated by government officials and government appointees, would be susceptible to British government influence. Thus, in speaking of the Britain–China–Hong Kong triangle, it is necessary from time to time to think of Hong Kong as public opinion in Hong Kong rather than as the Hong Kong government. As the Nationality Act incident illustrated, the colonial administration was not a reliable spokesman for Hong Kong.

### Sino-British Negotiations over Hong Kong's Future: 1982–84

Sir Edward Youde's four and a half years of service as governor (1982–86) were highly dramatic: they saw Hong Kong through the traumatic negotiations in Beijing on the territory's future and saw that future defined as a restoration of Chinese control in 1997, with Hong Kong being transformed into a special administrative region. But, sadly, Youde died in office during a visit to Beijing in December 1986.

Hong Kong, as historian Ming K. Chan suggested, "found itself in 1982 on the verge of the most drastic political change in its history."[23] Sir Edward Youde arrived in Hong Kong on May 20, 1982, at a time when "the colony's eyes [were] fixed with some anxiety on 1997."[24] London had already closed its doors to the people of Hong Kong with the 1981 Nationality Act. The Beijing government, apart from making reassurances to investors that they could put their minds at ease, had not made clear their position on Hong Kong. Some hints of things to come, however, had become evident for discerning observers. In 1981 the Chinese National People's Congress drafted provisions for the establishment of a special administrative region, which would enjoy "a high degree of autonomy," in the constitution. According to the *Times*, the Chinese government had even privately asked the British to look at the provision for the establishment of a special administrative region in relation to Hong Kong.[25]

The British and Chinese governments clearly had come to accept that formal discussions on the 1997 issue could not be delayed any further. Beijing leaders were indicating their intention to reclaim the sovereignty of Hong Kong and turn it into a special administrative region. In Governor Youde's inaugural speech he addressed the issue of Hong Kong's future and suggested that the view of the people of Hong Kong would be taken into account. A majority of the Hong Kong population, according to an opinion poll commissioned by the Hong Kong Observers in May and June 1982, favored the continuation of British administration in the colony. The poll was seen as an important document reflecting public feelings in the colony.[26]

High hopes were put on British Prime Minister Margaret Thatcher's visit to China in September 1982 for finding a solution to the 1997 Hong Kong question. Instead of bringing better understanding between Britain and China, however, the first ever visit by an incumbent British prime minister to the People's Republic ushered in a period of intense strain among China, Britain, and Hong Kong. In the aftermath of the Falklands victory, a triumphant Thatcher took a tough stance on the legality of the treaties that ceded Hong Kong and parts of Kowloon to Britain and leased the New Territories and North Kowloon to Britain for ninety-nine years.[27] The British prime minister publicly announced that the treaties —long rejected by Beijing as unequal and invalid—were "valid in international law." The Chinese government took an equally uncompromising stance, insisting that China's sovereignty over Hong Kong was not negotiable.[28]

The so-called phase one of the Sino-British negotiations on Hong Kong's future began shortly after Thatcher's departure from Beijing. With both sides taking tough positions on the question of sovereignty, a deadlock ensued. The phase one talks were therefore merely "talks about talks" on procedural matters. It was only when the British side softened its position on the question of sovereignty that phase two talks on substantive matters began in July 1983. These talks proceeded amid a degree of secrecy and received widespread publicity internationally; the people of Hong Kong watched from the sidelines with great anxiety and frustration.[29]

After seven rounds of negotiations, the British government conceded in early 1984 that the continuation of British administration in Hong Kong beyond 1997 would not be possible. The remaining question therefore became the manner and conditions of the transfer of sovereignty. Sir Percy Cradock, a former British ambassador to China and the leader of the Hong Kong policy team in the Foreign Office, later suggested that the talks were "appallingly difficult," saying that the British had very few cards in the negotiations.[30]

The initialing of the Sino-British Joint Declaration on September 26, 1984, formally sealed the fate of the British colony. The two governments agreed that on July 1, 1997, China would resume sovereignty over Hong Kong. The territory would become a Special Administrative Region and the existing economic and political system in Hong Kong would remain unchanged for at least fifty more years under the formula of "one country, two systems."[31] In an analysis of the negotiations, Jaw-ling Joanne Chang described the outcome as "China's Hong Kong victory."[32]

As the British and Chinese negotiators searched for common ground and mutual understanding on the Hong Kong problem, the two governments turned their attention to the broader question of future Sino-British relations. In the search for a settlement for Hong Kong's future, Beijing and London were also "more subtly, laying the foundations for their own future relationship."[33] In fact, it was only in 1986, after the Joint Declaration obtained Chinese sanction for the British administration in the colony up to 1997, that the queen was able to pay her first visit to China, followed by a short stay in Hong Kong.

After almost a decade of developing closer relations with the United States, Beijing decided in 1982 that it was time for China to project a more independent and neutral image. The threat posed by the Soviet Union had declined considerably, and Chinese leaders were feeling uncomfortable about China's international image because of its association with Washington. Beijing had therefore already began to readjust China's foreign policy in 1982, but at the same time the Chinese leaders were also keen to see that the policy adjustments would not affect China's economic relations with the West, which were vital to Beijing's modernization effort. Improving relations with Britain, a key member in the European Community, would help China to project a more independent image and at the same time serve the purpose of maintaining close links with the West.[34]

For Britain, improving relations with China would meet general British interests in the Asia-Pacific region. Direct British political and strategic interests in the region had ceased to be significant in British foreign policy since the 1970s, but during much of the early and mid-1980s the Soviet Union was still perceived as a major threat to international security in East Asia by the West. The British government therefore shared the broader Western concern for the convergence of Chinese and Western strategic interests in the region. Another factor in British thinking about China was the economic dynamism of East Asia. Under the Thatcher government, driven by new economic policies and developments in international economic relations, Britain "returned" to Asia and the Pacific. Japan and the East Asian newly industrializing economies—South Korea, Taiwan, Singapore, and Hong Kong—were clearly key components in the economic vitality of the region, but China was also becoming increasingly important as an economic player after the initiation of Deng's new economic policies. A better Sino-British relationship would help British economic activities in East Asia in general and in China in particular. Maintaining friendly relations with China would also help British businesses to continue their links with Hong Kong after 1997.[35]

The Hong Kong people were largely denied a direct role in the negotiations about their future. Both the British and Chinese governments did attempt to influence public opinion in Hong Kong during the negotiations, however.[36] Lord Belstead's remark about the three-legged stool was seen as one such attempt. The Hong Kong government launched a campaign to solicit public opinion and tried to galvanize support from the existing political machinery of representation in the colony such as the district boards, and the Executive and Legislative Councils.

The Chinese government, while rejecting a formal role for Hong Kong in the negotiations, clearly attempted to cultivate public support for its position. It enlarged Hong Kong's political representation to the national and provincial level by appointing more Hong Kong and Macau delegates to the Chinese People's Political Consultative Conference, the Guangdong Provincial People's Congress, and the National People's Congress. Prominent businessmen in Hong Kong not traditionally associated with pro-Beijing groups were also invited by

Beijing to consult on Hong Kong's future. The Chinese government made extensive efforts to reassure different sectors of the Hong Kong public about China's intentions. Between November 1982 and September 1984, more than thirty-three delegations from Hong Kong were invited by Beijing to visit China; many of them were received by top-level leaders.

During the protracted negotiations on Hong Kong's future, the three-legged stool was most unstable, as two of the three legs, Britain and China, were at loggerheads. The third leg, Hong Kong's public, was suspicious of both China and Britain and at the same time was experiencing a keen sense of its own importance. The 1984 Joint Declaration simultaneously reaffirmed the importance of the three-legged stool before 1997 and changed its configuration in the long run, as the British leg was doomed to wither away.

Whereas the British role was predominant during much of the MacLehose era, the Joint Declaration provided for the gradual reduction of that role and it stipulated an enlarged role for Hong Kong. China, too, would become more visible and increasingly influential, since it would serve with Britain in such bodies as the Joint Liaison Group and the Land Commission in the years leading up to 1997. When the Joint Declaration was ratified by the British Parliament and the Chinese National People's Congress after having been found "acceptable" by the people of Hong Kong, the three-legged stool appeared to have regained its former firmness for the time being, but its life span was clearly limited.[37]

## Britain, China, and Hong Kong's Limited Democratization, 1984–86

For more than two decades after the abortive 1947 Young plan for constitutional reform, the British government made no further effort to introduce democratic political reform to Hong Kong.[38] Limited reforms were initiated by the MacLehose government. In May 1972 the government appointed the McKinsey consultants to review comprehensively the civil service system. The changes proposed by the McKinsey report, though not resulting in a dramatically different administration, at least represented an attempt by the MacLehose government to initiate changes to the civil service to meet new commitments to provide more public and social services.[39] The launching of the Community Plan in the early 1970s again represented the MacLehose administration's effort to broaden participation in public affairs.[40]

All these reforms, however, were limited, and the broadening of political participation was conducted primarily at the local level, with little direct influence on the central policy-making process. In the end, no proper democratic reforms were introduced during the MacLehose years despite the colony's spectacular economic performance in the 1970s and growing public pressure for participation in public affairs. The people of Hong Kong had to wait until the Youde years before the Hong Kong government took the issue of democratic reform more seriously.

One of the main provisions in the Joint Declaration was that Hong Kong was to be run by the people of Hong Kong after 1997. The Joint Declaration also promised that "the legislature of the Hong Kong Special Administrative Region shall be constituted by elections. The executive authorities shall abide by the law and shall be accountable to the legislature."[41] This provision suggested a democratic political system for Hong Kong, something the colony had never enjoyed during its more than 140 years as a British colony.

The British and Hong Kong governments began in 1984 to build up a system of representative government. It was the understanding of the British and Hong Kong governments, as well as of Parliament and the Hong Kong people, that such a system of representative government would be necessary for the implementation of the Joint Declaration. The British foreign secretary, Sir Geoffrey Howe, in announcing in April 1984 that the British administration was to end in 1997, also made clear Britain's commitment to the evolution of a more representative form of government for Hong Kong. The proposed political reforms took the form of a number of green and white papers on representative government. The green paper was released in July 1984, as the Sino-British negotiations on the future of Hong Kong were drawing to a close. Two months later, the Joint Declaration was initiated, and, two months after that, in November, a white paper on the further development of representative government was issued, reiterating the objective of setting up a system of government that would represent authoritatively the views of the people of Hong Kong.[42]

The green paper, *Further Development of Representative Government*, proposed "to develop progressively a system of government the authority for which is firmly rooted in Hong Kong, which is able to represent authoritatively the views of the people of Hong Kong, and which is more directly accountable to the people of Hong Kong." The green paper, therefore, made concrete proposals on making the government's central institutions more representative.[43] The publication of the white paper provided for enlarging the Legislative Council, introducing indirectly elected members to the council in 1985, and made positive suggestions about direct elections for a number of Legislative Council seats in 1988. The white paper reported: "With few exceptions the bulk of the public response from all sources suggested a cautious approach with a gradual start by introducing a very small number of directly elected members in 1988 and building up to a significant number of directly elected members by 1997."[44]

There were skeptics who questioned the government's sincerity. John Walden, a retired civil servant turned critic, called the democratization process "the grand illusion," a "Trojan Horse" to appease the people of Hong Kong, maintaining that the reforms amounted to little more than cosmetic democracy. He suggested that the purpose of the proposals was to ensure that the British Parliament would endorse the Joint Declaration, but not truly to introduce a democratic system for Hong Kong.[45] The democratization of a colonial system without a democratic tradition in a turbulent period of political transition clearly would not be an easy process. Nevertheless, the Hong Kong government appeared to have accepted that the public desire for building a more representative government could not be ignored.[46]

In the months following the 1984 green and white papers on representative government, China dissociated itself from the reforms by characterizing them as something that had nothing to do with China; Beijing did not say, however, that they were in violation of the Joint Declaration. As the British moved to develop representative government in Hong Kong, China moved to draft a Basic Law to govern the territory from 1997 on.

The Basic Law, under article 31 of China's 1982 constitution, provides the constitutional basis for the establishment of the Hong Kong Special Administrative Region in 1997 for fifty years and the legal principles and policies for the administration of Hong Kong after 1997 in accordance with the Joint Declaration. As Britain sought to involve the people of Hong Kong in running the Hong Kong government, so China appointed 23 people from Hong Kong to serve on the 59-member Basic Law Drafting Committee, set up in June 1985. The Chinese government also set up a 180-member Basic Law Consultative Committee —a Hong Kong based local organization—to collect and consult public opinion. Beijing exercised tight control over the drafting process, however, through "a combination of institutional, procedural, and personnel measures."[47]

At first, China refrained from public criticism of the British-sponsored political reforms, just as Britain stayed out of the Basic Law drafting process, each recognizing the other's prerogatives. In November 1985, however, almost a year after the Joint Declaration was formally signed, the Chinese finally made clear their unhappiness with the political reforms. The publication of the white paper on representative government apparently aroused suspicion on the Chinese side that Hong Kong might develop an independent tendency with a representative government. On November 21, in discussing the political reforms, the director of the Xinhua News Agency and China's chief representative in Hong Kong, Xu Jiatun, made a thinly veiled attack on Britain, accusing it of not abiding by the Joint Declaration. His now famous remarks were: "It is not difficult to detect that somebody has already deviated from the Joint Declaration."[48]

The Chinese position was that political reform in Hong Kong should converge with the Basic Law, the drafting process of which was dominated by Beijing. At first, Britain attempted to prevent China from involvement in the political reforms but ultimately had to yield to Chinese pressure and included the reforms on the agenda of the Joint Liaison Group. After all, if China strenuously opposed the reforms, it was not possible for them to go forward. Britain and Hong Kong by themselves could not keep a three-legged stool upright. By 1986 the Hong Kong government was often being taunted as a "lame duck" administration, having given up the initiative of political reform. The British government accepted that the democratization process had to be slowed down, if not immediately called to a halt.[49]

The years from 1982 to 1986 saw greatly increased political participation in the colony. Five elections at various levels were held, but not direct elections to the Legislative Council. Several political groups also gradually emerged on the scene. While the turnout rate at the elections remained relatively low, the actual number of voters increased significantly. The growing number of political groups also spurred more political activity and greater citizen involvement in the political process.[50] Hong Kong's democratization, however, was restricted by the pressure to converge with the Basic Law.

The last year of the Youde administration witnessed the nuclear disaster at Chernobyl in April 1986. It was followed by widespread apprehension in Hong Kong over the building by China of a nuclear plant at Daya (or Bias) Bay, fifty kilometers from Hong Kong. That development also helped illustrate the workings of the three-legged stool. On this issue the Chinese and the British were of one accord, while public opinion in Hong Kong was strongly opposed. Over a million people signed a petition urging the scrapping of the plans. An opinion poll also revealed strong public disapproval of the project. The Chinese government acknowledged Hong Kong's concern by asserting that extreme care would be exercised and offered assurances that every precaution would be taken. It did not accede to Hong Kong public opinion, however.[51]

The British, for all intents and purposes, cooperated with China. Despite strong Hong Kong opposition, the Daya Bay nuclear power plant proceeded according to plan. The Daya Bay controversy has been compared to the issue of direct elections: both polarized the community, resulted in rapid mobilization of public opinion, involved a decision by the Chinese government that ran counter to public opinion in Hong Kong, and led to public apathy when the people realized that their views were not properly taken into account.[52] By early 1987, local political commentary pointed to the possible de facto tendency of joint Sino-British administration of the territory. Although this view was not universally shared, the perception of Beijing's interference in Hong Kong's political development was clearly widespread.[53]

Political confidence in Hong Kong suffered as a result of the difficulties Hong Kong encountered in the development of representative government and the Daya Bay incident. On both issues, the three-legged stool was no longer standing on three legs; the Hong Kong leg was removed from decisions that affected the people of Hong Kong. Doubts about the colony's political future clearly contributed to increased emigration from Hong Kong to Western destinations, in particular, Canada, the United States, and Australia. A study by Ronald Skeldon on Hong Kong's emigration problem identified the year 1986 as the watershed. According to official estimates, emigration between 1980 and 1986 fluctuated but amounted to about twenty thousand people per year. After 1986, emigration accelerated to a peak of sixty-two thousand in 1990. Hong Kong's emigration, as Skeldon argued, should not be analyzed in simplistic terms; there were nonpolitical factors causing the "brain drain," and definite conclusions could hardly be drawn about the impact of the emigration on Hong Kong's future because of the many unknowns.[54] Nevertheless, the accelerating rate of emigration since 1986 could arguably be regarded as a case of "voting by feet," and the perceived problems created by the brain drain clearly had a major impact on the stability of Hong Kong.

In early December 1986, during a visit to Beijing, Governor Youde died in his sleep. He became the only governor in Hong Kong's history to die in office. People in Hong Kong greeted his death with deep grief when it was officially announced in Hong Kong on the morning of December 5. Thousands turned out to mourn the death of the governor who had served Hong Kong for only four and a half years. They were mourning not only the tragic death of their governor but also the passing away of an era.[55]

## The Britain–China–Hong Kong Economic Balance, 1971–86

Hong Kong's growing economic might could be thought to produce corresponding political clout. The fifteen years covered by this chapter constituted one of the most sustained periods of economic growth in Hong Kong's development. This period saw the opening of the cross-harbor tunnel, the inauguration of the Mass Transit Railway system, and the launching of the container terminal at Kwai Chung, which rapidly made Hong Kong the world's third most important container port. It also saw Hong Kong develop into one of the world's major financial centers, playing an increasingly crucial economic role in the region.

However, Hong Kong has not been able to translate its economic might into political muscle as far as its relations with Britain and China are concerned. The territory thrived under the British umbrella, and, since the continuation of that status was in Britain's, not Hong Kong's, hands, the colony could do little but seek the best possible bargain London was willing to offer, since independence was out of the question. In the 1970s, Hong Kong was given the right to manage its monetary reserves as it pleased. Certainly, without its economic success, Hong Kong would be much less of a prize, but even given economic success, Hong Kong's room to maneuver has always been relatively limited. The changing importance of China and Britain as Hong Kong's economic partners during the 1980s caused significant changes in the three parties' relations with each other.

During 1972, the first full year of the MacLehose era, Britain was Hong Kong's second most important market, after the United States, accounting for 14.4 percent.[56] China, meanwhile, constituted Hong Kong's second largest source of imports, after Japan. Thus, both countries played important roles in maintaining Hong Kong's economic well-being.

By the end of the fifteen-year period of the MacLehose–Youde years, the relative importance of Britain and China for Hong Kong had shifted dramatically. By 1986, the last year of the Youde administration, China's importance as the leading supplier for Hong Kong was unchallenged, with China having overtaken Japan five years previously. In terms of Hong Kong's exports, China had moved up from virtual insignificance in 1972 to become the territory's second most important market, topped only by the United States. During that time, Britain's relative importance declined, dropping from second place in 1972 to fourth place in 1986 in terms of Hong Kong's exports, and from fourth to seventh place in terms of Hong Kong's imports.

In the realm of reexports, China soared to the top spot in 1980 and remained there each year throughout the rest of this period.[57] During the fifteen-year period, Britain moved from tenth to eighth place. The reexport trade assumed increasing significance, so that by 1985 it accounted for 44.8 percent of total exports. In percentage terms, Britain's sales to Hong Kong accounted for 6.6 percent of Hong Kong's imports in 1972 and fell steadily to 3.4 percent in 1986. China's sales to Hong Kong soared from an already high 17.7 percent in 1972 to almost 30 percent in 1986.

Similarly, in terms of importance as a market for Hong Kong's products, Britain accounted for 14.4 percent of Hong Kong's exports in 1972 but only took 3.4 percent of Hong Kong's goods in 1986, and declined in importance as a market for Hong Kong reexports, accounting for 2.4 percent in 1972 but for a mere 2 percent in 1986. China, which was not even reckoned among the top ten in 1972, soared to second place in 1986, taking 11.7 percent of Hong Kong's exports and 33.4 percent of Hong Kong's reexports.

In overall terms, Hong Kong's trade with both countries has grown in the fifteen-year period. Britain and China each accounted for about HK$4 billion in Hong Kong trade in 1972. By 1986, Britain's share had grown to almost HK$22 billion. This was dwarfed by China's share, however, which stood at over HK$140 billion in 1986. By 1986, Hong Kong was doing more business with China than with any other country, including the United States. Thus, although Britain's role in Hong Kong's external economic relations by the end of the Youde administration was still substantial, it was diminishing, while China's role has shown sustained phenomenal growth.

The restructuring that took place in Hong Kong's economy in the mid-1980s has fundamentally altered Hong Kong's economic relations with Britain and China. The territory's renewed role as an entrepôt between China and the rest of the world, its extensive investment in China, and the increasing importance of southern China, especially the Pearl River Delta in Guangdong, as the manufacturing base for Hong Kong industrialists, have been clear signs that Hong Kong's economy has been integrating with the Chinese economy despite their different political and economic structures.[58] The implications of the changes in Hong Kong's external economic relations for the Britain–China–Hong Kong triangular relationship are very clear: The China–Hong Kong economic partnership has been strengthened, but, because of this strengthening, Britain's importance to Hong Kong has been further reduced.[59]

## Conclusion: Whither the Three-Legged Stool?

The three-legged stool manifested itself in Hong Kong's development during the MacLehose and Youde years. Both the London and Hong Kong governments exercised great care not to unduly provoke China, and Beijing accepted the British administration in Hong Kong. The people of Hong Kong also appeared to have accepted the continuation of an undemocratic British colonial rule. Toward the end of the Youde years, however, as Britain and China sought consensus on post-1997 arrangements for Hong Kong, the balance of the stool tilted toward the China leg, and it became unsteady.

The triangular Britain–China–Hong Kong relationship, as demonstrated by this study, is of a peculiar kind. In a true triangular relationship, there is constant competition to prevent any two parties from developing ties that are so close that they become inimical to the interests of the third party. Any change in one side of the triangle inevitably affects the two other sides. In the triangular relationship among Hong Kong, Britain, and China, the situation has been different: Hong Kong is not an equal player; it occupies a subordinate position to both Britain and China. Hence, its room to maneuver is much more restricted. Moreover, Hong Kong cannot afford to view either Britain or China as a potential opponent. Thus, Hong Kong has not been able to secure Britain's support by edging closer to China, or to flirt with Britain to entice China's backing. These options simply have not been available.

Hong Kong's dependence on Britain to conduct its external relations has been expressed in this way:

> Because of Hong Kong's status as a dependent territory, the Secretary of State for Foreign and Commonwealth Affairs is constitutionally responsible to the British Parliament for the actions of the Hong Kong government. He and officials of the Foreign and Commonwealth Office, on his behalf, have authority to give directions to the Hong Kong government. In practice, however, such formal directions are rarely issued, and the relationship between London and Hong Kong is essentially one of cooperation. For example, one important task routinely undertaken by the Foreign and Commonwealth Office is to ensure that Hong Kong's interests and views (which are not always identical with those of the United Kingdom) are properly considered within the British government machinery, particularly when new policies are being formulated by other Whitehall departments.[60]

Although Britain has promised to give Hong Kong's interests and views "proper consideration," developments under the MacLehose and Youde governorships showed that when the interests of Britain and its colony collided, British interests, not Hong Kong interests, prevailed. The British Nationality Act of 1981 showed that Hong Kong public opinion did not prevent Britain from acting in what it saw as its own interests.

Britain has not been alone in viewing Hong Kong as an unequal partner; China, too, has always viewed Hong Kong as part of its territory, and, after 1997, Beijing's relationship with Hong Kong will be that of central government to local government. China has never recognized Hong Kong as a diplomatic entity and refers to the present government as "the British authorities in Hong Kong," thus regarding the Hong Kong government as merely an instrument of Britain.[61] Although events in Hong Kong had repercussions in China and in Britain, decisions that affected Anglo-Chinese relations were made not in Hong Kong but in the capitals of those two countries.

Hong Kong's unequal status in relation to both Britain and China was starkly evident during the Sino-British negotiations on Hong Kong's future: Hong Kong was not even represented, though both parties claimed to speak for the people of Hong Kong. The Joint Declaration can be described as the formal enshrining of the three-legged stool concept, since it joined Britain and China in an agreement whose ratification required the acceptance of the people of Hong Kong. As this study has made clear, however, Hong Kong has not been an equal partner in the three-legged stool arrangement. On many occasions it was reduced to a bargaining chip in Britain and China's bilateral maneuvering. The Daya Bay incident certainly showed that Hong Kong public opinion, while constituting one of the three legs, is not sufficient in itself to veto decisions made by China.

Events after the 1984 Joint Declaration increasingly demonstrated the limitations of the three-legged stool as a concept in analyzing postagreement political developments in Hong Kong. The Hong Kong government's plans to introduce a more representative government was derailed by the Beijing government, with the people of Hong Kong again denied the opportunity to express their will. The three legs did not cooperate too well on the democratization of Hong Kong. As pointed out earlier, the political reforms ran into trouble in 1985 because, despite British and Hong Kong support, they encountered severe opposition by China, and Britain accepted the need for the convergence of political reforms in Hong Kong and the Basic Law.

As for the Basic Law, originally it was thought that China would not allow any Hong Kong representation on the drafting committee. The exclusion of Hong Kong participation would have severely shaken the three-legged stool. The inclusion of Hong Kong members and the setting up of an all–Hong Kong Consultative Committee had the effect of making the exercise more legitimate, involving two of the three legs. The third leg, Britain, was content to stay out. Although the Beijing government involved Hong Kong in the deliberations on the Basic Law, it dominated the drafting process, allowing rather limited scope for Hong Kong opinion.

But, just as China can torpedo the political reforms in Hong Kong by claiming that they violate the Joint Declaration, so Britain, too, could wreak havoc if it announced that, in its view, the Basic Law did not properly reflect the Joint Declaration. The active refusal of the British leg to go along with the Basic Law could seriously wobble the stool. In the pre-1997 period, although China, Britain, and Hong Kong are not equal partners, it is still crucial for the territory's political stability that each of the three parties continue to play a positive role. Neglecting the vital interests of any of the three parties will have the effect of seriously endangering the viability of the stool itself.

It is probably safe to say that after 1997, when Hong Kong becomes a Special Administrative Region, its room to maneuver as far as China is concerned is likely to be even more restricted. Britain will no longer play a meaningful part in the political development of the territory. However, this does not necessarily mean that the Beijing government will totally ignore public opinion in Hong Kong. It is by no means impossible that the polarization of Hong Kong politics between the "democrats" and the business conservatives would give rise to a new three-legged stool in post-1997 Hong Kong politics—a dominant leg in the form of the Beijing government and the shorter legs in the form of two major political groupings in Hong Kong. One thing is still far clearer: at the end of the Youde administration, Hong Kong's political system was, as in 1971, still undemocratic, but in 1986 the Britain–China–Hong Kong three-legged stool had lost its balance.

## Notes

1. The question of "decolonization without independence" has been an important theme in scholarly analysis on Hong Kong's political development. See, for example, Siu-kai Lau, "Decolonization without Independence: The Unfinished Political Reforms of the Hong Kong Government." Occasional Papers no. 19. Center for Hong Kong Studies, Institute of Social Studies, Chinese University of Hong Kong. See also Tang, "From Empire Defence to Imperial Retreat: Britain's Postwar China Policy and the Decolonization of Hong Kong." *Modern Asian Studies* (1993-94).

2. John Rear, "One Brand of Politics," in *Hong Kong: The Industrial Colony,* ed. Keith Hopkins (Hong Kong: Oxford University Press, 1971), p. 55.

3. For a discussion of how the Hong Kong colonial regime managed to resolve the legitimacy question and resisted introducing democratic changes to Hong Kong, see Ian Scott, *Political Change and the Crisis of Legitimacy in Hong Kong* (Hong Kong: Oxford University Press, 1989). Lau's conceptualization of Hong Kong politics is in Lau, *Society and Politics in Hong Kong* (Hong Kong: Chinese University Press, 1982), pp. 17–20.

4. Ambrose Yeo-chi King, "The Administrative Absorption of Politics in Hong Kong: Emphasis on the Grassroots Level." *Asian Survey* 15, no. 5 (May 1975).

5. See, for example, Hong Kong Observers, *Pressure Points: A Social Critique by the Hong Kong Observers* (Hong Kong: Summerson Eastern Publishers, 1981).

6. See reports in the *Hong Kong Standard* and the *South China Morning Post*, December 11, 1982.

7. Bray's remark is quoted in Nornan J. Miners, *The Government and Politics of Hong Kong*, 5th ed. (Hong Kong: Oxford University Press, 1991), p. 251, n. 3. Miners's own reference to his work as an extended commentary on Bray's remarks is on p. 8; his explanation of the book's framework is on p. 16.

8. Henry Kissinger, *The White House Years* (London: George Weidenfeld and Nicolson, 1979), pp. 165, 712.

9. For an account of Britain's recognition of the People's Republic and the establishment of chargé d'affaires diplomatic relations in 1954, see James Tang, *Britain's Encounter with Revolutionary China, 1949–54* (London: Macmillan, 1992). Other discussions on the recognition include Richie Ovendale, "Britain, the United States, and the Recognition of Communist China," *Historical Journal*, no. 1 (1983); and D.C. Wolf, "'To Secure a Convenience': Britain Recognizes China—1950," *Journal of Contemporary History* 18, no. 2 (April 1983).

10. F. S. Northedge, *Descent from Power: British Foreign Policy, 1945-73* (London: Allen and Unwin, 1974). See also Phillip Darby, *British Defence Policy East of Suez, 1947–1968* (London: Oxford University Press for the Royal Institute of International Affairs, 1973).

11. For an account of the normalization of Sino-British relations, see Robert Boardman, *Britain and the People's Republic of China, 1949–74* (London: Macmillan, 1976), chap. 8.

12. See the *South China Morning Post*, March 13, 1972.

13. *South China Morning Post*, December 23, 1972.

14. Boardman, *Britain and the People's Republic of China, 1949–74*, p. 146. See also, for example, John Gittings, "Red Carpet for Sir Alec," *Guardian*, October 27, 1972. The question of Hong Kong was entirely ignored in Gittings's analysis of the foreign secretary's to visit China. For more information on Hong Kong's release of prisoners, see Miners, *The Government and Politics of Hong Kong*, p. 213.

15. See *Hong Kong Standard*, April 29, 1976. A summary of the business community's concern about Hong Kong's status as reported by the local Chinese press is in the *Gist*, March 8, 1979.

16. Peter Wesley-Smith, *Unequal Treaty, 1898–1997: Hong Kong's New Territories* (Hong Kong: Oxford University Press, 1980), p. 82.

17. The account of what transpired when MacLehose met Deng was pieced together by Frank Ching from several sources, two of whom were present at the meeting. Also see Wen Wei Po, comp., *Jibenfa de dansheng* (The birth of the basic law) (Hong Kong: Wen Wei Publishing, 1990), p. 58.

18. Xue Monhong and Pei Jianzhang, eds., *Diplomacy of Contemporary China* (Hong Kong: New Horizon Press), p. 464.

19. *South China Morning Post*, April 7, 1979.

20. See *Far Eastern Economic Review*, September 15, 1978; *Beijing Review*, December 29, 1978, 6–16. Two accounts of China's policy changes are: Harry Harding, *China's Second Revolution* (Washington, D.C.:Brookings Institution, 1987); and Robert Kleinberg, *China's Opening to the Outside World* (Boulder, CO:Westview Press, 1990).

21. *South China Morning Post*, January 29, 1981.

22. The British Nationality Act received the royal assent on October 30, 1981, and its main provisions took effect on January 1, 1983.

23. Ming K. Chan, "Democracy Derailed: Realpolitik in the Making of the Hong Kong Basic Law, 1985-90," in Ming K. Chan and David J. Clark, eds., *The Hong Kong Basic Law: Blueprint for "Stability" under Chinese Sovereignty?* (Armonk, NY: M.E. Sharpe, 1991), p. 3.

24. *Times* (London), May 19, 1982.

25. *Times* (London), May 19, 1982.

26. *Far Eastern Economic Review*, August 20, 1992. See also *South China Morning Post*, August 13, 1992, and the editorial in *South China Morning Post* on August 14, 1992.

27. For an account of the treaties, see Wesley-Smith, *Unequal Treaty, 1898–1997*. For a Chinese perspective of the question, see Wang Shuwer, *Xianggang tebie xingzhhenggu*

*jibenfa daolun* (An introduction to the basic law of the Hong Kong special administrative region) (Beijing: Zhonggong zhongyang dangziao chubanshe, 1990), pp. 4–6.

28. See, for example, reports in the *South China Morning Post* and the *Hong Kong Standard*, September 24–28, 1982. For a discussion of the Sino-British negotiations, see Scott, *Political Change and the Crisis of Legitimacy in Hong Kong*, chap. 5.

29. Both the Chinese and British sides committed to keeping the talks confidential, and no arrangements were made for press coverage at first. There was no official press briefing before the first-round talks, and the venue was kept secret, generating intense rumors and speculation in the colony. James T.H. Tang covered the talks in Beijing as a journalist. See reports in the *Hong Kong Standard* and the *South China Morning Post*, July 12–14, 1984.

30. Peter Hennessy, "Cradock's People," *New Society*, October 11, 1984, p. 54.

31. The Joint Declaration of the Government of the People's Republic of China and the Government of the United Kingdom of Great Britain and Northern Ireland on the Question of Hong Kong is in *A Draft Agreement between the Government of the United Kingdom of Great Britain and the People's Republic of China on the Future of Hong Kong* (Hong Kong: Government Printer, September 26, 1984). Discussions on the "One Country, two systems" formula include Kuo-ch'iang Hsing, " 'One Country, Two Systems': Theory and Practice," in Yu-ming Shaw, ed., *Changes and Continuities in Chinese Communism. Vol. 1, Idology, Politics and Foreign Policy* (Boulder, CO: Westview Press, 1988); George Hicks, "Hong Kong After the Sino-British Agreement," in Jurgen Domes and Yu-ming Shaw, eds., *Hong Kong: A Chinese and International Concern* (Boulder, CO: Westview Press, 1988).

32. Jaw-ling Joanne Chang, "China's Hong Kong Victory: A Study of the PRC's Negotiating Style, 1982-1984." Paper prepared for the annual meeting of the Asian Studies Association, San Francisco, March 25-27, 1988.

33. Scott, *Political Change and the Crisis of Legitimacy in Hong Kong*, p. 174.

34. An analysis of the changing international strategic environment from a Chinese perspective is Chen Zhongjing, *Problems in International Strategy,* trans. Du Youliang and Liu Naiyuan (Hong Kong: Man Hai Language Publication, 1990). One account of the changes in China's relations with the United States and the Soviet Union is Harvey W. Nelsen, *Power and Insecurity: Beijing, Moscow, and Washington, 1949-1988* (Boulder CO: Westview Press, 1989). A general work on China's relations with Western Europe is Harish Kapur, *Distant Neighbours: China and Europe* (London: Pinter, 1990).

35. A useful discussion of Western interests in East Asian international security during the 1980s is Robert O'Neill, ed., *East Asia, The West and International Security* (London: Macmillan in association with the International Institute for Strategic Studies, 1987). For discussions of the Thatcher government's interests in East Asia, see Gerald Segal, "Asia and the West," in Peter Byrd, ed., *British Foreign Policy under Thatcher* (New York: St. Martin's Press, 1988), pp. 117–36. A more general discussion of British interest in East Asia is Lord Beloff, "Britain's Route to and from the Far East," in Michael Leifer, ed., *The Balance of Power in East Asia* (London: Macmillan, 1986)

36. Chang, "China's Hong Kong Victory."

37. The agreement had the support of many important commercial and business organizations, and the majority of the population seemed to have acquiesced to the Joint Declaration, but the people of Hong Kong were denied the expression of their views through the ballot box. See Scott, *Political Change and the Crisis of Legitimacy in Hong Kong*, pp. 206–16.

38. For a full account of the abortive Young plan, see Steve Yiu-sang Tsang, *Democracy Shelved: Great Britain, China, and Attempts at Constitutional Reformin Hong Kong, 1945-1952* (Hong Kong: Oxford University Press, 1988). See also Miners, "Plans for

Constitutional Reform in Hong Kong, 1946–52," *China Quarterly,* no. 107 (September 1986).

39. McKinsey and Company Inc., *Strengthening the Machinery of Government: Summary* (Hong Kong, 1972), and *The Machinery of Government: A New Framework for Expanding Services* (Hong Kong, 1973). For an analysis of the impact of the McKinsey reports, see Scott, *Political Change and the Crisis of Legitimacy in Hong Kong*, pp. 133–40.

40. *Annual Departmental Report by the Secretary of Home Affairs* (Hong Kong: Government Printer, 1974).

41. Joint Declaration, annex 1, sect. 1.

42. See Norman Miners, "Moves Towards Representative Government, 1984–1988," in Kathleen Cheek-Milby and Miron Mushkat, eds., *Hong Kong: The Challenges of Transformation* (Hong Kong: Center of Asian Studies, University of Hong Kong, 1989).

43. Hong Kong Government, *Green Paper: The Further Development of Representative Government in Hong Kong* (Hong Kong: Government Printer, July 1984), p. 4.

44. Hong Kong Government, *White Paper: The Further Development of Representative Government in Hong Kong* (Hong Kong: Government Printer, November 1984), p. 8.

45. John Walden, "Towards the Democratization of Hong Kong," in John Walden, ed., *Excellency, Your Gap Is Growing: Six Talks on a Chinese Takeaway* (Hong Kong: All Noble, 1987).

46. For an analysis of some of the problems for political reforms in Hong Kong, see Lau, "Decolonization without Independence."

47. Ming K. Chan and David J. Clark, *The Hong Kong Basic Law*, p. 9. Other discussions on the drafting process of the Basic Law and its implications for Hong Kong's political development include Michael C. Davis, *Constitutional Confrontation in Hong Kong: Issues and Implications of the Basic Law* (London: Macmillan, 1989); Peter Wesley-Smith and Albert Chen, eds., *The Basic Law and Hong Kong's Future* (Hong Kong: Butterworths, 1988). An account from a more pro-Beijing perspective can be found in Wen Wei Po, *Jibenfa de dansheng* (The birth of basic law). See also Wang, *Xianggang tebie xingzhhenggu jiberfa daolun.*

48. See, for example, *Hong Kong Standard*, November 10 and 22, 1985.

49. For discussions of the developments in this period, see Joseph Y.S. Cheng, "Hong Kong: The Pressure to Converge," *International Affairs* 63 (Spring 1987) and "Hong Kong: The Decline of Political Expectations and Confidence, " *Australian Journal of Chinese Affairs,* no. 19/20 (1988). See also James Cotton, "Hong Kong: Convergence or Divergence?" *Journal of Northeast Asian Studies* 6, no. 4 (Winter 1987).

50. See Shiu-hing Lo, "Decolonization and Political Development in Hong Kong: Citizen Participation," *Asian Survey* 28, no. 6 (June 1988).

51. See Herbert Yee and Yiu-chung Wong, "Hong Kong: The Politics of the Daya Bay Nuclear Plant Debate," *International Affairs* 63, no. 4 (Autumn 1987).

52. Scott, *Political Change and the Crisis of Legitimacy in Hong Kong*, p. 309.

53. See, for example, Tairan Wu, " 'Zhongying gongguang' de qushi" (The tendency toward "Sino-British joint administration"), *Jiushi Niandai* (The Nineties), August 1987, pp. 24–26.

54. Ronald Skeldon, "Emigration and the Future of Hong Kong," *Pacific Affairs* 63, no. 4 (Winter 1990-91). See also Charles R. Emmons, *Hong Kong Prepares for 1997: Politics and Emigration in 1987* (Hong Kong: Center of Asian Studies, University of Hong Kong, 1991).

55. See, for example, Denis Bray's reflections on the governor's death, *Hong Kong Standard*, December 12, 1992.

56. Trade figures are culled from Hong Kong annual reports for the relevant years.

57. See also Hong Kong Trade Development Council, *Survey on Hong Kong Re-ex-*

*ports: Summary Report* (Hong Kong, 1988).

58. One assessment of Hong Kong's economic prospects in the aftermath of the Sino-British agreement on Hong Kong's future is Y.C. Jao, "Hong Kong's Economic Prospects after the Sino-British Agreement: A Preliminary Assessment," in Hungdah Chiu, J.C. Jao, and Yuan-li Wu, eds., *The Future of Hong Kong: Towards 1997 and Beyond* (Westport, CT: Greenwood Press, 1987).

59. A.J. Youngson, *China and Hong Kong: The Economic Nexus* (Hong Kong: Oxford University Press, 1983). See also Yun-wing Sung, *The China–Hong Kong Connection: The Key to China's Open Door Policy.* (Cambridge: Cambridge University Press, 1991).

60. Government Information Services, *Hong Kong Annual Report, 1985,* p. 69.

61. For example, during the Cultural Revolution, when Chinese journalists in Hong Kong were arrested, China retaliated by putting the Reuters correspondent Anthony Grey under house arrest for two years.

# 4

# Judicial Development of Hong Kong on the Eve of 1 July 1997

*Berry F. Hsu*

In May 1984, a delegation of Chinese members of the Executive and Legislative Councils of Hong Kong expressed their concern in London about the continuation of the economic, political, and social systems in Hong Kong after 30 June 1997.[1] Their concerns included the commitment of the Beijing government to the political philosophy of communism.[2] Although their concern is well grounded, the question remains to what extent the delegation represented the Chinese population of Hong Kong, as none held an elected office. Throughout the Sino-British negotiations on the future of Hong Kong, the Beijing government took the view that no British officials nor their appointees represented the interests of the Chinese population of Hong Kong.[3] One of the items agreed on, however, is that the Common Law judicial system should be maintained in Hong Kong after 30 June 1997. This may be for commercial reasons as much as anything else.[4]

One of our previous studies clearly indicates a consensus in the opinion of the Chinese population of Hong Kong that the Common Law judicial system is acceptable (Table 4.1). An overwhelming majority of the Chinese population of Hong Kong believe that the Common Law judicial system should be retained in Hong Kong after 30 June 1997.[5] This support is necessary for the future success of the Common Law in Hong Kong. The judicial development of Hong Kong prior to 1 July 1997 is vital to the successful maintenance of the Common Law judicial system. Another important factor is the implementation of the 1984 Sino-British Joint Declaration,[6] which includes the enactment of the Basic Law

---

The original version of this chapter appeared in *The Common Law System in Chinese Context: Hong Kong in Transition*, by Berry Fong-Chung Hsu (Armonk, NY: M.E. Sharpe, 1992).

Table 4.1

**Common Law Indexes across Population Groups**

| Concepts | Chinese population | Legal profession | English population |
|---|---|---|---|
| Individual and Legal Rights | 72.44 | 92.02 | 80.47 |
| Rule of Law | 59.89 | 74.55 | 78.76 |
| Judicial Independence | 32.17 | 83.76 | 40.39 |
| Adversarial System and an Independent Legal Profession | 77.17 | 82.01 | 87.47 |
| Jury System | 73.45 | 70.58 | 73.14 |
| Presumption of Innocence | 53.37 | 77.64 | 62.36 |
| Common Law Indexes | 61.42 | 80.09 | 70.43 |

of Hong Kong by China.[7] This very much depends on the modernization within China prior to and after 1997.

Since the signing of the Joint Declaration, the authority of the British administration in Hong Kong has been diminishing and has the image of a "lame duck" government.[8] On 21 November 1985, the Beijing government expressed its concern over the Westminster government's tendency to deviate from the Joint Declaration, and stated that the future political system of Hong Kong was an internal affair of China.[9] Since then, in October 1987, Sir David Wilson, governor of Hong Kong, stated that the Basic Law[10] will "influence the evolution of our own systems before 1997."[11] Consequently, the British administration in Hong Kong has shown signs of increasing insecurity and low morale amid criticism by a few outspoken members of the Legislative Council.[12] This sense of insecurity, compounded by the quality of the civil service, can be demonstrated by the request made by the Chief Secretary, Mrs. Anson Chan, to the Chief Justice, Sir Ti-liang Yang, for his opinion on the Hong Kong Bill of Rights Ordinace.[13]

In spite of the setbacks, the British administration has attempted to establish an independent political system in Hong Kong that can resist Beijing's influence. But the judicial development of Hong Kong clearly depends on the Basic Law of Hong Kong.

## The Sino-British Joint Declaration and the Basic Law of Hong Kong

### *The Joint Declaration*

On 1 July 1997 when the Beijing government takes over Hong Kong under the Joint Declaration, it will cease to be a British Crown colony.[14] Accordingly, the application of Common Law in Hong Kong will lapse by operation of law, as the Royal prerogatives and acts of the British parliament will lose force in Hong Kong. The Joint Declaration was ratified by the Standing Committee of the National People's Congress for Beijing.[15] The implementation of the Joint Declaration on the Hong Kong Special Administrative Region will be carried out by the Basic Law of Hong Kong.[16] Therefore, the operation of the Basic Law will decide the fate of the Common Law system in Hong Kong after 30 June 1997.

Although the People's Republic of China is not a party to the 1969 Vienna Convention on the Law of Treaties, there are ample authorities to suggest that the Joint Declaration is a valid international treaty made under customary international law regardless of its designation.[17] Both British and Chinese representatives stated that it constitutes an international agreement.[18]

It is a cardinal doctrine at Common Law that an international treaty must be given legislative effect if it is to be enforced as law by English courts.[19] Like the constitutional practice in Great Britain, the Chinese constitution does not give any "self-executing" authority to international agreement. The internal application of treaties in mainland China is provided from time to time by "cover-all" legislation (e.g., Article 189, Law of Civil Procedure, 1982, and Article 16, paragraph 2, Law on Income Tax of Enterprises of Joint Venture, 1980). The Joint Declaration expressly provides that the basic policies as stated therein shall be stipulated in a Basic Law of Hong Kong that shall be enacted "in accordance with" the Chinese constitution.[20] The Joint Declaration, therefore, gives the Beijing government wide discretion in enacting the Basic Law of Hong Kong as any sovereign state has the exclusive power to interpret its constitution.

The Beijing government took the view that the drafting of the Basic Law is part of China's sovereign powers.[21] It has stated that the matter of Hong Kong is a domestic Chinese affair and no country or international organization can interfere after 30 June 1997.[22] It is also a long-standing view of the Taipei government that the question of Hong Kong is a domestic Chinese issue.[23] No Chinese government or regime will hurt the pride of its citizens by conceding that the issue of Hong Kong is an international affair. Accordingly, there are major doubts whether the Beijing government regards the Joint Declaration as an international agreement. There is little doubt that if the Westminster government were to raise breaches of the Joint Declaration after 30 June 1997 in an international forum, the Beijing government would deny that it was an international agreement and say that it was not a matter for international discussion. International law has no force within the jurisdiction of any sovereign state without that state's consent. As the Basic Law is a statute enacted by Beijing under Article 31 of the Constitution of the People's Republic of China, 1982,[24] its interpretation will inevitably be carried out in accordance with the legal practice of the Chinese Communist party. Therefore, any international adjudication over the violation of the Joint Declaration is seemingly unrealistic.

## *The Basic Law of Hong Kong under the Chinese Constitution*

Beijing's only legislative obligation under the Joint Declaration is to enact and promulgate a Basic Law of Hong Kong "in accordance with the Constitution of the People's Republic of China" stipulating that Hong Kong's previous capitalist system and life-style, including the laws in force, shall remain unchanged for fifty years and also stipulating other basic policies of the People's Republic of China regarding Hong Kong as provided thereunder.[25] Article 5 of the Chinese constitution provides inter alia that "no law or administrative rules and regulations shall contravene the constitution," and nothing in the constitution indicates that this article can be exempted or suspended.[26] Articles 31 and 62(13) of the same constitution under which the Hong Kong Special Administrative Region is created is rather vague.[27] Nevertheless, it is clear and unambiguous that this article and any statute enacted in mainland China, including the Basic Law, are subject to the rest of the constitution by virtue of Article 5.[28]

The laws in the Hong Kong Special Administrative Region cannot contravene the Basic Law,[29] and the Basic Law cannot contravene the Chinese constitution.[30] Therefore, in case of conflict between the Common Law judicial system in the Hong Kong Special Administrative Region and the Chinese constitution, the latter prevails. The National People's Congress can always amend the Basic Law or enact a statute to be applied in the Hong Kong Special Administrative Region.[31]

## *Common Law under the Socialist Legal System*

The socialist legal system, to which the Common Law judicial system in Hong Kong will be subservient after 30 June 1997,[32] adheres to the leadership of the Communist party, the guidance of Marxism-Leninism, and the thought of Mao Zedong, the people's democratic dictatorship, and the socialist road.[33] Accordingly, the dominant legal system should reflect the state's ideology of class struggle between the thesis, represented by the people, which gives rise to the antithesis, represented by the enemy of the people,[34] under the Marxist doctrine of dialectical materialism.[35] According to Marxist jurists, law serves class interest.[36] As such, the Common Law judicial system in Hong Kong serves the interest of capitalists. The practical value of the supremacy of the Chinese constitution over Hong Kong has been queried by some legal scholars in mainland China,[37] but no solution has been suggested. There does not seem to be any unless the present Chinese constitution is amended or interpreted unconventionally by the National People's Congress.[38] In resolving any conflict of law between the Hong Kong Special Administrative Region and mainland China, it appears that the paramount consideration is the supremacy of Chinese sovereignty.[39] Article 2 of the present Chinese constitution provides that "[a]ll power in the People's Republic of China belongs to the people." The question is how will the minority interest of the capitalists be allowed to encroach on the socialist sovereignty of mainland China? The Common Law judicial system is a product of a capitalist society, and its doctrine of precedent is flexible and adaptable to the changing needs of such society.[40] On the other hand, the socialist legal system in mainland China is dogmatic and ideological and is linked to its socialist economy. Its preliminary objective is to serve the interest of the Communist party.[41] In view of the differences between the Common Law system and Beijing's socialist judicial system, their coexistence under the same constitution is doubtful.[42]

### *The Legislative Process of the Basic Law of Hong Kong*

It is not an easy task to draft legislation in accordance with a socialist constitution and also maintain the capitalist system and preserve a Common Law judicial system. Needless to say, China has a vested interest in Hong Kong's success. As a center of trade and commerce, it is vital that the capitalist system shall be maintained in Hong Kong. The Joint Declaration itself is not only a compromise between the Beijing and Westminster governments, it is also a compromise among different factions within China itself. China's paramount leader, Deng Xiaoping, must contend with the Communist party ideologues who do not share his policy on economic modernization, conservative bureaucrats who do not wish to give up their powers, the rival factions in the Chinese military, and the regional interests in Guangdong Province.[43] Compromising these factional interests is already a major task.

Local business elites control the financial portfolios in Hong Kong and are ready to move capital out if their interests are at risk. Most of them want to maintain their position of influence and power as given them by the British colonial government. This is the group of people that the Beijing government tried to woo.[44] Local intellectuals, small businessmen, civil servants, workers, teachers, professionals, and other groups are the Beijing government's least concern. They can only vote by their feet if they can afford to.

On 28 April 1988, the first draft of the Basic Law of the Hong Kong Special Administrative Region was released by the Beijing government for solicitation of opinions. On 21 February 1989, the Standing Committee of the National People's Congress passed a resolution on the publication of the *Basic Law of the Hong Kong Special Administrative Region of the People's Republic of China (Draft)*. This is the second draft of the the Basic Law for Hong Kong, and the first time it was passed by such a high-level state organ in Beijing.[45] In this draft, certain issues over judicial authority and human rights have been improved.

On 16 February 1990, the third draft of the Basic Law was passed by the Drafting Committee for the Basic Law. The second round of consultation launched in 1989 received little enthusiasm in Hong Kong. Had it not been for the last-minute negotiation between Beijing and Westminster officials on the pace of democratic reform in Hong Kong, the second draft of the Basic Law would have been kept virtually intact by the Drafting Committee.[46] The third draft was passed by the Drafting Committee with twenty-four amendments made to the second draft.[47] On 4 April 1990, the third draft was enacted as the Basic Law of Hong Kong by the National People's Congress.

## Absorption of Common Law Notions by the Basic Law

The Basic Law of Hong Kong carries out the provision in the joint declaration that the "laws currently in force in Hong Kong will remain basically unchanged."[48] Article 8 of the Basic Law provides that "[t]he laws previously in force in Hong Kong, that is, the common law, rules of equity, ordinances, subordinate legislation, and customary law shall be maintained, except for any that contravene this Law, and subject to any amendment by the legislature of the Hong Kong Special Administrative Region."

Article 18 of the Basic Law provides that the law of Hong Kong shall be the Basic Law, those provided by Article 8 of the Basic Law, and the laws enacted by the legislature of the Region. This Article also provides a list of national laws stated in its Annex III to be applied to Hong Kong. Annex III merely concerns matters such as national anthem, territorial sea, nationality, and diplomatic privileges and immunities. Under this Article, however, the Standing Committee "may make additions to or deletions from the list of laws in Annex III." Much will depend on political developments in mainland China.

Under Article 18 of the Basic Law, the Central People's Government "may issue an order applying the relevant national laws in the Region" under certain circumstances. It is not unreasonable for this Article to allow the Central People's Government to adopt certain measures after the Standing Committee declares a state of war or, by reason of turmoil, decides there is a state of emergency in the region. This Article restricts the definition of "turmoil" by applying it to those activities that endanger "national unity or security." It appears that this restriction was intended to dispel the fear of Hong Kong's Chinese population after the 4 June 1989 massacre.

There is no provision in the Joint Declaration that restricts the inclusion of the above terms in the Basic Law. Because the Joint Declaration provides that the laws of the Hong Kong Special Administrative Region shall include the Basic Law,[49] such provisions, if enacted in the Basic Law, can be a source of law in the Hong Kong Special Administrative Region.

It was argued that the Joint Declaration does not allow for any extension of the laws of mainland China to Hong Kong, except in relation to foreign and defense affairs.[50] This argument is untenable because the Joint Declaration merely provides the region with executive, legislative, and independent judicial power,[51] which has never been intended to be exclusive. The "high degree of autonomy" provided by the Joint Declaration[52] means that the "autonomy" is not absolute.[53] Powers are still subservient to the Chinese constitution.[54] This seems to be more a concession intended by the Westminster government than an oversight by the legal officers of the Crown.[55]

This raises concern as to the meaning of "national unity or security." It is broad enough to include any issue that the State Council thinks fit.[56] It should be noted that "national stability and unity" has been invoked by the Beijing government in the condemnation of the January 1987 demonstrations and the anti-government rioting in the Tibet Autonomous Region.[57] The interpretation, however, will more likely be in accord with the prevailing policy of the Chinese Communist party at the time.[58] Beijing's approach to the interpretation of statutes differs fundamentally from the Common Law approach, and the doctrine of *stare decisis*, generally speaking, has not been formally accepted by the socialist legal system in China.[59] Moreover, judicial decisions in any country are inevitably influenced by political ideology.[60]

For the time being, the meanings of "laws previously in force in Hong Kong"[61] and "the judicial system previously practiced in Hong Kong"[62] under the Joint Declaration and the Basic Law of Hong Kong are questionable. Are the customary law and judicial system stated therein intended to be those at the time when the Joint Declaration was signed, when the Basic Law was enacted, or when China takes over Hong Kong on 1 July 1997? This is somewhat similar to the question of what Chinese law and custom should be recognized as the law of Hong Kong, which has been the topic of several cases.[63]

Notwithstanding the above, the Basic Law has entrenched the basic framework essential to the operation of a Common Law judicial system. The six legal concepts used for our Common Law Indexes have essentially been entrenched in the Basic Law. The defects of the present Common Law framework should be addressed, however. Otherwise they may be considered as part of "the laws previously in force in Hong Kong" under the Joint Declaration,[64] and may set an undesirable precedent for the government of the Hong Kong Special Administrative Region to follow.

### *Individual and Legal Rights*

Under the socialist legal system in mainland China, the people's rights cannot be taken for granted as they can only be provided by laws or by the state in order to fulfill the state's ideology of class struggle and a people's democratic dictatorship.[65] Article 27 of the Basic Law provides that "Hong Kong residents shall have freedom of speech, of the press, and of publication; freedom of association, of assembly, of procession, and of demonstration; and the right and freedom to form and join trade unions and to strike." It should be noted that Article 35 of the Chinese constitution has an almost similar provision. How the Common Law courts of the Hong Kong Special Administrative Region will interpret this Article of the Basic Law has yet to be seen.[66] The question still remains how these freedoms are to be interpreted and what they will mean in practice.

Article 39 of the Basic Law provides that the International Covenant on Civil and Political Rights, the International Covenant on Economic, Social, and Cultural Rights, and international labor conventions as applied to Hong Kong shall be implemented through legislation by the region. As such, these covenants and coventions have no constitutional effect. This Article also provides that the restrictions imposed against the rights and freedoms cannot contravene these international covenants and conventions. Therefore, judicial review of legislation that contravenes these covenants and conventions is not impossible. "The rights and freedoms as provided for by the laws previously in force in Hong Kong" in the Joint Declaration[67] are less than impressive in that Hong Kong still has to rely on Common Law for the protection of rights and freedoms.[68] The future development in Hong Kong with regard to the protection of basic rights prior to 1 July 1997 has yet to be seen.

Great Britain is a signatory state to both the above covenants, and they are applicable to Hong Kong subject to certain expressed reservations.[69] The provisions of these two covenants, however, have never been incorporated into the constitutional law of Hong Kong through amendment to the Letters Patent or Royal Instructions, nor until June 1991 had any provisions of these covenants been incorporated as the laws of Hong Kong. They have been observed by convention and, arguably, by domestic reception of customary international law.[70]

The general rule is that subscription to any international covenants is regarded at Common Law as giving rise to a moral, rather than strictly legal, obligation,[71] although the court takes these covenants into account in interpreting a statute as it is presumed that statutes should not conflict with treaties.[72] Only a signatory state to the above covenants, and not an aggrieved individual, can file a complaint of a violation of the covenants to the Human Rights Committee of the United Nations unless the state adopts the protocol on direct application.[73]

Under the auspices of the International Covenant on Civil and Political Rights, a signatory country must make regular reports. During the hearings on 3 and 4 November 1988 concerning the report on Hong Kong, the Human Rights Committee of the United Nations sharply criticized the Westminster government for lack of direct elections in Hong Kong, excessive police powers, restrictions on freedom of the press, and film censorship.[74] It should be noted that after 30 June 1997, there will be no mechanism for continued monitoring of this covenant by the United Nations in Hong Kong as the Beijing government is not a signatory state to this covenant.

The Common Law doctrine of public interest privilege (or Crown privilege) of withholding documents or refusal to answer any questions in judicial proceedings on the ground that disclosure or answer would be injurious to public interest has established undesirable precedents for Hong Kong,[75] although the courts have residual power to inspect documents privately in order to determine whether the interests of the parties to proceedings and unfettered administration of justice should be outweighed.[76] The *ratio decidendi* for public interest privilege is not very clear.[77] Although there are exceptions to the rule, the authority of the Hong Kong government has seldom been challenged in courts.[78] Therefore, the extent of abuse of this privilege in Hong Kong is difficult to measure. The localized Common Law of Hong Kong can clearly set out provisions to protect the interests of the state and the civil liberties of the individual as the public interest privilege will become state privilege.[79]

On 16 March 1990, the Hong Kong government belatedly released the *Commentary on the Draft Hong Kong Bill of Rights Ordinance 1990.*[80] This was enacted by the Legislative Council of Hong Kong on 5 June 1991 with six legislations to be immune from its operation for a year. The Bill of Rights has twenty-three articles, borrowed from the International Covenant on Civil and Political Rights, including inter alia the protection of privacy, family, home, correspondence, honor, and reputation; freedom of opinion and expression; right of peaceful assembly; and freedom of association.[81] The Bill of Rights, however, will not be entrenched into the constitutional law of Hong Kong and is subject to certain reservations as provided by Part III therein. The Letters Patent has been amended on 6 June 1991 to provide that all laws of Hong Kong be subject to the Bill of Rights and that some fifty-eight ordinances be revised to ensure conformity to the Bill. The fundamental flaw is that the Bill of Rights is merely an ordinance enacted by the Legislative Council and the Letters Patent shall cease to operate on 1 July 1997.

The Bill of Rights, however, has met with opposition from certain interested groups that called for special considerations.[82] The Heung Yee Kuk, an organization of landowners and businessmen in the New Territories, went so far as to argue against sexual equality in order to maintain male-line inheritance in the New Territories as stated in traditional Chinese law,[83] notwithstanding that the majority of the people in Hong Kong and the New Territories did not approve the exclusive male succession law.[84] Some worry that the law and order will decline as the power of the police is curbed.[85] Some established members of the legal profession may not be ready for a bill of rights.[86] The Beijing government warned against having a bill of rights with supremacy over other laws in Hong Kong as it would violate the tenets of the Basic Law,[87] and two pro-Beijing legislators voted against a motion that supports the enactment of the Hong Kong Bill of Rights Ordinance.[88] All these concerns seem untenable, as two academic lawyers remarked: "The net result [of having a bill of rights] will be the modernization of the law appropriate to a modern Chinese community in the 1990s and will assist in presenting Hongkong to the world as a credible financial centre."[89]

The existing constitutional documents of Hong Kong do not provide any protection to the Hong Kong citizens from the government in confiscating their property. The present Legislative Council has full power to enact legislation to take away any person's home without any compensation. This is, however, not possible under the Basic Law. Article 6 of the Basic Law provides that the "Hong Kong Special Administrative Region shall protect the right of private ownership of property in accordance with law" and Article 105 of the Basic Law provides that no person can be deprived of their property without fair compensation in accordance to the real value of the property.

### *The Rule of Law*

The Basic Law has specific provisions providing the Common Law doctrines of the Rule of Law. Article 25 of the Basic Law provides that "[a]ll Hong Kong residents shall be equal before the law." Article 28 of the Basic Law provides that no Hong Kong resident shall be subjected to arbitrary or unlawful arrest, detention, imprisonment, or search. Under this Article, torture is expressly prohibited. The Joint Declaration makes provision for judicial review of administrative action in the Region.[90] Article 35 of the Basic Law enables the citizens "to institute legal proceedings in the courts against the acts of the executive authorities and their personnel." It should be noted that Articles 5, 33, and 37 of the Chinese constitution have somewhat similar provisions.

Article 22 of the Bill of Rights provides inter alia "[a]ll persons are equal before the law." Article 3 of the Bill expressly prohibits torture. Articles 5, 6, 10, and 11 of the Bill entrench the Common Law doctrine of the Rule of Law and specify provisions for observing due process of the law. These Articles provide inter alia freedom from arbitrary arrest and detention, equality before the courts and the right to a fair and public hearing, and the right to legal assistance for the accused person in criminal proceedings. All of the above Articles in the Bill will be carried out by Article 39 of the Basic Law.[91] The considerable wide power of arrest provided to the Royal Hong Kong Police under the Police Force Ordinance[92] and the Immigration Ordinance[93] may well be inconsistent with Article 5 of the Bill as being arbitrary power. In the meantime, the Hong Kong government has decided to repeal judicial corporal punishment.[94]

The present Hong Kong government has seldom exercised its power in an arbitrary and authoritarian way, as it has to account to a democratic government and parliament in Great Britain.[95] British constitutional conventions and the Rule of Law are basically practiced in Hong Kong. After 30 June 1997, there is no guarantee that such conventions will be observed, as the government of the region will account to a highly centralized socialist government in China. This government recently massacred its own citizens who rallied for democratic rights in front of the world media.[96] Notwithstanding the above, the Basic Law has provided a schedule for a directly elected legislature in Hong Kong.[97] The developments of a democratic political system, freedom of the press, and the certainty of the law prior to 1 July 1997 would strengthen the framework of the Rule of Law.

*Democracy in Hong Kong*

A democratically elected legislature is an important check and balance for the Rule of Law and for judicial independence. The American experience during the Watergate crisis in the early 1970s has proven the importance of a directly elected congress to ensure the Rule of Law, and an independent judiciary to uphold the privilege of the congress. At present, all Common Law countries that observe the Rule of Law are democratic.[98] This is a rule rather than an exception. In Hong Kong, the problem of the Rule of Law is not a serious issue as the Hong Kong government is accountable to a democratic government in Great Britain. The successful operation of the Joint Declaration on judicial appointment and removal[99] relies on the future of democracy in Hong Kong, as well as the document of the Basic Law of Hong Kong.

In its editorial of May 1987, the *Hong Kong Law Journal* called for "direct elections to the Hong Kong legislature by means of universal adult suffrage."[100] The editor considered that "such elections are an essential element of the Rule of Law, they are consistent with the terms of the Joint Declaration on Hong Kong, and they are an effective means of preserving public order in a free society." The International Commission of Jurists, in its 1965 Declaration of Bangkok, laid down inter alia that "[t]he Rule of Law can only reach its highest expression and fullest realization under representative government."[101]

According to the *White Paper on Democratisation* released on 10 February 1988, the present Hong Kong government has made it clear that there will only be partial democracy.[102] As *The Economist* noted, "it [the white paper] could have been written in Beijing."[103] On a more positive side, our results show that a directly elected local legislature has the support of 80 percent of the Chinese members of the legal profession[104] although the present Legislative Council reserves one seat to be elected by the legal profession. Even the Hong Kong government's survey office reported that 75 percent of the Chinese population favor direct elections.[105] On 26 July 1989, the Executive and Legislative Councils of Hong Kong endorsed a proposal to increase the proposed number of directly elected legislative seats to twenty by 1991.[106]

The meaning of "constituted by elections" under the Joint Declaration[107] and the Basic Law[108] is also subject to different interpretations. Although one can safely assume that the word "elections" mean universal adult suffrage, some groups in Hong Kong have suggested that in preserving the present system direct elections must be ruled out.[109]

Article 68 of the Basic Law provides that "[t]he ultimate aim is the election of all the members of the Legislative Council by universal suffrage." Under Annex II of the Basic Law, however, changes in the election procedures, which include implementing a directly elected Legislative Council, are possible only after 2007. As the third term of the Legislative Council expires on 30 June 2007, a direct election is not possible until 2011.[110] This will materialize only if the bill is passed by a two-thirds vote in the Legislative Council and approved by the chief executive. The flaw is that there is no guarantee of a direct election. It should be noted that Clause 13 of the Bill of Rights ''does not require the establishment of an elected Executive or Legislative Council in Hong Kong.''

Under the Joint Declaration, the chief executive of the region ''shall be selected by election or through consultations held locally and be appointed by the Central People's Government.''[111] This will be carried out by Article 45 of the Basic Law, which also provides that ''[t]he ultimate aim is the selection of the Chief Executive by universal suffrage upon nomination by a broadly representative nominating committee in accordance with democratic procedures.'' Again, there is no guarantee of a direct election.

In the meantime, the conservative business groups in Hong Kong have done their best to please the Beijing government.[112] In alliance with the pro-Beijing labor unions, they lobby against universal suffrage, which they claim would threaten the stability and prosperity of Hong Kong.[113] There is evidence to suggest that the business tycoons in Hong Kong are vying for positions of influence and power, particularly after the chief executive position of the region.[114] Universal suffrage will defeat their intention. Their antidemocracy campaign is well financed.[115] The reality is, however, that one is unlikely to devote all one's time and energy to politics when there is no future in it.[116]

In recent times, the future of Hong Kong's Legislative Council has been the subject of contention. The "through train" for the Legislative Council has met a dead end.[117] China alleges that this is because 1994–95 reforms to the electoral system and thus the Legislative Council composition are inconsistent with the spirit of the Basic Law. For this reason, the present legislature will be dismantled on 1 July 1997. The formation of the new legislature will be the task of the Preparatory Committee, to be set up in January 1996.

### *Freedom of the Press*

Freedom of the press is a powerful check in support of the Rule of Law. The press can protect the public by exposing the authority's abuses of power and thus enhancing public awareness of the Rule of Law. An independent press is essential for the judicial development of Hong Kong, and should be well established prior to 1 July 1997. Presently, there are limits to freedom of the press in Hong Kong. An example is the Royal Hong Kong Police's suppression of a news report criticizing their fairness.[118] This type of action is counterproductive to future judicial development in Hong Kong.

Additional doubts concerning the observance of the Rule of Law by the present Hong Kong government arose when the attorney general refused to grant leave to prosecute a pro-Beijing magazine that had obviously violated the then enforceable Section 27 of the Public Order Ordinance[119] only a few months after the above action of the Royal Hong Kong Police.[120] There is mounting concern arising from contrasting governmental reactions to wrongdoings by politically influential groups and the government's approach to illegal conduct by others. This double standard does not produce positive attitudes toward the Common Law judicial system by the Chinese population of Hong Kong. It is therefore undesirable for this type of selective application of the law to recur, although pressure from the Beijing government is understandable.[121]

### *The Certainty of the Law*

The doctrine of *stare decisis*, which is essential to the notion of Common Law, has historical roots at Common Law.[122] Most of the Common Law doctrines were developed when the judiciary was small in number and homogeneous in thought.[123] As a result, the Common Law doctrines from England were not necessarily sufficient for the new colonies' different cultural circumstances. In the United States, the doctrines underwent separate judicial development.[124] After 30 June 1997, Hong Kong will undergo its own separate judicial development. A codified criminal law in Hong Kong is conducive to the certainty of the law and will reduce the reliance on case law.[125]

In Canada, a Common Law country, the criminal law was codified in 1892 under the Criminal Code, and the code provides that no person shall be convicted of an offense outside the code with the exception of provincial statutes.[126] Therefore, it is desirable to have all laws in Hong Kong codified prior to 1 July 1997 with criminal law as a priority.[127] Codification assures a citizen of knowing what he may or may not do and is regarded to be the idea behind the Bill of Rights.[128]

In a lecture delivered at the School of Oriental and African Studies, London, on 28 May 1986, Mr. Michael Thomas, then attorney general of Hong Kong, claimed that codification of the entire law of Hong Kong would be impossible to undertake.[129] He admitted, however, that "criminal offenses must be defined precisely."[130] There is evidence that Hong Kong intends to follow the Canadian model on criminal liability[131] and to consider the successful codifications of laws in other Common Law countries.[132] The Hong Kong government is considering codification of decisions and principles on the law of arrest.[133] The Law Reform Commission of Hong Kong is presently considering codifying the criminal law and a report on the matter is expected to be forthcoming at the end of 1990.[134] Such tasks are a step in the right direction. The present Hong Kong government may consider establishing a commission to study the feasibility of codifying all the laws of Hong Kong.

The localized Common Law can fill in the gaps as to what has been absent in Hong Kong in order to prove its effectiveness. Some of the archaic features of Common Law, which tolerate the abuse of police power, can be expressly excluded by the localized Common Law of Hong Kong. For example, illegally obtained evidence is admissible at Common Law.[135] Most Common Law countries, e.g., the United States, have abandoned such practices,[136] and, to a degree, Great Britain has followed this path.[137]

Both the present Laws of Hong Kong and the Basic Law of Hong Kong should incorporate provisions against retroactive legislation. Otherwise the Rule of Law cannot operate as the law is uncertain. The War Damage Act of 1965 was passed by the British Parliament to reverse a judicial decision of the House of Lords with retroactive effects for a civil case.[138] Had there been a written constitution in Great Britain guaranteeing the existence of certain rights, the reversal of judicial decisions by legislative process would have had to pass a judicial review. Article 12 of the Bill of Rights provides that there shall be no retrospective criminal offenses or penalties. This will also be carried out by Article 39 of the Basic Law. This is a step in the right direction.

### *Judicial Independence*

Article 85 of the Basic Law provides that ''[t]he courts of the Hong Kong Special Administrative Region shall exercise judicial power independently, free from any interference'' and that ''[m]embers of the judiciary shall be immune from legal action in the performance of their judicial functions.''

#### *Judicial Appointment and Removal*

The present system of government in Hong Kong is archaic by Western standards.[139] In keeping with the spirit of the Common Law, however, judicial independence has been preserved to a certain extent.[140] Under the Judicial Service Commission Ordinance,[141] although there is a consultative process, there is no independent body that can ultimately decide on judicial appointments. The presence of the attorney general on this commission was criticized as being inconsistent with the concept of judicial independence.[142] The majority of the magistrates are employed on ''contract terms'' as civil servants.[143] As there is a lack of tenure for most magistrates, their independence is observed only by convention. Prior to 1 July 1997, it is unlikely that this convention would be severely breached, as Hong Kong is under the direct control of a democratic government in Great Britain.[144] In the meantime, the present Hong Kong government is considering changes in legislation so that judicial officers would no longer be subject to civil service regulations.[145]

The Joint Declaration makes provisions for an independent commission for judicial appointments and the chief executive of the region will be bound to act in accordance with the commission's recommendations.[146] Article 88 of the Basic Law carries out this provision of the Joint Declaration for appointing judges of the region. The Common Law practice for the removal of judges is provided under the Joint Declaration,[147] and this is implemented by Article 89 of the Basic Law.

Article 92 of the Basic Law makes a distinction between ''[j]udges and other members of the judiciary.'' Under the present legal system in Hong Kong, magistrates are not considered as judges.[148] Therefore, the Basic Law does not provide full judicial independence for the magistrates.[149] Article 91 retains the present system for their appointments, which contravenes the principle of judicial independence. In practice, appeals from magistrates' courts are expensive and rare. The decisions of the magistrates are often conclusive. Therefore, their independence is necessary.

Article 10 of the Bill of Rights provides inter alia that "everyone shall be entitled to a fair and public hearing by a competent, independent, and impartial tribunal established by law." It may be argued that as the magistrates cannot be said to be independent by reason of their appointments, this Article is violated. The present Hong Kong government will then have to enact an ordinance to ensure their independence and reconsider Section 5 of the Magistrates Ordinance.[150]

As more than 95 percent of criminal cases are tried by magistrates,[151] the impartiality of the majority of judicial decisions is at least open to question, if not openly doubted. This is reflected in the opinion of 60 percent of the Chinese members of the legal profession.[152] Although there is a perception of judicial partiality, the judiciary as a whole is conceived to be independent.[153] As in any jurisdiction, administrative interference with the judiciary is not unknown in contemporary Hong Kong.[154] It is the responsibility of the present Hong Kong government, however, to ensure full impartiality of the judiciary. The burden placed on the present Hong Kong government is great as the level of acceptance of the concept of judicial independence by the Chinese population of Hong Kong is rather low.[155]

### *Separation of Powers*

The doctrine of separation of powers has been rejected by Marxist jurists in mainland China. They view judicial independence as an outcome of the victory in the power struggle between capitalists and feudal rulers, and as capitalist machinery to adjust the distribution of benefits so that the working class can be more effectively subdued.[156] Although Article 126 of the Chinese constitution provides for judicial independence, Article 128 of the same constitution requires the Supreme People's Court to be responsible to the National People's Congress and its Standing Committee.

The Standing Committee of the National People's Congress,[157] not the judiciary, has the constitutional authority to interpret the constitution and statutes of the People's Republic of China,[158] including the Basic Law of Hong Kong. The National People's Congress can in turn alter or annul decisions of its Standing Committee.[159] Therefore, the power of final judgment vested in the Court of Final Appeal of the region can only be qualified. This alone immediately raises the issue of conflict of laws in which the socialist legal system in China will be dominant over the Common Law judicial system in Hong Kong.

The Standing Committee can declare a statute enacted by the National People's Congress to be unconstitutional, but the National People's Congress, in its judicial capacity, can reverse the decision of its Standing Committee by the same simple majority vote used to enact a statute.[160] There is always the possibility, however, that the Standing Committee will consider that none of the Basic Law provisions are unconstitutional.[161]

It was suggested that the constitutionality of laws passed by the legislature of the Hong Kong Special Administrative Region should be adjudicated conclusively by the Court of Final Appeal of the Region[162] in accordance with the Common Law tradition as provided by the Joint Declaration.[163] This would require constitutional changes in the People's Republic of China.[164] There is no provision in the Joint Declaration that requires Peking to amend its constitution to preserve the Common Law judicial system in Hong Kong, but rather that the Basic Law shall be enacted in accordance with its constitution.[165] Accordingly, the authority of the Standing Committee over the courts of the Hong Kong Special Administrative Region was intended by the Joint Declaration.[166] This major constitutional issue may well have been overlooked by the legal officers of the Crown.

It was suggested that some sort of constitutional court or arbitral tribunal can be set up in the region with British and Chinese judges to decide the questions arising from the Joint Declaration.[167] Such a suggestion is out of touch with the reality that no Chinese government or regime would hurt its citizens' pride by such an arrangement nor would they attract criticism from nationalists regardless of political belief. A better solution was proposed by Jill Barrett at a SOAS seminar:

> The danger of conflict could be greatly reduced if the Standing Committee were to delegate its power to interpret the *Basic Law* (except those provisions relating to defense and foreign affairs) to the Court of Final Appeal in Hong Kong. . . . A national judicial or mediation body capable of resolving such disputes [i.e., those on foreign or defense concerns of the central government] is crucial. It must be truly national. . . . and it must enjoy the confidence of both sides.[168]

Article 158 of the Basic Law appears to have resolved the technicality involving the jurisdiction of the Court of Final Appeal in the region. This article provides a mechanism whereby the Standing Committee "shall authorize the courts of the Hong Kong Special Administrative Region to interpret on their own, in adjudicating cases, the provisions of the Law which are within the limits of the autonomy of the Region." The power of the Standing Committee, however, is limited. Under Article 62(11) of the Chinese constitution, all decisions of the Standing Committee that are inappropriate can be altered or annulled by the National People's Congress. The National People's Congress will more likely take political considerations into account in exercising its "legislative interpretation" power, and the outcome will very much depend on political developments. The question is how willing Beijing officials will be to accept the exclusive role of the courts in interpreting laws and regulations.[169]

Article 158 of the Basic Law provides that the Standing Committee has the statutory authority to interpret it. The Standing Committee can interpret a provision of the Basic Law at any time, which will bind the courts of the Hong Kong Special Administrative Region but will not affect judgment already rendered. The courts of the region can only interpret the Basic Law "in adjudicating cases" before it. This allows possible intervention by the Standing Committee in any judicial process as the courts of the region are bound by the interpretation of the Standing Committee, which can be made at any time prior to or after the appeal channels are exhausted. In the task of interpreting the Basic Law, the courts of the region have some final authority, as their judgment rendered prior to an interpretation made by the Standing Committee is not affected.

Articles 17 and 160 of the Basic Law empower the Standing Committee to adjudicate, at any time, on any law of the region that is "not in conformity with the provisions of this Law regarding affairs within the responsibility of the Central Authorities or regarding the relationship between the Central Authorities and the Region," and to return it. The law then becomes immediately invalidated. Although the jurisdiction of the courts of the region is not ousted, the Standing Committee can intervene at any stage of the legal proceedings. Moreover, Article 160 can operate retroactively to render void existing legal arrangements[170] if they contravene the Basic Law.

Article 158 of the Basic Law provides that all cases involving the interpretation of the provisions of the Basic Law "concerning affairs which are the responsibility of the Central People's Government, or concerning the relationship between the Central Authorities and the Region" shall be referred to the Standing Committee by the courts of the Region for an "interpretation" before making their final judgments, which are not appealable, on the cases if the interpretation will affect the judgments. In the task of interpreting these matters, the courts of the Region no longer have any final authority.[171] Article 19 of the Basic Law also provides that the courts of the Hong Kong Special Administrative Region have no jurisdiction over cases relating to inter alia the "Acts of State" of the Beijing government. The Central People's Government has the ultimate right to certify whether an act is an "Act of State" of the Beijing government.[172]

At Common Law, Acts of State, which include the declaration of war and the field of external affairs, are prerogative acts.[173] But the judges of the Common Law courts have the right to determine the limits of the prerogative.[174] Once the prerogative is established, the Common Law courts cannot further inquire into the matter. The Crown is entitled to determine conclusively matters of State, however, and the court accepts as conclusive a certificate entered by the Crown on these matters.[175] Therefore, the protection of state interest in the sphere of defense and foreign affairs is sufficient at Common Law as the state can act freely without any judicial review once the prerogative is established by the court.

The separation of powers in Hong Kong was undermined when on 17 November 1995, the Chief Justice, Sir Ti-liang Yang, submitted to the authority of the Chief Secretary, Mrs. Anson Chan, and prepared a statement which espoused his opinions about the controversy he had created over the Hong Kong Bill of Rights Ordinance.[176] The entire episode is not so much about the conversation between Sir Ti-liang Yang and Mr. Zhang Junsheng, the vice-director of the New China News Agency in Hong Kong, which resulted in such request made by the Chief Secretary, rather it is about the intrusion of judicial independence by the executive branch of the Hong Kong government. The matter is aggravated by the prompt submission of the Chief Justice to the authority of the Chief Secretary. This episode is not conducive to the judicial development of Hong Kong.

### *Human Resources for Judges*

In November 1988, Mr. Simon Li, a retired judge of the Hong Kong Court of Appeal and a member of the Basic Law Drafting Committee, expressed his concern about the quality of the judiciary in the Court of Final Appeal of the Hong Kong Special Administrative Region because of the quality of the present legal profession in Hong Kong.[177] He estimated it would take at least twenty years to produce a judiciary of good quality in Hong Kong among the Chinese lawyers.[178] Sir Ti-liang Yang, chief justice of the Supreme Court of Hong Kong, was also concerned with ''whether suitable ethnic Chinese candidates can be found to fill these [judicial] positions by 1997.''[179]

The Joint Declaration provides that the Court of Final Appeal in the region may, as required, invite judges from other Common Law jurisdictions to sit on the Court of Final Appeal.[180] Article 90 of the Basic Law provides that only ''[t]he Chief Justice of the Court of Final Appeal and the Chief Judge of the High Court'' of the region shall be Chinese citizens who are permanent residents of the region with no right of abode in any foreign country. Article 92 of the Basic Law provides that ''[j]udges and other members of the judiciary'' of the region shall be chosen on the basis of their judicial and professional qualities and may be recruited from other Common Law jurisdictions. It was noted by a legal academic that there is no mention of legal qualification for judicial appointment.[181] As not all Common Law judges and lawyers are qualified to practice law in Hong Kong, this Article may leave room to alleviate the human resources problems. The question is whether any lawyers of good quality will want to serve in a judicial system where their future is uncertain.[182]

It should also be noted that there is a system of lay justices in England and Wales[183] and, under the Magistrates Ordinance,[184] the governor of Hong Kong may appoint special magistrates with limited powers of punishment.[185] Two lay justices of the peace have the same powers as a special magistrate in adjudicating minor offenses.[186]

The results of the survey of the Chinese members of the legal profession indicate that only 37 percent of the sample stated positively that they will stay in Hong Kong after 30 June 1997.[187] A recent survey conducted after the 4 June 1989 massacre has shown that 33 percent of Hong Kong lawyers intend to stay and practice law in Hong Kong after 1997,[188] and 79 percent are pessimistic about the political future of Hong Kong.[189] This is not a promising figure in view of the present shortage of lawyers in Hong Kong, and a vacuum may be created if most of the expatriate members of the legal profession and judiciary depart.[190] Consequently, the choice of qualified individuals for judicial appointments, particularly those in whom Hong Kong's Chinese population will have confidence, will be further limited.

The present Hong Kong government may consider selecting promising young lawyers to assist or undergo articles under the judges at High Court or higher levels of courts in England for a number of years, with a view that they will eventually be appointed to the judiciary in Hong Kong prior to 1 July 1997. The valuable experience they will bring back to Hong Kong will enrich the delivery of Common Law justice. At the same time, more extensive training courses for the judiciary should be offered locally by prominent members of the judiciary from the Common Law world. This production line approach is not unreasonable in view of the severe shortage of Chinese judges in Hong Kong. It was suggested that experience must be accumulated and that judges' quality would depend on the legal knowledge they themselves possess.[191] This appears to have overlooked the fact that some of the brightest United States Supreme Court justices received their appointments before they were forty-five years old.[192]

### *The Adversarial System and an Independent Legal Profession*

The Basic Law provides a framework for the future of the adversarial system and an independent legal profession in Hong Kong. The successful operation of this framework very much depends on human and financial resources. The present Hong Kong government has a heavy burden to strengthen these components of the localized Common Law judicial system prior to 1 July 1997.

#### *An Independent Prosecuting Authority*

The Joint Declaration provides that "[a] prosecuting authority of the Hong Kong Special Administrative Region shall control criminal prosecutions free from any interference."[193] Although the first draft of the Basic Law implemented this provision,[194] Article 63 of the Basic Law provides that "[t]he Department of Justice of the Hong Kong Special Administrative Region shall control criminal prosecutions, free from any interference." Article 48(5) of the Basic Law provides that the chief executive of the region shall nominate and report to the Central People's Government for appointment of, or to recommend the removal of, the Secretary of the Department of Justice.

The Director of Prosecutions in Hong Kong is part of the Legal Department.[195] As such, it is not independent from administrative and political influences. Faced with the uncertainty of Hong Kong's future, the attorney general was recently criticized for refusing to enforce criminal laws against the financial elite because of possible adverse effects on commercial transactions[196] and the possible abuse of the use of *nolle prosequi*.[197] To avoid the public perception that there may be political motivation in the administration of justice, there is a need to ensure a minimum level of independence for Crown counsel in the conduct of criminal prosecutions. An independent prosecuting authority would make it more difficult for the administration of justice to be meddled with on political grounds.[198] During this transitional period the morale of the expatriate Crown counsel is bound to decline as indicated by a series of scandals developed recently.[199] Some lawyers suggested that these scandals had caused almost irreparable damage to public confidence in the legal system.[200]

The results of our study suggest the need to enhance prosecuting procedures for a better adversarial system.[201] The results indicate that the majority of the Chinese members of the legal profession do not believe that Crown counsel cooperate with the defense or reveal evidence that favors the defense, and a substantial minority of them take the view that Crown counsel are under pressure to secure a conviction and that they treat English more favorably than Chinese.[202] As such, the independent prosecuting authority of the Hong Kong Special Administrative Region under the Joint Declaration[203] should be created as soon as it is practical under the model of the United States District Attorney. Although this model has its weaknesses, it is a step toward impartial criminal investigations.

### *Human Resources for Lawyers*

The Joint Declaration provides that the region shall "make provision for local lawyers and lawyers from outside the Region to work and practice in" the region.[204] Article 94 of the Basic Law provides that "[o]n the basis of the system previously operating in Hong Kong," the above provision will be carried out. Therefore, steps should be taken to ensure a quality legal profession during and after this transitional period.

The increased intake of undergraduates by the law faculty of the University of Hong Kong is a positive step[205] as it is a faculty of good quality. There are reservations, however, about the rapid expansion of the law degree and PCLL courses without considering the quality of the students. Amid the uncertainty of the future of the judicial system of Hong Kong, the need for a second law school was questioned as students might end up there only because places are being created.[206] The extramural studies for the University of London's external LL.B. and LL.M. programs and C.P.E. and PCLL courses offered by the University of Hong Kong are a welcome step in ensuring well-qualified law graduates.[207] The successful operation of the adversarial system and an independent legal profession depends on both the quality and the quantity of lawyers.

In England, conveyancing services can be provided by licensed conveyancers under the Administration of Justice Act of 1985. Hong Kong may consider following this English practice to alleviate the work load of the practicing solicitors.[208] In January 1987, the then attorney general of Hong Kong, Michael Thomas, admitted that there is a shortage of experienced lawyers in Hong Kong,[209] and that the government would attempt to attract qualified overseas lawyers who can contribute to Hong Kong. He also stated that the interests of young lawyers should be protected. Unfortunately, the term ''overseas lawyers,'' according to past practice, refers to those trained in British Commonwealth countries. The Hong Kong Bar Association, however, has been concerned with the influx of English lawyers who are less permanent than those whose roots are in Hong Kong and who may not be there after 30 June 1997.[210]

According to rough estimates, there are more than two thousand Chinese practicing lawyers and more than thirty Chinese judges in the United States.[211] There is no reason, other than professional protectionism, that these talents are not welcome in Hong Kong. It should be noted that a number of Crown counsel in Hong Kong are not qualified barristers or solicitors.[212] American lawyers have to undergo far more training and pass much more rigorous examinations than their Hong Kong counterparts.[213] This leaves little doubt about the competency of the Chinese lawyers who have made their way to sit on the bench in the United States.

The proposal to allow foreign law firms to hire local lawyers or take them on as partners, however, should be considered more carefully regardless of the motive of the Hong Kong legal profession.[214] The independence of the legal profession may be eroded if foreign law firms include those in mainland China as they are controlled by the state. Law firms from mainland China would have a commercial and political advantage over other foreign and local law firms as they have the right connection with the Beijing authorities. It is a welcome step that the Hong Kong government has abandoned this proposal.[215]

### *Financial Resources for Legal Services*

Article 35 of the Basic Law provides the people in the Hong Kong Special Administrative Region the right to confidential legal advice, choice of lawyers for timely protection of their legitimate rights and interests, representation in the courts, and judicial remedies. The rights to legal advice can only be guaranteed by widespread legal aid for all types of legal advice. Presently, the legal profession in mainland China is not completely independent from the state.[216] A defense lawyer is regarded as an independent party representing the administration of justice to protect his client's legitimate interest, and cannot be dictated to by his client.[217]

It may be better for legal aid to be administered by the law society or an independent body rather than by the government. In England, legal aid has been administered by the Law Society for more than forty years, with funding from the government. Its Legal Aid Act of 1988 provides for the setting up of the Legal Aid Board with mostly lay members.[218] Thus, the legal aid administration in England and Wales can ensure its independence from the government and the legal profession, and it is essential particularly in cases where the interest of the state or the legal profession is involved. In 1986, a working party of the Hong Kong government recommended that the Legal Aid Department be transformed into an independent Legal Aid Commission,[219] but despite similar calls for independence and another review in 1992, there has in fact been no substantial change to the situation. The Legal Aid Department is still a part of the government, and the proposed Legal Aid Services Council[220] has little power to rectify this problem.[221]

Although legal aid can be viewed as lawyer's aid by some,[222] one way to eliminate the economic barrier to obtaining justice is to raise the income and property qualifications, i.e., the means test, for legal aid eligibility,[223] and to introduce the prorata concept so that middle-income people can obtain legal aid for all cases by paying a reasonable fee. The state would then have to subsidize the market adjustments between actual and reasonable legal fees. This cost to society would have to be endured if an independent legal profession is to be maintained and if economic barriers to obtaining justice are to be eliminated until the supply-and-demand side of the economy can be resolved.

### *Jury System*

The Basic Law suggests no change in the present jury system of Hong Kong. Articles 8 and 18 of the Basic Law enable the continuation of this system in Hong Kong after 30 June 1990 as part of the "laws previously in force in Hong Kong," and Article 86 of the Basic Law provides that "[t]he principle of trial by jury previously practiced in Hong Kong shall be maintained."

### *The Right of Silence and Presumption of Innocence*

Regarding the right of silence and presumption of innocence, the Basic Law provides no change and the present laws on this area will be maintained under the same source of law for the jury system. Article 11 of the International Covenant on Civil and Political Rights provides that an accused person has the right to be presumed innocent until proven guilty according to law, and this Article is applied to Hong Kong. In the meantime, the Bill of Rights has incorporated this Article of the Covenant.[224] Accordingly, certain existing ordinances, e.g., the Dangerous Drugs Ordinance[225] and Prevention of Bribery Ordinance,[226] may have to be amended.

## Conclusion

The judicial development of the Common Law system depends very much on the present Hong Kong government. If a strong legal framework and a healthy localized Common Law are established prior to 1 July 1997, it will at least be more difficult for the executive branch of government in the Hong Kong Special Administrative Region to meddle with it. Conversely, if the present legal framework and Common Law continue after 30 June 1997, opportunities for interference will undoubtedly arise.

The Basic Law of Hong Kong is part of the implementation of the Joint Declaration. It is an important factor for the successful operation of the Common Law judicial system after 30 June 1997. Much will depend on the resolve of the Beijing government to implement the declaration. The document of the Basic Law serves as a barometer for the future of the Common Law in Hong Kong.[227] Regardless of what the Basic Law will guarantee the people of Hong Kong, mutual trust becomes the decisive factor.

The Basic Law seems to be the best document that the Beijing government can reasonably offer the Chinese population of Hong Kong within its power under the Chinese constitution. It has provided Hong Kong with a greater degree of autonomy than was provided by its first draft. The Beijing government does not want its citizens in the Chinese mainland to demand similar rights. Its determination is evidenced by the 4 June 1989 massacre. The Basic Law has 160 articles and 3 annexes, and makes a clear effort to maintain the Common Law judicial system and to observe the Joint Declaration. From the outset, the ''high degree of autonomy'' provided by the Joint Declaration[228] to the Hong Kong Special Administration Region depends on how the Chinese constitution is interpreted.[229] Under the Joint Declaration, the Westminster government expressly agreed that the Basic Law cannot contravene the Chinese constitution.[230] The Beijing government has the exclusive right to interpret its constitution.

## Notes

1. *Financial Times*, London, 10 May 1984.
2. Ibid.
3. David Bonavia, *Hong Kong 1997* (Hong Kong: *South China Morning Post*, 1983), pp. 121–22; *The Times*, 25 and 26 June 1984.
4. Alvin Rabushka, *The New China* (Boulder, CO: Westview Press, 1987), pp. 152–53; Ian Kelly, *Hong Kong: A Political-Geographic Analysis* (Honolulu: University of Hawaii Press, 1986), pp. 101–3.
5. Item 78, Appendix C–1.

6. The Joint Declaration of the Government of the United Kingdom of Great Britain and Northern Ireland and the Government of the People's Republic of China on the Question of Hong Kong (1984).

7. Article 3(12) and Paragraph I, Section I, Annex I, of the 1984 Sino-British Joint Declaration.

8. Ian Scott, *Political Change and the Crisis of Legitimacy in Hong Kong* (Hong Kong: Oxford University Press, 1989), p. 219; Emily Lau, "Peking Rules Out British Role in Formation of Future Government," *Far Eastern Economic Review*, 22 October 1987, p. 21; Philip Bowring, "Ear to Peking, an Eye on Whitehall," *Far Eastern Economic Review*, 7 April 1988, p. 54; *Asian Magazine* (*ah-chou chou-k'an*), 5 February 1989, pp. 13–14.

9. Emily Lau and Philip Bowring, "Laying Down the Law," *Far Eastern Economic Review*, 5 December 1985, pp. 12–15.

10. This future miniconstitution of Hong Kong was enacted by the Peking National People's Congress on 4 April 1990.

11. Lau, "Peking Rules Out British Role."

12. Scott, *Political Change*, pp. 322–26; Bowring, "Ear to Peking," pp. 53–54; For example, the chief secretary of Hong Kong, David Ford, accused two legislators who criticized the Hong Kong government as "lame-duck," and warned them that they will "have a tiger by the tail." See *Sing Pao Daily*, San Francisco, 13 November 1987.

13. "Sparks Fly as Chief Justice States Case," *South China Morning Post*, Hong Kong, 18 May 1995.

14. The Hong Kong Act (1985) makes provision for and is in connection with the ending of British sovereignty and jurisdiction over Hong Kong on 1 July 1997.

15. As empowered by Article 67(14) of the Constitution of the People's Republic of China, 1982. Also see *Beijing Review*, "The Hong Kong Solution," in *China and the World* (Peking, 1985), p. 47.

16. Article 3(12) and Paragraph I, Section I, Annex I, Joint Declaration.

17. Georg Ress, "The Hong Kong Agreement and Its Impact on International Law," in *Hong Kong: A Chinese and International Concern*, ed. Jurgen Domes and Yu-ming Shaw (Boulder, CO: Westview Press, 1988), p. 135; Roda Mushkat, "The Transition from British to Chinese Rule in Hong Kong: A Discussion of Salient International Legal Issues," *Denver Journal of International Law and Policy* 14 (1986), p. 191; and "The International Legal Status of Hong Kong under Post-Transitional Rule," *Houston Journal of International Law* 10 (1987), p. 9.

18. Mushkat, "International Legal Status," p. 9.

19. *The Parlement Belge* (1879) 4 *P.D.* 129.

20. Article 3(12) and Paragraph I, Section I, Annex I.

21. *Guangming Daily*, Peking, 16 February 1990.

22. Emily Lau, "No More Concessions," *Far Eastern Economic Review*, 30 November 1989, p. 13.

23. Yu-ming Shaw, "An ROC View of the Hong Kong Issue," in *Hong Kong: A Chinese and International Concern*, ed. Jurgen Domes and Yu-ming Shaw, p. 100.

24. Article 3(1), Joint-Declaration; Article 11, Basic Law of Hong Kong.

25. Article 3(12) and Paragraph I, Section I, Annex I.

26. Paragraph 3 of this section provides inter alia "[a]ll acts in violation of the constitution and the law must be looked into." This imposes a constitutional duty to investigate any possible violation. Articles 62(2) and 67(1) of the constitution provide constitutional power to enforce the constitution.

27. Article 31 provides: "The state may establish special administrative regions when necessary. The systems to be instituted in special administrative regions shall be prescribed by law enacted by the National People's Congress in light of the specific condi-

tions." Article 62(13) provides: "The National People's Congress exercises the functions and powers to decide on the establishment of special administrative regions and the systems to be instituted there."

28. Notwithstanding this, it has been argued that it is inappropriate to adopt a strict approach in interpreting the Chinese constitution. A fortiori, the Common Law notion of ultra vires should not be applicable. See W. S. Clarke, "Hong Kong under the Chinese Constitution," *Hong Kong Law Journal* 14 (1984), pp. 77–79. Such argument is not supported by Professor William Wade, Q. C., *The Draft of Hong Kong Basic Law* (opinion drafted for the Law Society of Hong Kong, Cambridge, 1988), pp. 4–5; Also see Edward Epstein, "China and Hong Kong," in *The Future of the Law in Hong Kong*, ed. Raymond Wacks (Hong Kong: Oxford University Press, 1989), p. 54.

29. Paragraph I, Section II, Annex I, Joint Declaration; Article 11, Basic Law of Hong Kong.

30. Paragraph I, Section I, Annex I, Joint Declaration; Article 5, Constitution of the People's Republic of China; Clarke, "Hong Kong under the Chinese Constitution," pp. 74–77.

31. Article 18 of the Basic Law of Hong Kong can always be amended by virtue of Article 159.

32. Paragraph I, Section I, Annex I, Joint Declaration.

33. Preamble, Constitution of the People's Republic of China, 1982.

34. The preamble of the Constitution of the People's Republic of China, 1982, reaffirms the state's ideology of class struggle and considers the enemy of the people as those elements in the world that try to undermine China's socialist system.

35. R. N. Carew Hunt, *The Theory and Practice of Communism* (London: Penguin Books, 1971), pp. 39–67.

36. Chang You-yu, *A Few Questions on the Socialist Legal System* (*kuan-yu she-hui chu-i fa-chih te jo-kan wen-ti*) (Peking: Fa-lu Publishing Co., 1982), pp. 8–9, 32–63; R. W. M. Dias, *Jurisprudence*, 5th ed. (London: Butterworths, 1985), p. 398.

37. Xu Chong-de, "One Country, Two Systems (*i-kuo liang-chih te hsin-ke-ti*)," *Law* (*fa-hsueh*) 10 (1987) pp. 24–25.

38. Jill Barrett, "The Relationship between the Two Legal Systems" (paper presented at the Seminar on the Draft Basic Law for Hong Kong, School of Oriental and African Studies, London, 15 June 1988); Clarke, "Hong Kong under the Chinese Constitution," pp. 77–79.

39. Xu Guo-jian, "My Humble Opinion on Resolving the Conflict of Law between the Interior of Our Country and Hong Kong," *Law Science Quarterly* 32.2 (1987), pp. 236–38.

40. Ronald Jack Walker, *Walker and Walker's English Legal System*, 6th ed. (London: Butterworths, 1985), p. 143.

41. Preamble and General Principles, Constitution of the People's Republic of China, 1982.

42. Raymond Wacks, "Can the Common Law Survive the Basic Law?" *Hong Kong Law Journal* 18 (1988), p. 444; Timothy Gelatt, "Review of Amnesty International's China—Violations of Human Rights," in *China Rights Annals*, ed. James Seymour (Armonk, NY: M. E. Sharpe, 1985), pp. 183–84.

43. Bruce Bueno de Mesquita, *Forecasting Political Events: The Future of Hong Kong* (New Haven: Yale University Press, 1985), p. 58.

44. Scott, *Political Change*, pp. 173–75.

45. The first draft had been endorsed only by the Drafting Committee for the Basic Law for solicitation of opinions.

46. Emily Lau, "Backroom Betrayal," *Far Eastern Economic Review*, 1 March 1990, p. 14.

47. The amendments are mostly related to matters on national security, nationality issues, and the pace of democratic reform.

48. Article 3(3). Note the word "basically."

49. Paragraph III, Section II, Annex I.

50. Martin Lee, "How Much Autonomy?" In *Basic Law, Basic Questions*, ed. William McGurn (Hong Kong: Review Publishing Company, 1988), p. 46.

51. Subsection 3(3) and Paragraph II, Section I, Annex I.

52. Subsection 3(2) and Paragraph II, Section I, Annex I.

53. See Hungdah Chiu, "The Agreement on Hong Kong and Its Implications on China's Unification," *Issues & Studies* 21 (1985), pp. 13–20. For other views, see Ress, "The Hong Kong Agreement," pp. 142–43; Mushkat, "Transition from British to Chinese Rule, pp. 181–83; "International Legal Status," pp. 1–24.

54. For another viewpoint, see Wade, *Draft of Hong Kong Basic Law*, pp. 2–6. Wade suggested that the constitutional difficulties can simply be obviated by amending the Constitution of the People's Republic of China, which is wishful thinking.

55. There is evidence to suggest that the British government knew from the outset that a "cast-iron guarantees" agreement was not possible. See Scott, *Political Change*, p. 201.

56. Lee, "How Much Autonomy?" p. 46.

57. Robert Delfs, "Talking Out of School" *Far Eastern Economic Review*, 16 June 1988, p. 18; Delfs, "Repression Repeated," ibid. (16 March 1989), pp. 10–11; *Asian Magazine* (*ah-chou chou-k'an*), 14 February 1988, p. 53.

58. Albert Chen, "The Developing Legal System in China," *Hong Kong Law Journal* 13.3 (1983), p. 309.

59. Philip Baker, "Theories of Legislation, Codification, and Interpretation in China and the West" (paper presented at the Symposium on Chinese and European Concepts of Law, Hong Kong, 1986) pp. 6–7; Jeanette Pinard, *The People's Republic of China: A Bibliography of Selected English-Language Legal Materials* (Washington: Library of Congress, 1985), pp. 11–12; Tao-tai Hsia and Constance Johnson, *Law Making in the People's Republic of China: Terms, Procedures, Hierarchy, and Interpretation* (Washington: Library of Congress, 1986), pp. 19–23; and Standing Committee of National People's Congress, Resolution on Strengthening the Legal Interpretation of Law (10 June 1981).

60. Dennis Lloyd, *The Idea of Law* (London: Penguin Books, 1977), pp. 212, 219–20; Glendon Schubert, "Political Culture and Judicial Ideology," *Comparative Political Studies* 9 (1977), pp. 363–408; J. A. G. Griffith, *The Politics of the Judiciary* (London: Fontana/Collins, 1979), pp. 187–216; Roger Cotterrell, *The Sociology of Law* (London: Butterworths, 1984), pp. 228–58.

61. Paragraph III, Section II, Annex I, Joint Declaration; Article 8, Basic Law of Hong Kong.

62. Paragraph I, Section III, Annex I, Joint Declaration; Article 81, Basic Law of Hong Kong.

63. See section 2.3.2.

64. Paragraph III, Section II, Annex I; Article 8, Basic Law of Hong Kong.

65. Chang Hsin, "The Influence of Chinese Legal Perceptions on the Basic Law," *Ming Pao Monthly* 23:2 (1988), pp. 33–36; Chapter 2, Constitution of the People's Republic of China, 1982.

66. Raymond Wacks, "The Judicial Function," in *The Future of the Law in Hong Kong*, pp. 140–44.

67. Paragraph I, Section XIII, Annex I.

68. Nihal Jayawickrama, "Hong Kong and the International Protection of Human Rights," in *Civil Liberties in Hong Kong*, ed. Raymond Wacks (Hong Kong: Oxford

University Press, 1988), pp. 38–40; Nihal Jayawickrama, "Protecting Civil Liberties," in *The Future of the Law in Hong Kong*, pp. 148–53.

69. Jayawickrama, "Hong Kong and the International Protection of Human Rights," pp. 38–40; Albert Chen and Johannes Chan, *Human Rights and the Rule of Law—The Challenges of Hong Kong's Transition* (in Chinese) (Hong Kong: Wide Angle Press, 1987), pp. 64–68.

70. W. S. Clarke, "Messrs. Wong and Ng and the Universal Declaration of Human Rights," *Hong Kong Law Journal* 15.2 (1985) pp. 139–41.

71. Norman Anderson, *Liberty, Law and Justice* (London: Stevens and Sons, 1978), pp. 66–67.

72. *R v. Secretary of State for Home Affairs, ex parte Bhajan Singh* [1976] Q.B. 198–207.

73. Great Britain did not sign the Optional Protocol to the covenant that would allow individuals to file direct complaints. See Jayawickrama, "Protecting Civil Liberties," p. 153; Chen and Chan, *Human Rights and the Rule of Law*, p. 66.

74. Jayawickrama, "Protecting Civil Liberties," pp. 153–58; David Porter, "A Blast from Geneva," *Far Eastern Economic Review*, 24 November 1988, pp. 26–27.

75. See *Duncan v. Cammell, Laird & Co.* [1942] A.C. 624.

76. *Conway v. Rimmer* [1968] A.C. 910.

77. Stanley A. deSmith, *Constitutional and Administrative Law*, 5th ed., ed. Harry Street and Rodney Brazier (London: Penguin Books, 1985), pp. 639–40.

78. See the few cases in which Crown privilege was challenged in Peter Wesley-Smith, *Constitutional and Administrative Law in Hong Kong*, vol. 2 (Hong Kong: China and Hong Kong Law Studies, 1988), pp. 296–97.

79. See also "Acts of State" under Article 19 of the Basic Law of Hong Kong.

80. Also see *Sing Pao Daily*, 18 March 1990; Emily Lau, "Law unto Itself," *Far Eastern Economic Review*, 29 March 1990, pp. 10–12.

81. Articles 14, 16, 18, and 19.

82. "ICAC Withdraws Call for Rights Bill Exemption," *South China Morning Post*, 12 June 1990.

83. "Bill of Rights 'a legacy of chaos'—kuk," *South China Morning Post*, 13 July 1990; "Rights Bill Study Requested," *South China Morning Post*, 16 June 1990; *Sing Pao Daily*, 29 June, 1990.

84. "Repeal Archaic Succession Law, Says Survey," *South China Morning Post*, 30 July 1990.

85. "Law and Order Decline Feared," *South China Morning Post*, 28 June 1990.

86. Henry Litton, Q.C., "A Conflict of Interests," *South China Morning Post*, 14 May 1990; Andrew Brynes and David Clark, "In Defense of the Bill of Rights," *South China Morning Post*, 18 May 1990; Letter dated 6 June 1990 by Henry Litton, Q.C., to the *South China Morning Post*.

87. Emily Lau, "Law unto Itself," *Far Eastern Economic Review*, 29 March 1990, p. 10; "Chinese May Repeal Hong Kong Charter," *The Independent*, London, 7 June 1991.

88. "Opposition to Rights Bill Motion," *South China Morning Post*, 28 June 1990; *Sing Pao Daily*, 29 June, 1990.

89. David Clark and Andrew Byrnes, "Letters to the Editor," *South China Morning Post*, 9 June 1990.

90. Paragraph II, Section XIII, Annex I.

91. Articles 7, 9, 10, and 14 of the International Covenant on Civil and Political Rights.

92. Cap. 232, Laws of Hong Kong, 1984 ed.

93. Cap. 115, Laws of Hong Kong, 1987 ed.

94. Corporal Punishment Ordinance (Cap. 222, Laws of Hong Kong, 1982 ed.); Subsection 33(2), Public Order Ordinance (Cap. 245, Laws of Hong Kong 1987 ed.); "Legco to Repeal Law on Flogging for Rights Bill," *South China Morning Post*, 22 June 1990.

95. Joseph Y. S. Cheng, "The Political System," in *The Basic Law and Hong Kong's Future*, ed. Peter Wesley-Smith and Albert Chen (Hong Kong: Butterworths, 1988), p. 169; N. J. Miners, "Disallowance and the Administrative Review of Hong Kong Legislation by the Colonial Office 1844–1947," *Hong Kong Law Journal* 18.2 (1988) 218–48.

96. The 4 June 1989 Massacre. See Albert Chen, "The Suppression of China's Democracy Movement and Hong Kong's Future," *Hong Kong Law Journal* 19.3 (1989), pp. 283–89.

97. Albert Chen, "From Colony to Special Administrative Region: Hong Kong's Constitutional Journey," in *The Future of the Law in Hong Kong*, pp. 124–26.

98. The Economist, *The World Human Rights Guide* (London: The Economist, 1986), pp. xiv–xv.

99. Paragraph III, Section III, Annex I.

100. W. S. Clarke, "The Need for Direct Elections to the Hong Kong Legislature," *Hong Kong Law Journal* 17.2 (1987), p. 139.

101. Ibid.

102. *The Development of Representative Government: The Way Forward* (Hong Kong: Government Printer, 1988), sections 27–29, chapter 3.

103. "The Other, Better Chinas," *The Economist*, 13 February 1988; Scott, *Political Change*, p. 25.

104. Item 78, Appendix C–1; Scott, *Political Change*, pp. 30–31.

105. *Sing Pao Daily*, 6 November 1987.

106. *South China Morning Post*, 27 July 1989. The Electoral Provisions (Amendment) Bill (1990), which will lay the foundation for the direct elections of eighteen seats, has been gazetted by the Hong Kong government on 20 July 1990. See "Bills Seek to Ensure Clean 1991 Elections," *South China Morning Post*, 20 July 1990.

107. Paragraph III, Section I, Annex I.

108. Article 68.

109. Clarke, "Need for Direct Elections," p. 140.

110. Article 69, Basic Law of Hong Kong.

111. Paragraph III, Section I, Annex I.

112. Emily Lau, "The Political Line-up," *Far Eastern Economic Review*, 9 February 1989, pp. 16–17; "The Gloves Come Off," *Far Eastern Economic Review*, 17 May 1990, pp. 22–23.

113. Ibid; Scott, *Political Change*, pp. 205–6, 289.

114. Lau, "The Political Line-up"; "The Gloves Come Off."

115. Ibid.

116. Ibid.

117. Paragraph 6, Decision of the National People's Congress on the Method for the Formation of the First Government and First Legislative Council of the Hong Kong Special Administrative Region (4 April 1990).

118. Philip Bowring, "Start Shredding the News," *Far Eastern Economic Review*, 26 March 1987, p. 12.

119. Cap. 245, Laws of Hong Kong, 1987 ed.

120. Scott, *Political Change*, p. 315; Emily Lau, "Sense and Censorship," *Far Eastern Economic Review*, 23 July 1987.

121. For example, the letter dated 23 October 1989 from Hong Kong government political adviser Mr. William Ehrman to the Beijing authorities in Hong Kong. See "April

Fifth Prosecutions 'Politically Motivated,' " *South China Morning Post*, 5 December 1989.

122. A. K. R. Kiralfy, ed., *Potter's Historical Introduction to English Law*, 4th ed. (London: Sweet and Maxwell, 1958), pp. 274–80.

123. Griffith, *Politics of the Judiciary*, pp. 25–26.

124. See William Nelson, *Americanization of the Common Law* (Cambridge: Harvard University Press, 1975).

125. Michael Jackson, "The Criminal Law in Hong Kong," in *The Future of the Law in Hong Kong*, pp. 202–18; Dias, *Jurisprudence*, pp. 324–27, 383, 388.

126. Section 9, Criminal Code, R.S.C. 1985, chapter C–46.

127. Codification has its weakness, but its benefits outweigh its disadvantages. Moreover, the objections do not stand. See Roscoe Pound, *Jurisprudence*, vol. 3 (St. Paul: West Publishing Co., 1959), pp. 728–32.

128. Ibid, p. 679.

129. This speech is almost identical to the "Closing Address" (paper presented at the Symposium on Chinese and European Concepts of Law, Hong Kong, 1986), p. 11.

130. Thomas, ibid., p. 4.

131. Notwithstanding, Mr. Thomas said, "To a limited extent, areas of the Common Law have been codified and refined in Statute Law. But for the most part we still rely on the precedents reaching back hundreds of years for our law governing crimes, . . ." ibid., p. 6.

132. For examples, see Pound, ibid., pp. 705–23.

133. Thomas, ibid., p. 11.

134. "Codifying the Criminal Law," *The New Gazette*, May 1990, p. 9; The report is entitled *Topic 26, Codification of the Criminal Law* (Hong Kong: Government Printer, 1989).

135. *Kuruma, Son of Kanui v. The Queen* [1955] A.C. 197.

136. *Coolidge v. New Hampshire* [1971] 403 U.S. 443.

137. Section 78, Police and Criminal Evidence Act, 1984.

138. *Burmah Oil Co. v. Lord Advocate* [1965] A.C. 75; Also see deSmith, *Constitutional and Administrative Law*, p. 34.

139. Kelly, op. cit., p. 12–15; John Walden, "Accountability: Past, Present, and Future," in *Basic Law, Basic Questions*, ed. William McGurn (Hong Kong: Review Publishing Company, 1988), pp. 53–68.

140. Eric Barnes, "The Independence of the Judiciary in Hong Kong," *Hong Kong Law Journal* 6.1 (1976), pp. 7–26.

141. Sections 3–5 (Cap. 92, Laws of Hong Kong, 1984 ed).

142. Henry Litton, Q.C., "Editorial," *Hong Kong Law Journal* 13.2(1983), pp. 129–32; Albert Chen, "Editorial" *Hong Kong Law Journal* 18.3 (1988), pp. 364–69.

143. Barnes, "Independence of the Judiciary," p. 22n; see section 5.7.

144. For a few recent cases involving the nonrenewal of magistrates' contracts and possible breach of this convention, see "The Scales of Injustice?" *South China Morning Post*, 23 March 1990.

145. "Judicial freedom 'vital,'" *Hong Kong Standard*, 9 January 1990.

146. Paragraph III, Section III, Annex I.

147. Paragraph III, Section III, Annex I.

148. Subsection 5(4) of the Magistrates Ordinance (Cap. 227, Laws of Hong Kong, 1984 ed.) provides that "[a]ny magistrate appointed under this section shall be a justice of the peace by virtue of his office." Article XIV of the Letters Patent 1917–1986 (dated 14 February 1917 [amended 12 times] passed under the Great Seal of the United Kingdom) makes distinctions among "Judges, Justices of the Peace, and other public officers."

149. Articles 8, 88, and 89, Basic Law of Hong Kong. Under note 7, p. 90, first draft of the Basic Law, other members of the judiciary include magistrates of magistrates' courts and presiding officers at special tribunals.

150. Cap. 227, Laws of Hong Kong, 1984 ed.

151. Hong Kong Government, *Hong Kong 1987* (Hong Kong: Government Printer, 1987), Appendix. Between 1984 and 1988, the total number of cases heard in the magistrates' courts is 3,332,764. See David Clark, "Are All Appointments of Magistrates Since January 1984 Invalid?" *Hong Kong Law Journal* 19.3 (1989), p. 332.

152. In answering whether judges in Hong Kong are fair and impartial, 38 percent of the Chinese members of the legal profession were not sure ('neither nor') and more than 21 percent positively disagreed with this notion. Only 40 percent of them did not believe affirmatively that judges in Hong Kong treated English more favorably than Chinese when making judicial decisions. See Items 53 and 57, Appendix C–4.

153. Items 42 and 48, Appendix C–4.

154. "Showdown Looms for Magistrate," *South China Morning Post*, 20 December 1987; Emily Lau, "Sharpening Up the Beaks: Magistrates Come Under Pressure to Step Up Conviction Rate," *Far Eastern Economic Review*, 3 November 1988, pp. 29–30; Barnes, "Independence of the Judiciary," p. 15n.

155. See Table 4.1, p. 66.

156. Gu Chun-de, "Why the System of Separation of Powers Is Not Being Implemented in China," *Studies in Law* 6 (1987), p. 25; Tao-Tai Hsia, "The Concept of Judicial Independence," (paper presented at the Symposium on Chinese and European Concepts of Law, Hong Kong, 1986); *Asian Magazine* (*ah-chou chou-k'an*), 15 May 1988, p. 7.

157. The Standing Committee is also an administrative and legislative body. See Article 67, Constitution of the People's Republic of China.

158. Article 67(1) and (4), Constitution of the People's Republic of China, 1982. Baker, "Theories of Legislation,"; Albert Chen, "The Developing Legal System in China," pp. 307–10.

159. Article 62(11), Constitution of the People's Republic of China, 1982.

160. Articles 62(11), 64, and 67(1) and (4), Constitution of the People's Republic of China, 1982.

161. Wade, *Draft of Hong Kong Basic Law*, p. 5.

162. Lee, "How Much Autonomy?" p. 45.

163. Article 3(3); Paragraph II, Section I, Annex I; Section III, Annex I.

164. The Standing Committee, however, has delegated some of its judicial authority to subordinate judicial organs by virtue of its "Resolution on Strengthening the Legal Interpretation of Law" (10 June 1981).

165. Article 3(12) and Paragraph I, Section I, Annex I.

166. Article 169 of the first draft provided that the power of interpretation of the Basic Law should be vested in the Standing Committee. This is in accordance with the Joint Declaration.

167. Wade, *Draft of Hong Kong Basic Law*, p. 20.

168. Barrett, "Relationship between the Two Legal Systems."

169. Baker, "Theories of Legislation," p. 19.

170. Documents, certificates, contracts, and rights and obligations.

171. Compare with the place of the European Court of Justice in the English legal system. See L. Neville Brown and Francis Jacobs, *The Court of Justice of the European Communities* (London: Sweet and Maxwell, 1977), pp. 131–49; Walker, *English Legal System*, pp. 183–86.

172. Article 19.

173. deSmith, op. cit., pp. 157–63.

174. Case of Proclamations (1611), 12 *Co. Rep.* 74.

175. deSmith, *Constitutional and Administrative Law*, pp. 154–57.

176. "Sparks Fly as Chief Justice States Case," *South China Morning Post*, Hong Kong, 18 May 1995.

177. *Sing Pao Daily*, 26 November 1988.

178. Ibid.

179. Emily Lau, "The Judiciary Faces Major Task in 1997 Run-up," *Far Eastern Economic Review*, 20 April 1989, p. 21; see chapter 6, 200n; "Shortage of Magistrates Met by UK," *South China Morning Post*, 20 February 1991.

180. Paragraph IV, Section III. Annex I.

181. Wacks, "The Judicial Function," p. 135n. Note: Section 9 of the Supreme Court Ordinance (Cap. 4, Laws of Hong Kong, 1987 ed.) spells out the professional qualification of judges and this will be part of "[t]he laws previously in force in Hong Kong."

182. The "Findlay affair" has brought tension as a result of the localization to the surface. It was suggested that some senior expatriate judges might violate Section 12 of the Judicial Service Commission Ordinance (Cap. 92, Laws of Hong Kong, 1982 ed.) for meddling with the decision of the Judicial Service Commission in its attempt to push for the appointment of an expatriate Crown counsel to the bench. See Emily Lau, "The Government Reneges on High Court Appointment," *Far Eastern Economic Review*, 3 May, 1990, p. 18.

183. Magistrates' Courts Act, 1952.

184. Section 5, Cap. 227, Laws of Hong Kong, 1984 ed.

185. The delegated power of the Chief Justice of Hong Kong to appoint magistrates was questioned by academic lawyer. See David Clark, "Are All Appointments of Magistrates Since January 1984 Invalid?" *Hong Kong Law Journal* 19.3 (1989), pp. 330–44; The Letters Patent was amended on 16 April 1991 to cover this possible defect. See "Department Denies Claims by Lecturer," *South China Morning Post*, 25 April 1991.

186. Subsection 7(2) (Cap. 227, Laws of Hong Kong, 1984 ed.).

187. Item 79, Appendix C–8.

188. Survey Research Hongkong Ltd., *Survey on Manpower Planning of Lawyers Report*, prepared for the Law Society of Hong Kong (Hong Kong: Survey Research Hongkong Ltd., December 1989), Table 5; "Lawyers' Brain Drain," *The New Gazette*, February 1990, pp. 37–39.

189. Survey Research Hongkong Ltd., ibid., p. 5.

190. See Berry Hsu, *The Common Law System in Chinese Context: Hong Kong between China and Britain, 1842–1992* (Armonk, NY: M. E. Sharpe, 1992), sections 6.3.2 and 6.5.5.

191. *Hong Kong Economic Journal*, 30 December 1989.

192. William O. Douglas at forty, Potter Stewart at forty-three, Byron R. White at forty-four, and William H. Rehnquist at forty-seven.

193. Paragraph V, Section III, Annex I.

194. Article 63, first draft of the Basic Law.

195. David Lyons, "The Role of the Attorney General's Chambers in Hong Kong," *Hong Kong Law Journal* 13.3 (1983), pp. 288–90.

196. Philip Bowring, "Ear to Peking, an Eye on Whitehall," *Far Eastern Economic Review*, 7 April 1988, p. 54.

197. Albert Chen, "The Powers and Accountability of the Attorney General," *Hong Kong Law Journal* 20.1 (1990), pp. 7–8.

198. The attorney general has to publicly exercise his prerogative power, e.g., *nolle prosequi*.

199. Mr. Christopher Harris, a senior Crown counsel, was convicted of sexual offenses. *Ta Kung Pao*, Hong Kong, 22 February 1990; Chen, ibid., p. 7; Mr. Warwick

Reid, a Deputy Director of Public Prosecutions, was convicted of corruption and several lawyers were also implicated. "Reid Pleads Guilty to Corruption Charge," *South China Morning Post*, 21 June 1990; "Lawyers in the Dock," *Far Eastern Economic Review*, 28 June 1990, pp. 18–19; "Prosecution Still a Law unto Itself," *South China Morning Post*, 2 September 1990.

200. "Step to Repair 'Incalculable Damage,'" *South China Morning Post*, 7 July 1990.

201. See Hsu, *The Common Law System in Chinese Context*, section 6.5.1.

202. See Ibid., Table 6.16, p. 84.

203. Paragraph V, Section III, Annex I.

204. Paragraph VI, Section III, Annex I.

205. See *The New Gazette*, February 1990, p. 38.

206. W. S. Clarke, "Does Hong Kong Really Need So Many More Lawyers?" *Hong Kong Law Journal* 17.3 (1987), pp. 286–87.

207. "Postgraduate Studies in Law Receive Boost," *South China Morning Post*, 23 July 1990; "HKU Bid for More Lawyers," *South China Morning Post*, 13 January 1991.

208. Michael Sandor, "The Legal Profession," in *The Future of the Law in Hong Kong*, pp. 226–27.

209. *Sing Pao Daily*, 14 January 1987.

210. W. S. Clarke, "Overseas Barristers and the Independence of the Bar," *Hong Kong Law Journal* 16.1 (1986), p. 1.

211. *Edmonton Chinese Times*, July 1987.

212. William Turnbull, "What Can Hong Kong Do for the Overseas Lawyers?" *Papers of the Seventh Commonwealth Law Conference* (1983), p. 478.

213. According to an international review, thirty-two of the top sixty-five law schools in the world are in the United States. See Jack Gourman, *Gourman Report: A Rating of Graduate and Professional Programs in American and International Universities*, 2d ed. (Los Angeles: National Education Standards, 1983), pp. 76–77; 4th ed. (Los Angeles: National Education Standards, 1987), pp. 71–78.

214. "Competition Healthy, Even for Lawyers," *South China Morning Post*, 22 July 1990; Philip Bowring, "The Politics of Greed: Hongkong Lawyers Play with Fire to Preserve the Status Quo," *Far Eastern Economic Review*, 8 December 1988, pp. 72–73; Sandor, "The Legal Profession," pp. 222–23.

215. "Foreign Lawyer Plan to Be Abandoned," *South China Morning Post*, 20 July 1990.

216. Jenkin Chan Shiu-fan, "The Role of Lawyers in the Chinese Legal System," *Hong Kong Law Journal* 13.2 (1983), pp. 157–73; Philip Baker, "Some Comments on the Chinese Criminal Justice System" (paper presented at the 2d North American Conference on Human Rights and Democracy in China, Toronto, 5 April 1991), p. 4.

217. Chan, "The Role of Lawyers," p. 165.

218. Section 3 and Schedule 1.

219. Albert Chen, "Legal Aid in Hong Kong: The Way Ahead," *Hong Kong Law Journal* 18:1 (1988), pp. 1–2.

220. Legal Aid Services Council Bill, 1995.

221. The recommendations are that the Legal Aid Service Council have a supervisory role, but with no power to interfere with day to day administration. Nor will it be able to hear any appeals against the Legal Aid Department. Its role will effectively be confined to policy making and advising.

222. Ibid., pp. 3–5.

223. Emily Lau, "Lawyers Hold out Against Reform Proposals," *Far Eastern Economic Review*, 20 April 1989, p. 23.

224. Article 11.

225. Cap. 134, Laws of Hong Kong, 1982 ed.

226. Cap. 201, Laws of Hong Kong, 1987 ed.

227. *The Economist*, London, 5 November 1988, p. 22.

228. Subsection 3(2) and Paragraph II, Section I, Annex I.

229. See the sections in this chapter, "Common Law Under the Socialist Legal System," p. 68, "Separation of Powers," p. 79, and note 27.

230. Paragraph I, Section I, Annex I.

# 5

# The Decolonization of Hong Kong Education

*Gerard A. Postiglione*

As Hong Kong confronts an uncertain future, its education system is attempting to position itself within the transitional process leading to the recovery of sovereignty by China. Education is expected to play a part in cementing the reunification. New educational reforms have the potential to act as vehicles for negotiating a smooth social transition, as well as instruments for resisting decolonization.

Educational institutions and society's expectations of them are transformed dramatically only when a society's vision of its own future changes or when the conditions for the realization of that vision are perceived to change.[1] Societies approaching decolonization share a vision of their future as one in which they will gain autonomy from the colonial metropole.[2] This applies especially to the institution of education, which often spearheads the task of nation-building.[3]

With the formal signing of the Sino-British Declaration in 1984, Hong Kong's predominant vision of its future was one of continued stability and prosperity within a framework that would permit a great degree of autonomy under the sovereignty of the mother country. Until June of 1989, the conditions to carry out that vision existed, and were to be reflected in the Basic Law of the post-1997 Special Administrative Region (SAR) government. After June 4, 1989, the Basic Law Drafting Committee temporarily suspended work, revealing that the conditions for the fulfillment of the post-1997 vision had indeed changed.[4] Accordingly, the society's expectations of education also began to show signs of transformation, as the problem of reconciling capitalism, socialism, and patriotism became more pronounced. Over a hundred thousand secondary and

The original version of this chapter appeared in *Education and Society in Hong Kong: Toward One Country and Two Systems*, ed. Gerard A. Postiglione (Armonk, NY: M.E. Sharpe, 1992).

postsecondary students, teachers, and administrators joined demonstrations to express their sentiments toward events in China.[5] Education Department officials ignored enforcement of the long-standing ban on politics in schools, and school principals and teachers wrestled with how to react to students' poster displays in schools and their participation in territory-wide demonstrations.[6] Months after the Tiananmen crisis in Beijing, Hong Kong still found itself in a severe confidence crisis as cooperation between the British and Chinese governments became strained.

Such events added a new dimension to the already unusual nature of Hong Kong's decolonization process. Power had gradually shifted to the local elite and the new middle class, yet most power still resided with the British government. Hong Kong's people looked to the British government to press for a speedier pace of democratization even while Beijing denied its appropriateness. Some referred to the transfer of sovereignty as the replacement of one hegemonic force with another because the future degree of autonomy gained by the territory would not be determined by the colonial metropole or even by the people of the territory itself, but rather by Beijing. Confidence in the Sino-British agreement on Hong Kong's future was won or lost within a plural society which favored decolonization and supported Chinese sovereignty, yet remained apprehensive in the face of interference by Beijing in Hong Kong's affairs. The degree to which decolonization, as opposed to the replacement of one force by another, was taking place became a complex question that could only await the outcome of struggles over representative government in Hong Kong, and the direction of future events in China. The precise nature and characteristics of Hong Kong as a transitional society became inseparable from the evolution of these factors during the crucial period before 1997.

Education plays a role in Hong Kong's transitional period insofar as it shapes the thinking of the generation that will lead Hong Kong after 1997. It influences the selection criteria for recruitment into important positions within the civil service of the transitional government; it works to maintain a highly skilled labor force in the face of the large-scale emigration of talented people from the territory; it determines, to some extent, the degree of interaction between the educational systems of Hong Kong and other parts of China; it influences school socialization processes that build a cultural identity essential for reuniting people in Hong Kong with the rest of China; and, finally, it bolsters or restrains the general process of democratization in the society.

## From Colonial Development to National Development: The Role of Education

For most of Hong Kong's history, educational developments occurred within a colonial society built upon an *entrepôt* trade economy.[7] Beginning after 1949, skills and technology transferred from Shanghai, a steady immigration from the adjoining region of Guangdong, and increasing amounts of local investment combined with a laissez-faire economy and a British-style colonial government to promote Hong Kong's industrial foundation.[8] Successful textile manufacturing, followed by new international investments in other infant industries—through the 1960s and 1970s, including electronics—contributed to the socialization of a work force.[9] Government land sales, efficient infrastructural planning, and a growth rate averaging 10 percent each year further improved the investment climate, even as the British government entered into negotiations with the People's Republic of China on the question of sovereignty over Hong Kong. By 1990 Hong Kong had become a major international financial center with the second highest living standard in Asia, a key regional center for semiconductor manufacturing, and an important point for technology transfer to China.[10]

Hong Kong's burgeoning position as a textile trader within the European community in the 1970s led to pressure on the governor to ensure that child labor was not a factor in the territory's economic success. The implementation of free and compulsory schooling was used to indicate compliance. The rapidly expanding educational system, funded through both public and private efforts and managed through a combination of voluntary, government, and semi-government arrangements, was increasingly brought under the authority of the government's Education Department. The British tradition of elite education combined well with the Chinese tradition of examination-oriented selection for positions in government. By the early 1980s, Hong Kong had a highly bureaucratized, well-monitored, and tightly structured system of schools.

Education in Hong Kong has deviated little from its traditional colonial role. With the exception of minor revisions to the content of some school textbooks, schooling continues to socialize children in almost the same way that it has for over 140 years.[11] Moreover, China has no plans to implement an explicit educational strategy of nation-building in Hong Kong after 1997. Nevertheless, as is noted above, education is increasingly seen as a key institution in the transitional period. Specific decisions about the expansion of higher education and the introduction of civics are just two examples.[12] Also, without a military acting to strengthen a particular brand of patriotic socialization, education may take on a more important ideological function.

## Education for a Special Administrative Region: Autonomy under the Basic Law?

With the signing of the Sino-British Declaration in 1984, the territory was provided with a blueprint for its future. Although the agreement provides little detail aside from declaring the return of sovereignty over Hong Kong to China, it nevertheless permits Hong Kong to maintain its capitalist system, along with the general life-style of its people. According to the Sino-British Agreement and the Basic Law of the Hong Kong Special Administrative Region, education will maintain a great degree of autonomy.

> The Hong Kong Special Administrative Region Government shall on its own decide policies in the field of culture, education, science, and technology, including policies regarding the education system and its administration, the language of instruction, the allocation of funds, the examination system, the system of academic rewards and the recognition of educational and technological qualifications.[13]

> Community organizations and individuals may, in accordance with law, run educational undertakings of various kinds in the Hong Kong Special Administrative Region. Educational institutions of all kinds may retain their autonomy and enjoy academic freedom. They may continue to recruit staff and use teaching materials from outside the Hong Kong Special Administrative Region. Schools run by religious organizations may continue to provide religious education, including courses on religion. Students shall enjoy freedom to choose between educational institutions and pursue their education outside the Hong Kong Special Administrative Region.[14]

These statements place the control over education in the hands of the SAR government. Some groups in Hong Kong doubt that the SAR government will be autonomous and representative of the wishes of Hong Kong people. Nevertheless, in 1997 the government of the People's Republic of China will inherit a government–education relationship that is, in one way, similar to its own. In both societies educational policy has been the province of a small group of elites.[15]

## Transitional Dimensions in Comparative Perspective: The Hong Kong Factors

Although Hong Kong has little overall resemblance to most transitional societies, a number of similarities exist regarding education.[16] In colonial-to-postcolonial transitional settings, pre-independence education may remain largely unchanged throughout the transition, an exception being the specific role schools play in affirming national identity. Educational changes are found more in the content of education than in the form or structure of the system. For instance, social studies, history, and language curriculae may be revised. Colonial social structures may remain almost intact through the early postcolonial period, with the colonial power vacuum being filled by a national bourgeoisie. Hong Kong's economic system is to be retained through the transition, and the colonial elite have already been replaced by the local bourgeoisie. Nevertheless, continued emigration of large numbers of local bourgeoisie prior to 1997 could result in a totally new set of circumstances. One scenario depicts the ever-increasing Beijing-sponsored capital within the territory coupled with new immigrants from China—born and educated under socialism—replacing the present bourgeoisie with a new "socialist bourgeoisie." This is bound to have a measurable influence on the cultural ethos of Hong Kong schools.[17] Another scenario depicts increasing internationalization of many spheres, including education, as a way to discourage Beijing's explicit interference after 1997.

The conditions of education in states where a socialist transition is underway are unique.[18] Here changes in the education system are complete and comprehensive, taking on the form, structure, and philosophical foundations of the system. But socialist transition theory may have limited relevance to Hong Kong's initial transition phase. It may take at least four decades as a Special Administrative Region before Hong Kong's transition to socialism could begin. It would be a transition for which, not unlike that of 1997, Hong Kong would need ten years to prepare. Such a situation is far too remote for most Hong Kong residents to consider now. However, even if one believes that socialist transition will occur in 2047, then today's primary schoolchildren will be at the helm of the territory's socialist transition. For this reason, the education system might well begin to consider the question of how it should prepare students. Furthermore, there are indications that a socialist bourgeoisie may begin to gain greater influence in government departments—where the recruitment ban on graduates from the so-called patriotic secondary schools has been lifted—and in the government-run, post-secondary teacher training colleges, which have followed suit.[19] The patriotic secondary schools began to enter the mainstream in 1989 as they bid to join the government's proposed direct subsidy scheme for private schools.[20] The rejection by these schools of a formal curriculum in the 1960s and early 1970s, when the Cultural Revolution had spilled over into Hong Kong, had led to their exclusion from the colonial education system. There has also been further consideration of educational qualifications from China (including Taiwan) as they relate to Hong Kong's occupational structure. The emigration of talented members of the Hong Kong work force and the territory's 1 percent unemployment rate led the American Chamber of Commerce and the Institute of International Education in Hong Kong to lobby both the Hong Kong and British governments to permit recruitment of Chinese students not returning to China after completing their studies in the United States. These students would be recruited to firms in Hong Kong as a temporary step before their eventual return to China. This supplies much-needed professionally and technically skilled labor for Hong Kong. These are some of the factors affecting Hong Kong's transitional process and the role of educational institutions within that transitional period.[21]

Hong Kong begins to inform the study of education within transitional societies with such new factors as the expansion of externally sponsored national socialist capital, the increasing numbers of immigrants born and raised under socialism, and the further integration of patriotic elements into government organs and the occupational structure. At the same time, there has been an expansion of liberal groups in the territory, some going so far as to advocate the downfall of the Beijing government or of communism itself.[22] These developments become even more important when they are viewed in the context of

Hong Kong's evolving cultural ethos and the dual identities it reflects, that of Chineseness and Hong-Kongeseness.[23] As a Chinese society with a long history of colonial rule, Hong Kong has structural features distinguishable from those of both traditional and modern China. This has fostered an ethos which represents "at once a departure from dominant Chinese values and a continuation of Chinese heritage."[24] Its dual nature is visibly a postwar phenomenon and has been particularly salient with the advent of the 1997 issue and the rise to prominence of the younger generation. Furthermore, the sharp value differences that are reflected in these two identities become more distinct in the education system, which differs on such important cultural, social, and political features as the medium of instruction (English, Cantonese, or Mandarin), the political leaning of the school (in support of Beijing or Taipei), the connection of the school with various clansmen and provincial associations in China, and the school's social class composition.[25] The plurality of Hong Kong schools has existed and flourished alongside a highly centralized educational policymaking bureaucracy. For most of Hong Kong's history bureaucratic polity has enjoyed a high degree of insulation as part of a government not directly representative of the people. Nevertheless, through a variety of formal and informal consultative channels, the educational policy process maintained a threshold level of legitimacy within the Chinese community, even though schools with stronger ties to the colonial elite enjoyed greater influence.

## Trajectories for Educational Change: Limited Options

We can identify three broad options or orientations relating to school politics and educational change in Hong Kong's transitional period. Each deals in a different way with reconciling emerging problems. The first option, most likely in the short run, sees a maintenance of the status quo. The second hinges on increased democratization of the society, which would bring the pluralism of Hong Kong schools more into the forefront of the reform process, resulting in a less consensus-bound, more conflict-prone reform process. The third option envisions the replacement of the influence of one central government by another, and sees the shoring up of traditional consultative mechanisms for ensuring support for educational changes, with greater influence exerted by those individual schools and groups of schools having or building closer ties with mainland institutions.

The potential role of education in Hong Kong in solving the complex problems that will emerge during the recovery of sovereignty by China will be determined by the specific characteristics of the transitional society. Whether education will work toward reconciling or heightening the contradictions between capitalism, socialism, and patriotism, and whether schools will assume a new role in political socialization and the preparation of popular political leaders will also depend in part on the dual identities reflected in the cultural ethos of Hong Kong, as well as on how selected contextual features are brought to bear on education. Before examining these contextual features, we will review the basic characteristics of Hong Kong education, including the organization of selection, governance, policy, and reform.

## Hong Kong Education: Governance, Policy, and Reform

Throughout Hong Kong's history, a combination of government, government subsidized, and private forms of education flourished.[26] For most of its history, education in Hong Kong generally followed a colonial pattern, although Chinese education was always an accepted part of the system.[27] However, after the Second World War, a gradual move away from traditional colonialism took place as educational influence shifted slightly away from total dependence on developments in the United Kingdom. Hong Kong's population is 98 percent Chinese, and aside from the schools established for the children of expatriates and which the children of Hong Kong families who have returned from overseas increasingly attend, the school system is designed to serve the needs of the local populace.

In 1978, Hong Kong achieved a nine-year universal, free, and compulsory education system.[28] About 87 percent of the student population continues beyond nine years, with most studying in government or government-aided schools and the rest in self-financing private schools. The number of private schools declined continually until 1988, when a Direct Subsidy Scheme was proposed as a measure by which more private schools could survive. Twelve schools were admitted to the scheme in the first three years.

Under the Education Ordinance, the director of education controls all government schools and supervises all other kindergarten, primary, secondary and postsecondary institutions in the territory—with the exception of the universities and polytechnics.[29] The ordinance provides the director with broad-ranging powers over the life and practice of schooling, its staff and pupils, and in particular anything that seems like politics in schools. Most of the schools in the territory are publicly funded but privately operated. Each school has an unpaid management committee and supervisor appointed by the sponsoring body. In most cases, members of the committee are people who are not involved in policymaking or the day-to-day affairs of the school. The supervisor has considerable legal responsibility and usually works closely with the school principal in policy and personnel decisions. School principals, who have absolute power over the staff and pupils, are appointed to government schools by the education department and to other schools by the sponsoring agencies. In 1993 over a hundred schools participated in an iniative to provide for greater participation by parents, teachers, and former students in decision-making and management.

Educational policy in Hong Kong has been characterized as lying somewhere between a centralized and a decentralized system. It would be more accurate to say that decision making and policy are part of the centralized system, yet there is a broad and complex consultative process that has evolved since the late 1970s. Although the educational system is modeled closely on that of the United

Kingdom in its structure, organization, admission and examination regulations, and curriculum, it is far from a duplicate of that or any other system. Traditionally, educational policy has been the province of an influential elite of the colony who are not representative of the people as much as reflective of the powers that be. As the system expanded in the 1960s and 1970s, the policy process became more complex, with a variety of education associations, unions, and pressure groups all entering into the consultative process.

In general, the highest decision maker is the governor-in-council. Four committees advise the governor on educational matters. The Board of Education concerns itself with education from kindergarten to sixth form, the University and Polytechnic Grants Committee is responsible for funding and development of university education, and the Vocational Training Council is responsible for technical education. A lack of coordination led to the founding of a fourth committee, the Education Commission, composed of appointed members of the community and representatives from the other three committees. It provides consolidated advice to the governor on the overall development of the education system.[328]

A key feature of educational policy in Hong Kong as it bears on transitional processes concerns the maintenance of legitimacy. Colonial societies carry with them an inherent suspicion of government and an opposition to its policies. The Hong Kong government has skillfully minimized this problem of maintaining support for its educational policies by building an extensive consultative network. Having the chance to be heard by government increases the satisfaction of groups, which thereby yields a threshold level of legitimacy to the government's policies. This occurs within a system that has a marked degree of pluralism under a centralized, non-representative structure of territory-wide educational governance.

## Educational Transformations: The Shifting Social Context

Educational changes during most of Hong Kong's history have occurred within the context of a minimally integrated sociopolitical system. A British-controlled autonomous bureaucratic polity has existed alongside an atomistic Chinese society.[31] Until the latter part of the 1980s, the government was able to remain largely secluded from Chinese society. However, more activism from society, particularly in the struggles for more representative government, has brought a new sociopolitical context to bear on educational issues. It is to this context that we now turn.

### *Decolonization and the Transformation of the Length of University Education*

Educational issues during decolonization have long been a serious problem in former British colonies such as India, Kenya and Malaysia, where history shows that events leading to drastic changes in tertiary education have been repeated again and again. Political observers and educational reformers have suggested that in the past, education was used as a powerful tool for Britain to keep control over its colonies following decolonization. The elite education system allowed the British government to continue its influence on those who received tertiary education and would become community leaders. This would ensure a favorable link with the territory after British withdrawal.[32]

The Hong Kong Education Commission has worked toward a continuation of British-style higher education. Its most controversial educational reform proposal had a direct bearing on the issue of decolonization.[33] This reform was directed at sixth form education, but had major implications for Hong Kong's two universities. The reform's stated intention was to standardize sixth form education (high school grade 12), reduce examination pressure, and unify the admission scheme to universities. Its effect was to bring the issue of length of university education to the forefront.

Prior to the Education Commission's recommendations, the University of Hong Kong had recognized the problem of sixth form education as it affected the quality of the pool of candidates from which it drew its students. The university decided to develop a foundation year, which would be attached to the beginning of the already existing three-year program.[34] The foundation year was designed to provide new students with a broad curriculum and language improvement opportunities. This change would have brought the University of Hong Kong into line with the Chinese University of Hong Kong, thus eliminating the need for sixth form students to surmount the dreaded Advanced Level examinations before entering the University of Hong Kong.

The Education Commission's report cited the narrowness of sixth form education and how it fostered students "who lack maturity, initiative, and innovation."[35] However, the commission favored broadening the sixth form rather than making modifications at the university level. A major reason cited was the high financial cost of extending university education and the concern with finding competent lecturers to staff it.

This reform was unique in the way that it broke the past pattern of consensus-bound educational reform and delivered the policymaking process into a conflict-prone mode of educational reform. At one time, 4,000 university students marched on the government in protest against the plan. Many educational groups in Hong Kong entered the fray, revealing a deep split in preference for and against the reform.[36] Although the heads of the major postsecondary institutions were opposed to the reform, the Legislative Council voted, by a narrow margin, in favor of it.

The government's strong ties to British higher education were enough to stifle any movement toward a four-year university system. With encouragement from the government, the influential subsidized secondary schools council came out in favor of the proposal, tipping the balance in favor of maintaining upper sixth form schooling. The proposal had important resource implications, thus acting to unite secondary school principals who received government subsidies for the upper year of their secondary schools. The funding for this year stood to be eliminated if a four-year university structure came into being.

The issue of truncating the Chinese University program from four to three years was not new.[37] Although it had been debated before, the context of the deliberations surrounding the latest debate was different in that the Sino-British Declaration added strength to the case for bringing Hong Kong university education into line with that in China. At one time, opposition groups even appealed, although unsuccessfully, to China's quasi-ambassador in Hong Kong, asking him to become involved and support the four-year structure of higher education since it coincided with that in the rest of China. Thus, some have come to view this case as signifying neither an abandonment of the Chinese character of the Chinese University of Hong Kong, nor the embracing of colonial values, but rather an acknowledgment that groups in Hong Kong are prepared to exercise their right, as spelled out in the Joint Declaration, to resist following the model of education in China.

The way in which government handled this reform highlighted a break with the past tradition of activating the elaborate consultation network and soliciting outside expertise in order to create the legitimacy needed to carry out its reforms more smoothly.[38] Moreover, since that time the government has seemed less concerned about its legitimacy in educational matters. This was evident more than a year later when it acted without consultation and proposed to double the number of places in tertiary education by 1996.[39] In contrast to the earlier reform, the government neither seemed concerned about the cost of financing the dramatic expansion, nor the difficulty of finding competent lecturers to staff the expanded system. While some have seen this as a way of rewarding tertiary institutions for their compliance with the earlier reform, others saw it as a form of crisis management and confidence building in the wake of the large emigration of talented people that followed the June 4 incident.

## Transforming Political Socialization and Preparing Political Leaders

The schools have never been a force in democratizing Hong Kong, and, if anything, have hindered the process. The school curriculum has, until the late 1980s, virtually ignored raising political consciousness. The planned return of sovereignty changed that to some degree by leading to minor modifications of the school curriculum. However, political democracy remained a topic to be avoided. Nevertheless, the government is concerned with doing what it can to ensure that popular political disruptions do not mar the return of sovereignty.[40]

Changes in the school curriculum, as noted by Paul Morris, provide much-needed legitimacy to a colonial government that has often been accused of dragging its feet for many years before introducing opportunities for representative government.[41] In this sense, people view the curriculum as an instrument to bolster their attempts at expanded representative government.

After the signing of the Joint Declaration in 1984, the number and range of school curriculum topics dealing with political awareness increased. Although this may be associated in any society with a general trend toward more affluence and a growing middle class, it derived at least equally from the expected return of sovereignty in 1997. The greatest stress is placed on the responsibilities of good citizenship, while activities that encourage political involvement are minimized. Two quotations from the government guidelines for civic education reflect this: "In light of Hong Kong's recent political development, evolution should be the watch-word and the emphasis in this guide will be on civic education as a politically socializing force for promoting stability and responsibility," and, "Democracy means different things to different people . . . so education for democracy per se would be difficult to interpret."[42]

Education officials have also lifted the taboo on teaching about post-1949 China. However, many school principals want to teach children about modern China but are encountering difficulties. In particular, it is difficult to get teachers to analyze the present regime. Teachers are reluctant to discuss post-1949 history of China, with the result that Hong Kong is fostering a generation of young people who have only the slightest understanding of their future as Chinese citizens. New government guidelines on civic education to be issued before 1997 are set to address this problem.

Following the recommendation of the *Education Commission Report No. 3,* a working group named the Working Group on Sixth Form Education was set up in June 1988 to consider the curriculum reform.[43] In July 1989, the working group submitted its report to the Secretary for Education and Manpower, who endorsed the recommendations. One recommendation was the introduction of a new course entitled "Liberal Studies," which would be offered beginning in September 1992 as a way of broadening the curriculum and making it more relevant to Hong Kong's future. The main modules included in the course were entitled Hong Kong Studies, Environmental Studies, The Modern World, Science Technology and Society, China Today, and Human Relationships.[44] Despite the benefits of such a long-overdue reform, the curriculum's restriction to the sixth form and its status as an optional course act to relegate this reform to the backwaters. Its successful implementation has been further threatened by the universities which have refused to make it an admission requirement.

These curriculum changes occurred against a backdrop of important changes in the political culture of Hong Kong during the late 1980s. The sociopolitical landscape has been gradually transformed from its traditionally apolitical orientation. Rapid economic growth, expanded educational opportunity, and a younger population have led to a decline of traditional institutions and social customs. Social and economic issues have been pushed into the political arena, leading to demands for more government action. After a long period in which a secluded bureaucracy existed apart from the Chinese society, there have been new efforts to formalize government–people relationships. An increasing number of people believe that the government is responsible for solving their personal and family problems. The people of Hong Kong are fast adopting an active, even interventionist concept of government, and they would like to see the government measure up to their expectations. Moreover, as the growth of political pressure groups continues, it is apparent that the people of Hong Kong are becoming more favorably disposed toward many kinds of political activism. A prominent Hong Kong political scientist notes that "tactics which involve a quantum of confrontation or violence are increasingly rated as effective means to compel the government to give in."[45] This is no small change. However, there is still a lack of adequate local structures for social and political participation, including areas of educational decision making. Nevertheless, the curriculum changes discussed, coupled with the general move toward more political activity within schools and the increasingly activist role played by teachers in grass-roots politics, point to a move away from a status quo orientation that prevents schools from taking a more visible role in territorywide education reforms.

Political leaders are slowly beginning to emerge from the school system. In fact, educators had a pronounced role in the first direct elections to the Legislative Council in September of 1991.[46] Teaching professionals have an edge over others because they can make use of longer holiday periods to organize campaigns and canvass for support. Moreover, the nature of the profession, and the knowledge among the public that teacher salaries are not nearly as high as for other occupations that command an equal level of educational qualifications, contribute to the image of the teacher as a dedicated politician.

However, in order for schools to become more effective in producing popular political leaders, they will have to integrate themselves into their surrounding communities. They are now isolated units. A 1982 report by a visiting panel stated:

> At the school level, there is little sense of community despite the fact that many schools can be found clustered together geographically. Even when the citing of new facilities has been premeditated, these can not be regarded as community schools in the usual sense of the phrase. The extensive devolution of authority and responsibility of voluntary agencies in the education portfolio and the fact that these agencies are not federated on a neighborhood basis makes it impractical to contemplate "local control" beyond that currently being contemplated in the school net schemes.[47]

The schools' isolation from the surrounding community is intensified by the lack of parental involvement in their operations. Parental involvement within schools is usually limited to formal parent–teacher association meetings (where they exist) and to rare school visits when a child's problems prompt the teacher to call for a parent. There is a strict and still widely accepted separation of roles between parents and teachers, and between home and school, deriving partly from the alienation many parents feel due to their own lack of schooling. Education authorities introduced a school management initiative in March 1991 that could be used to increase parental involvement in school affairs.

Despite the densely populated nature of the Hong Kong community, and the geographic position of schools within residential areas, the schools are not integrated into the communities. The social distance of the school from the surrounding community derives not only from the lack of contact between teachers and parents, but also from the lack of contact between school leaders and the community. School management boards do not see themselves as directly accountable to the surrounding community. The only perceived accountability is to the Education Department, which makes financial allocations and inspects the schools. Although they are essentially powerless, District Board officials are elected by members of the community and could provide a way for residents to channel their opinions about school problems to the government. However, District Board officials are seldom approached on educational matters.[48]

During the territorywide demonstrations of May and June 1989, some popular leaders did emerge from the schools because they embodied the sentiments of many Hong Kong people. Moreover, these demonstrations were also an opportunity for some young leaders to emerge from the ranks of the large number of secondary and tertiary school students.

### Decolonizing the Selection System: Language as Cultural Capital

Localization, a process in which local people are increasingly given priority in appointments to high-level posts in government and industry, was never taken as a serious objective until the signing of the Joint Declaration on Hong Kong's future in 1984. Before then, expatriates were clearly favored for recruitment to upper-level government posts. Just prior to the Sino-British Joint Declaration, the political scientist Myron Mushkat expressed the following view:

> A more subtle explanation for the extent of expatriate recruitment is that it dovetails with the higher objectives of "colonial control." Hong Kong, after all, is a British dependent territory and in order to fulfill its role with a measure of effectiveness the United Kingdom must have at its disposal reliable mechanisms for providing societal direction. The presence of a fairly large number of Britons in key policy-making posts may thus be construed as a factor which facilitates "colonial management." One could argue, however, that this legitimate objective no longer requires the balancing of each local appointment with an expatriate one and that a ratio more favorable to the local component need not detract from the U.K.'s grip over Hong Kong.[49]

The Hong Kong government officially adopted localization of the civil service as official policy as early as 1947, but by the mid-1980s a significant number of high-level positions continued to be held by expatriates.[50] Expatriates comprised almost half of all directorate officers and almost one-third of those at the top of the Master Pay Scale.[51] According to the Sino-British Declaration on Hong Kong, after 1997, "The government and legislature of the Hong Kong Special Administrative Region shall be composed of local inhabitants."[52] Furthermore, while foreign nationals may be employed by the future Hong Kong civil service, they may not hold posts as heads of major government departments, including the police department, or as deputy heads of some of those departments.[53] In his study of government planning with respect to government localization policy, John Burns concluded that

> it indicates a failure of the government's policy of localization over the years. Coherent plans to localize problem grades and departments are urgently needed. Hong Kong must develop a confident, forward-looking civil service for the years up to and beyond 1997. Much needs to be done.[54]

Since then, however, the government appointed the first non-expatriate as director of education.[55] Local Hong Kong Chinese are increasingly appointed to top posts in other government departments as well. Nevertheless, because of the great exodus following the Sino-British agreement, the pace of localization has slowed, particularly in the middle-level civil service. In an effort to stall the exodus of key individuals, the British government is proposing to make available 50,000 "insurance" passports, carrying the right to live in the United Kingdom, and is encouraging other nations with large interests in Hong Kong to do the same.[56] This may confound the educational policy process by creating strong loyalty to the United Kingdom, even after 1997. China has already asserted that it will not recognize the overseas passports of local residents of Chinese descent, and will undoubtedly develop countermeasures throughout the transitional period for what it sees as an illegitimate means to limit its sovereignty.

By gearing up to teach English-language courses that encourage success on linguistically based civil service examinations, educational changes have been increasingly fashioned to dovetail with the recruitment of native Hong-Kongese to the civil service. This has been accomplished through a policy process that reflects the colonial support for elite schools and the preservation of the University of Hong Kong as a wholly English-medium institution. English-language facility and cultural consonance are essential for the recruitment and promotion of graduates from the University of Hong Kong in the civil service.

This emphasis also led to the creation of a large Anglo-Chinese system of secondary schools. By the early 1980s this sector of the educational system peaked, surpassing the number of Chinese instruction schools by nine to one.[57] However, although the official medium of instruction in the Anglo-Chinese schools was English, the limited number of competent English-speaking teachers led to many variations in the quality of language instruction. Even when competent English-speaking teachers were available, a great many students were not able to learn in English. Parents resisted pleas by educators to reconsider educating their children in Anglo-Chinese schools instead of Chinese instruction schools. The Education Department eventually took steps to increase the number of schools in the Chinese sector by providing incentives to those questionable Anglo-Chinese schools to convert to Chinese instruction. This, it was hoped, would result in an increase in the number of Chinese-medium secondary schools, and a corresponding influence on the ethos of many Hong Kong secondary schools.

The medium of instruction in most secondary schools in Hong Kong is still officially English, which places a tremendous burden on students since most have little contact with native English speakers. The effects of this practice on culture and identity is of more interest to researchers than parents, most of whom continue to opt for as much English-medium education for their children as possible.[58] Children who attend elite English-medium schools are at an advantage in being recruited to government civil service posts. Public policies do not seek to redress this, as noted again by a visiting panel.

> There also seems to be an element of safeguarding privilege by an elite whose children are more or less bilingual. Everyone should try by the best legitimate means to secure the best start for his own child, but we feel the public policies should look particularly to the needs of those whose starting positions are not so favorable.[59]

This pattern may be reinforced further by a new set of language-policy proposals the government is considering. These would make entrance into English-language secondary education dependent on an examination administered after primary six.[60] The proposals' stated aim is to improve competency in at least one language and eliminate the use of "Chinglish," a mixture of English and Chinese words in the teaching–learning process.

However, all past government-initiated language proposals have fallen short of implementation. The medium-of-instruction controversy dates back to the end of World War II, the government forever being in the bind of eliminating either parental choice or sound educational practice. Some accuse the government of being halfhearted. In the case of Putonghua (Mandarin) teaching, the government recommended the language as an option but failed to make it a requirement. In 1984, the Education Commission recommended that the schools teach Putonghua either before or after hours or as an extracurricular activity, but few schools adopted it as the main medium of instruction.[61] It was not until December 1995 that the Education Commission recommended that, in the long term, Putonghua should become part of the core curriculum for all primary and secondary school students. Some researchers are confident that Putonghua will replace English and Cantonese as the language of power and the official language of government, and that everyone will be required to learn it.[62]

Growing business opportunities in the China trade and investment area, along with an expansion of interactions between China and Hong Kong, have added to a new ground swell favoring schooling in the Chinese mother tongue over English-language schooling. In fact, the battle to preserve Hong Kong's status as an English-speaking territory is far from won. At the same time, many educators in China have criticized Hong Kong's return to Chinese mother tongue education because Hong Kong Chinese consider Cantonese, rather than Putonghua, to be their lingua franca.[63] Many educators strongly resist the use of Mandarin as a learning medium in their schools. This represents yet another example of how the dual identity of Hong Kong's cultural ethos manifests itself within educational issues, even as it impinges on localization and recruitment into the government civil service. Thus, school language policy, and the extent to which individuals can function competently in Putonghua, Cantonese, and English, can easily come to influence the legitimacy of emerging political leaders and the orientation that educational reform will take.

**Social Stratification and the Transformation of Elite Education**

There is a staggering degree of income inequality in Hong Kong. While the average citizen enjoys the third-highest living standard in Asia, many still live without running water or legal electricity.[64] In most societies, such levels of inequality generate class conflict and industrial hostilities. However, when industry, trade, and commerce are prosperous and the labor market is active, the wages of workers in Hong Kong are still much better than those of their counterparts on the mainland. Except for the sporadic unrest in 1956, 1967, and 1984, the territory has been stable, with little overt social conflict since the end of World War II. There are signs indicating the emergence of a politically conscious middle class that is beginning to play a more active role in organizing itself in community political affairs. This emerging class is gaining more control over the educational system, which helps ensure that their children inherit their middle-class status. A future concern with regard to China's regaining sovereignty over Hong Kong is less its willingness to tolerate capitalism than its tolerance of the great gaps that exist among social classes in Hong Kong.

Access to opportunity has increasingly been placed within the domain of formal education. Chinese tradition holds education in high esteem, and the idea of having a scholarly examination system as a key determinant for access to high positions, especially in government, is not new to the Chinese.[65] However, the character of the school selection process in Hong Kong has been extremely competitive. Even though education is compulsory (and free) until age fifteen, only 8 percent were able to secure a university place in 1989. The extent of equity within this system is questionable although, as is often the case in other industrial societies, the meritocratic ideology (at least the notion that anyone who is capable and works hard in school, regardless of social class factors, can achieve success) has remained quite durable.

Research on educational success in Hong Kong has consistently confirmed what has been all too evident in the Western developed nations—that family background, however measured, is a major predictor of school achievement.[66] However, school characteristics also play a large role. In this regard, there is a great disparity among schools, as confirmed in the visiting panel's report:

> There are striking variations indeed. Hong Kong has some of the best schools in the world in terms of student attainment . . . most of the schools however, leave something to be desired. Facilities, teacher qualifications, examination results and other indicators of quality rank low. Students are allocated to these schools for various reasons, including their test performance and lack of opportunity owing to the educational and economic status of their parents.[67]

Little has been done to relieve this problem. If the economy goes through a period of crisis, this could highlight the gap between the social classes and increase the likelihood that the schools will become an arena of social class conflict. Whether or not social class conflict can work itself into the cultural fabric of the Chinese society in Hong Kong in such a way as to avoid becoming dangerously divisive remains an important question. If it cannot, then it may pose yet another threat to the realization of extended democratic educational changes.

## Interdependence and Academic Exchange

There has been a growing interdependence, both economically and politically, between Hong Kong and the People's Republic of China. China is well-justified in its assertion that it is responsible for the economic success of Hong Kong. Through immigration, it provides the indispensable manpower needed to fuel Hong Kong's industrialization. China also subsidizes a large percentage of Hong Kong's foodstuffs and provides relatively inexpensive clothing. Moreover, the mainland provides the colony with 35 percent of its water supply. Hong Kong remains a useful contact point with the West for China. The most common explanation for China's position with respect to Hong Kong has been, and remains, mutual advantage. The points of interdependence between China and Hong Kong are unique to ideologically opposed economic systems. Hong Kong is the largest market for China's exports, while China has become the second-largest export market for Hong Kong.[68] In short, Hong Kong is a major source of China's investment capital and will continue to play a major role in financing China's modernization.

The cultural system of the Hong Kong Chinese is heterogeneous. Among the 98 percent ethnic Chinese majority, according to Lau, there are "variations in dialect, customs, and styles of living as well as lingering hostilities among locality groupings which would be readily available cleavage lines to divide society into antagonistic frameworks."[69] Hong Kong's Chinese society is the product of a continual adjustment process in a society of Chinese people who are divided by ethnic, territorial, dialectical, and ideological identifications. The urbanization of Chinese regional groups within the Hong Kong context seems to have converted these regional groups into ethnic groups. This process has been noted in detail with three Chinese regional groups in Hong Kong—the Shanghainese, Fujianese, and Chao Zhouese.[70] As long as we do not consider ethnicity to be a rigid set of beliefs, behaviors, or customs, but rather one dimension of beliefs, behaviors, and customs that articulate closely with other dimensions of life and culture, then we can more easily see how Chinese regional groups take on the characteristics of ethnic groups when they migrate to an urban area like Hong Kong. Instead of viewing ethnicity as isolated, we see it as part of a process and a situational construct. As such, it exists only as a specific adaption and orientation to a given set of circumstances during a given period of time. Chinese regional groups who migrate to Hong Kong, such as the Shanghainese, Fujianese, or Chao Zhouese, engage in such a process of adaption and develop situational orientations, allowing them both to become a part of and remain apart from the Hong Kong Cantonese culture.

Nevertheless, the diversity of regional groups in Hong Kong is not outwardly reflected in a varied regionally based school system. With the exception of the handful of Chinese secondary schools that draw students from particular regions, most are heterogeneous. Therefore, the schools cannot be viewed as institutions that preserve regional ethnic cultures. Except for the few secondary schools that use Putonghua (Mandarin) as the medium of instruction, Cantonese mixed with varying amounts of English is the norm. Schools expose students of non-Cantonese origin to local Cantonese culture. This does not eliminate regional subcultures and the identities that derive from them, but it provides students from other regions with sufficient access to the local cultural milieu.

Economic interdependence with China has not been accompanied by educational or academic interdependence. There is virtually no structural interdependence between the two educational systems. Formal institutional agreements have been signed between universities in Hong Kong and those in other parts of China. The number and diversity of Chinese universities would make it difficult to choose only a few with which to set up formal arrangements, since agreements with many institutions could easily become overwhelming given the size of Hong Kong's two universities. Informal exchanges allow links to be maintained with a large number of higher educational institutions in China. Thus, most formal academic exchanges and research projects are conducted through faculty or academic department agreements, although each university sets aside funds that members of departments and faculties can use in academic exchange.

Since the early 1980s there has been an increasing amount of academic exchange between Hong Kong and the rest of China.[71] The early phase brought university staff together but resulted in little substantive cooperative work. The later phase initiated joint cooperative projects between departments or faculties of different institutions, including those facilitated by the World Bank and other international agencies. There are also organizations within Hong Kong, such as the Beijing–Hong Kong Academic Exchange Center and the Peihua Foundation, which encourage and sponsor academic exchange between universities in Hong Kong and other parts of China.[72] Student exchanges in both directions have also increased. Special scholarships have led the way for an increasing number of Hong Kong students to study at China's leading universities, although the number dropped after June 4, 1989. By June 1990, postgraduate enrollment had decreased by 75 percent. China's State Education Commission coordinated the selection of Hong Kong students for admission to graduate study and scholarships were provided to cover expenses at more than forty tertiary institutions in China, including key-point universities such as Beijing University and Qinghua University.[73] This adds to the already large number of Hong Kong students attending universities in South China, in close proximity to Hong Kong. More students from China are enrolled in graduate than undergraduate programs in Hong Kong's two universities, and their numbers have steadily increased.

Hong Kong's interdependence goes beyond linking itself with China. As an international trading center, it has developed economic interdependence with many other nations, and this has made itself felt in the educational arena. Over 90 percent of university staff in Hong Kong earned their doctorates outside of the territory. Furthermore, there are at least 30,000 Hong Kong students earning postsecondary degrees outside of Hong Kong.[74]

Given that it is strengthening ties with universities in other parts of China where academic freedom is often limited, there has been surprisingly little concern expressed within Hong Kong's universities over academic freedom. Moreover, in an international survey of higher-education faculty views, Hong Kong ranked below its East Asian neighbors, Japan and South Korea, in response to the question of whether academic freedom is strongly protected in the society.[75] The tenure system in Hong Kong's universities protects the critical scholar. However, a large number of non-tenure, three-year renewable contracts offered to new recruits have shown their potential to make critical academics more vulnerable. Unlike Hong Kong's journalists, who have steadfastly battled the forces that threaten their future openness, the universities have yet to bring this issue to the forefront.

Interdependence with the rest of China has a tremendous potential to influence the educational reform process in Hong Kong and in China as well. The extent of Beijing's influence will be determined by whether it is mediated through an educational reform process that is essentially democratic, or exerted through a restructured consultative system designed to align educational developments with mainland interests.

## Cultural Tradition, Educational Transformation, and the Hong Kong Identity

Traditional Chinese society was perpetuated by a state-dominated social order, which has existed for one hundred and fifty years in colonial Hong Kong. However, a different conception of the state–society relationship has appeared. Only in the last two decades has this conception undergone changes, while the basic nature of the political order has remained intact. Thus, the state-dominated society of Hong Kong is different in many ways from that of traditional Chinese society and of mainland China.

Governance in Hong Kong is characterized by such elements as authoritarianism, benign and enlightened rule, separate but blurred public and private spheres, and the rule of law. As Lau Siu-kai and Kuan Hsin-chi state:

> The establishment of colonial rule in Hong Kong was based until several decades ago on military force. In the long span of colonial rule, subtle versions of the doctrine of the economic prowess and cultural superiority of the white people, and the civilizing mission of the colonizer, had occasionally emerged to justify colonial dominance. Still, there has not been an elaborate, systematic theory, explicitly articulated, to buttress the legitimacy of authority in Hong Kong.[76]

Confucianism, for instance, disappeared from the content of Hong Kong civil service examinations. This deprived the residual Confucian presence of instrumental value and relegated it to cultural backwaters. The Confucian influence lingers, but is contingent more on the natural influence of social customs and family socialization than on any institutional underpinning, such as schooling.

Hong Kong Chinese society differs from traditional and modern Chinese society in a number of ways: its high degree of modernization, industrialization, and urbanization; its dominance by market forces; the erosion of tradition; the adapted changes in the family and other primary and quasi-primary structures; the lack of a moralizing elite; and the dominance of an economic elite. Furthermore, the values embodied in the Hong Kong Chinese elites differ from their counterparts in China.

Hong Kong's history has left the school system with the task of resolving the tensions that have resulted from a long colonial period. Dora Choi Po-king recognizes in the identity crisis of Hong Kong students the strains between cultural tradition and modern education. She goes part way toward explaining the source of this tension in the 1970s:

> The post-war generation was, therefore, bombarded with Western cultural influence both in and outside the school. Yet they were constantly reminded of their Chinese cultural heritage, and they did acquire a national cultural identity which was, however, never substantiated by any concrete ties, nor even candid discussion of relevant political developments. Caught in this ambiguous situation, the Hong Kong–born post-war generation met with a severe crisis of cultural identity.[77]

Lau and Kuan also note the distinctive ethos of the Hong Kong people as a post-war phenomenon that has become more salient with the onset of the transition to 1997, and the rise of the younger, more educated generation. They suggest the existence of two identities in Hong Kong, Chinese and Hong-Kongese:

> Sudden and dramatic confrontation with one's fellow "compatriots" who differed from oneself in many significant ways willy-nilly forced one to ask the soul-searching question of "Who I am?" . . . Hong Kong Chinese are made more conscious of their distinct identity when placed in juxtaposition with the mainland Chinese people.[78]

These local scholars continue to raise questions about the implications of the reincorporation of Hong Kong in 1997, especially as it relates to the apparent tension in the cultural identity of Hong Kong students. They identify the educational challenge of 1997 as socialization into a "one country, two system" society. Hong Kong education will be beset with a major dilemma, that of building an educational system that can reconcile the ideological contradictions between capitalism, socialism, and patriotism, and preparing local political leaders who can guide Hong Kong through the postcolonial transition.

## Conclusion: Education and Social Transformations

As decolonization proceeds and Hong Kong becomes closer to China, the potential for social transformation will become more closely tied to the ability of educational institutions to prepare popular political leaders. This will require a fundamental change in the manner of political socialization in secondary schools and tertiary institutions. The government's guidelines on civic education, the modification of the ban on political activity in schools, and the liberal studies curriculum go part way to this end. Moreover, an increasing number of teachers and school principals are becoming active in local elections aimed at guaranteeing more representative government. However, much more will have to be done to have any effect upon the factors, noted by Lau, that have impeded such leadership. These include the nature of colonial governance; the character of the Chinese community; the institutional features of the local sociopolitical system; time constraints; the inconsistent and incoherent leadership policy of the British and Chinese governments; and elusive and erratic mass support for leaders.[79] The educational changes discussed above have only begun to approach this important challenge. However, future educational reforms can be expected to pay increasing attention to this issue.

Each of the three broad orientations identified earlier in this chapter has the potential to reconcile or heighten contradictions. The likelihood of any single one prevailing will depend on the way in which the other macroscopic social transformations affect education during the period before and after 1997. At a minimum, the contextual processes outlined above reveal a tension developing between each of these orientations. The apparent increased vulnerability of the policy process places the long-term future of the first orientation in serious doubt. Hong Kong's ability to secure its preferred model of representative government from Beijing before 1997 is certain to shape events in favor of the second policy option. However, the degree to which the people of Hong Kong can acquire, accept, and work within the conflict-prone policy process of a more representative government will determine whether or not a centralizing force will be asserted after 1997. Such a centralizing influence would rebuild the traditional consultative mechanism for maintaining the legitimacy of the educational policy process. Given the uncertainty of future events, each option remains a possibility.

The degree to which each of the three broad orientations reconciles or heightens the contradictions between capitalism, socialism, and patriotism will also be determined in large measure by the way in which the macroscopic social transformations affect education. As is apparent from the experience of Eastern European societies, the contradictions between capitalism and socialism is reconciled when the citizenry becomes actively engaged in social transformation. This leaves only the second policy option as holding out any real hope for reconciliation. The challenge will be to show that patriotism must be harmonized in such a way as to allow opposition groups to thrive within a democratic framework.

How Hong Kong's educational system handles this situation in years to come will be of interest to scholars of social change. Unfortunately, the colonial history of Hong Kong shows some cause for disappointment. It supports the idea that the Hong Kong educational system of the 1990s will resist the changes necessary to reconcile such contradictions, specifically in the area of more popular democratic participation in the educational reform process. Hong Kong will have a strong tendency to shy away from significant reforms because of its long-standing economic success under the colonial government. This is understandable to an extent. However, carrying on as usual will only lead Hong Kong education into a greater dilemma. The territory will have to show greater flexibility—channels for active participation by all sectors of the society in educational matters must be widened, and resulting conflicts must be viewed in a constructive manner as part of a mature reforming society, not just as threats to stability and prosperity.

## Notes

I would like to thank Lee Wing On for his useful comments.

1. See Robert Church, *Education in the United States: An Interpretive History* (New York: Free Press, 1976).

2. See Philip G. Altbach and Gail P. Kelly, eds., *Education and Colonialism* (New York: Longman, 1978).

3. See Ingemar Fagerlind and Lawrence J. Saha, *Education and National Development: A Comparative Perspective* (Oxford: Pergamon Press, 1983).

4. Among the first to resign from the Basic Law Drafting Committee were the outspo-

ken liberal legislative councilors Lee Chu Ming and Szeto Wah. The editor of the *Ming Bao* daily newspaper, Louis Cha, who formerly had supported the Beijing government, also resigned after June 4, 1989.

5. See *Hong Kong Standard* and *Wen Hui Bao*, June 5, 1989.

6. See "Call to End Politics Ban in Schools," in *South China Morning Post*, June 7, 1989. On June 16, 1989, the University of Hong Kong Faculty of Education conducted a territorywide meeting of school teachers and principals in which accounts of student activism within and outside of schools were discussed. Most students were involved in territorywide demonstrations; however, many had organized activities at school such as speeches, political poster displays, letter writing, and student assemblies.

7. See Anthony E. Sweeting, *Education in Hong Kong, pre-1841 to 1941: Fact and Opinion* (Hong Kong: University of Hong Kong Press, 1990).

8. See Wong Siu-lun, *Emigrant Entrepreneurs: Shanghai Industrialists in Hong Kong* (Hong Kong: Oxford University Press, 1988).

9. See Edward K.Y. Chen, *Multinational Corporations, Technology, and Employment* (London: Macmillan, 1983).

10. See Jeffrey Henderson, "Hong Kong: High Technology Production and the Makings of a Regional Core," in Jeffrey Henderson, ed., *Global Option: Society, Space, and the Internationalization of High Technology Production* (London: Croom Helm, 1987).

11. See Lau, *Society and Politics in Hong Kong* (Hong Kong: Chinese University of Hong Kong Press, 1982).

12. "Academic Hits Out at Crisis Intervention," in *South China Morning Post*, November 5, 1989; and, "Tertiary Doors Will Open to More Students," in *South China Morning Post: Year in Review*, January 14, 1990.

13. *A Draft Agreement between the Government of Great Britain and Northern Ireland and the Government of the People's Republic of China on the Future of Hong Kong* (Hong Kong: Government Printer, 1984).

14. The Secretariat of the Consultative Committee for the Basic Law, *Draft Basic Law of the Hong Kong Special Administrative Region of the People's Republic of China* (Hong Kong: The Secretariat of the Consultative Committee for the Basic Law, 1988). See also those Chinese sources on the subject of the "one country, two system" policy: Zhao Qiuyi, *Yiguo liangzhi gailun* (Jilin University Press, 1988); Zhao Xiaowang, Deng Yun, and Zhou Bingyin, *Yige guojia liang zhong zhidu* (Liberation Army Press, 1989); *Xianggong wenti wenjian: xuanji* (Beijing: Renmin chubanshe, 1985); *Xianggong jiaoyu mianguan* (Guangdong renmin chubanshe, 1988); and Lei Qiang, Wu Fuguang, Zhong Guang, and Zheng Tainxiang, *Xianggong gaodeng jiaoyu* (Guangdong gaodeng jiaoyu chubanshe, 1988).

15. See *The Hong Kong Education System* (Hong Kong: Education Department, 1981). For an earlier historical account, see Sweeting, *Education in Hong Kong, pre-1841 to 1941: Fact and Opinion*, and Bernard Luk Hung-Kay, "Chinese Culture in the Hong Kong Curriculum," paper presented at the Annual Conference of the Comparative and International Education Society, Harvard University, March 31, 1989.

16. See Philip G. Altbach and Gail P. Kelly, eds., *Education and Colonialism*, pp. 1–52.

17. See Lau Siu-kai and Kuan Hsin-chi, *The Ethos of the Hong Kong Chinese* (Hong Kong: The Chinese University of Hong Kong Press, 1988).

88. See Martin Carnoy, *The State and Political Theory* (Princeton: Princeton University Press, 1985).

19. "Leftist School Leavers Gain Acceptance," *South China Morning Post*, October 2, 1989. What distinguishes these so-called patriotic, leftist, or pro-China schools is that they have traditionally supported the Beijing government's policies. During the Cultural

Revolution, for instance, they rejected the formal curriculum of the Hong Kong education department. These schools have the strongest links with schools in mainland China.

20. See "Pro-China Schools in Subsidy Bid," *South China Morning Post*, October 8, 1989.

21. See *Returning to Hong Kong: 1990*, Glen Shive, ed. (Hong Kong: American Chamber of Commerce with the Institute of International Education, 1991).

22. See *South China Morning Post*, January 1, 1990.

23. See Lau and Kuan, *The Ethos of the Hong Kong Chinese.*

24. Ibid., p. 187.

25. See *Xianggong jiaoyu shouce* (Xianggong: Shangwu shuguan, 1988); Huo Guoqiang, *Xianggong zhongxue gailan* (Xianggong: Xianggong zhonghua jidujiao qingnianhui, 1988).

26. See Anthony E. Sweeting, "The Reconstruction of Education in Post-War Hong Kong) 1945–54: Variations in the Process of Policy Making," Ph.D. dissertation, University of Hong Kong, 1989.

27. See Ng Lun Ngai-ha, *Interaction of East and West: The Development of Public Education in Early Hong Kong* (Hong Kong: The Chinese University of Hong Kong Press).

28. Hong Kong Government, *Hong Kong: 1984* (Hong Kong: Government Printer, 1985).

29. See Bernard Luk Hung-Kay, "Education," in Tsim Tak-lung and Bernard Luk Hung-kay, eds., *The Other Hong Kong Report* (Hong Kong: The Chinese University of Hong Kong Press, 1989).

30. See Hong Kong Government, *A Perspective on Education in Hong Kong: Report by a Visiting Panel* (Hong Kong: Government Printer, 1982).

31. See Lau, *Society and Politics in Hong Kong.*

32. See Frank Choi, "Education Report Criticized for Promoting Elitist System," *Hong Kong Standard*, October 25, 1988.

33. See Education Commission, *Education Commission Report No. 3* (Hong Kong: Education Department, 1988).

34. See documents of the University of Hong Kong's planning committee for the foundation year 1987–88.

35. *Education Commission Report No. 3*, p. 230.

36. See "Split over Educational Reforms," *South China Morning Post*, October 27, 1988.

37. A.E. Sweeting, "The Cat among the Pigeons: Education Commission Report Number 3," in A. E. Sweeting, ed., *Differences and Identities: Educational Argument in Late Twentieth Century Hong Kong* (Hong Kong: Faculty of Education).

38. Kai Ming, Cheng, "Educational Policy-Making in Hong Kong" (Working paper, University of Hong Kong, Department of Education, 1988).

39. See the speech of Sir David Wilson, governor of Hong Kong, regarding the expansion of higher education, in November of 1989; see also "Academic Hits Out at Crisis Intervention," *South China Morning Post*, November 5, 1989; and, "Tertiary Doors Will Open to More Students," *South China Morning Post: Year in Review*, January 14, 1990.

40. Morris, "Effects on the School Curriculum," p. 514.

41. See Paul Morris, "Preparing Pupils as Citizens of the Special Administrative Region of Hong Kong: An Analysis of Curriculum Change and Controls," in Gerard Postiglione and J.Y.M. Leung, eds., *Education and Society in Hong Kong: Toward One Country and Two Systems* (Armonk, NY: M. E. Sharpe, 1991).

42. See Education Department, *Guidelines on Civic Education in Schools* (Hong Kong: Government Printer, 1985). The government will issue new guidelines before 1997.

43. Education Department, *Report of the Working Group on Sixth Form Education* (Hong Kong: Government Printer, July 1989).

44. See Curriculum Development Council, *Liberal Studies* (Hong Kong: Curriculum Development Council of the Hong Kong Government Education Department, 1991).

45. See Cheng " The Changing Political Culture of the Hong Kong Chinese," pp. 37–38.

46. See Andy Ho and Daphne Cheng, "Educators Set to Dominate Legco Polls," in *South China Morning Post,* August 10, 1980.

47. Llewelyn Commission, *A Perspective on Education in Hong Kong* (Hong Kong: Government Printer, 1982), p. 17.

48. *See Spencer Liu Wing-kei,* "The Role of Teachers as a Political Force in the Period of Transition: A Case Study of the Professional Teachers Union," Master's thesis, University of Hong Kong, Faculty of Education, 1990.

49. M. Mushkat, *The Making of the Hong Kong Administrative Class* (Hong Kong: Center of Asian Studies, University of Hong Kong, 1982) p. 60.

50. See Civil Service Branch, "Civil Service Personnel Statistics," mimeo (Hong Kong, Civil Service Branch, Government Secretariat, 1986), pp. 11–12.

51. Ibid.

52. Hong Kong Government, *A Draft Agreement between the Government of the United Kingdom of Great Britain and Northern Island and the Government of the People's Republic of China on the Future of Hong Kong* (Hong Kong: Government Printer, September 26, 1984), p. 17.

53. Ibid.

54. John Burns, "Succession Planning and Localization," in J. Burns and I. Scott, eds., *The Hong Kong Civil Service and Its Future* (Hong Kong: Oxford University Press, 1984).

55. Mr. Michael Leung became the director of education.

56. See *South China Morning Post*, January 31, 1990.

57. See Education Department, *Report of the Working Group Set Up to Review Language Improvement Measures* (Hong Kong: Government Printer, 1989).

58. See John Gibbons, "The Issue of the Language of Instruction in the Lower Forms of Hong Kong Secondary Schools," *Journal of Multilingual and Multicultural Development*, no. 3, pp. 117–128.

59. Llewelyn Commission, *A Perspective on Education in Hong Kong*, p. 36.

60. See *Report of the Working Group Set Up to Review Language Improvement Measures.*

61. See Ora Kwo, "Language Education in a Changing Economic and Political Context: The Teaching of Putonghua in Hong Kong Schools," paper presented at the First Hong Kong Conference on Language and Society, Hong Kong, April 1989.

62. Herbert Pierson, "Language Attitudes and Use in Hong Kong: A Case For Putonghua," paper presented at the First Hong Kong Conference on Language and Society, Hong Kong, April 1989; Robert Bauer, *The Hong Kong Cantonese Speech Community*, manuscript, Center of Asian Studies, University of Hong Kong.

63. S.W. Wai, "Secondary Schools Favor Teaching through Chinese," *South China Morning Post*, November 12, 1986, p. 3.

64. See Benton, *The Hong Kong Crisis*, p. 19.

65. See Max Weber, *The Religion of China* (New York: The Free Press, 1951); J.M. Menzel, *The Chinese Civil Service* (Boston: D.C. Heath, 1963); and E.A. Kracke, "Religion, Family and Individual in the Chinese Examination System," in John K. Fairbank, ed., *Chinese Thoughts and Social Institutions* (Chicago: University of Chicago Press, 1957).

66. See Alan Brimer and Patrick Griffin, *A Study of Mathematics Achievement in Hong Kong* (Hong Kong: Center of Asian Studies, University of Hong Kong, 1985); R.E. Mitchell, *Pupil, Parent and School: A Hong Kong Study* (Taipei: The Orient Culture Service, 1972); Pedro Ng, *Access to Educational Opportunity: The Case of Kwun Tong* (Hong Kong: The Chinese University of Hong Kong Social Research Center, 1975); David Post and Pong Suet-ling, "Socio-economic Indicators and Higher Education Access in Hong Kong," paper presented at the Comparative and International Education Assocation Annual Meeting, Harvard University, March 31, 1989.

67. *A Perspective on Education in Hong Kong*, p. 58.

68. See Lau Pui-king, "Economic Relations between Hong Kong and China," in Joseph Y.S. Cheng, ed., *Hong Kong in Transition* (Hong Kong: Oxford University Press, 1986), pp. 235–267.

69. Lau, *Society and Politics in Hong Kong*, p. 4.

70. See Siu-lun Wong, *Emigrant Entrepreneurs: Shanghai Industrialists in Hong Kong* (Hong Kong: Oxford University Press, 1988); Gregory Guldin, "Overseas at Home: The Fujianese of Hong Kong," Ph.D. dissertation, University of Wisconsin at Madison, 1977; D.W. Sparks, "The Teochiu of Hong Kong," Ph.D. dissertation, University of Texas at Austin, 1978.

71. See Bai Jierui, *Jinggong xueshu jiaoliu xiankuang yu qiandan* (Xianggong: Jinggong Xueshu Jiaoliu Zhongxin, 1985).

72. See various issues of the monthly journal *Mainland–Hong Kong Academic Exchange*, published by the Beijing–Hong Kong Academic Exchange Center in Hong Kong.

73. See "Neidi jinliushijian gaodengyuanxiao shuoshi boshi kecheng shou gangao sheng," in *Da Gong Bao*, Hong Kong, January 4, 1991.

74. See Mary Louise Taylor, ed., Institute of International Education, *Annual Report, 1986* (New York: Institute of International Education, 1987).

75. See Ernest L. Boyer, Philip G. Altboch, and Mary Jean Whitelaw, *The Academic Profession: An International Perspective* (Princeton, NJ: The Carnegie Foundation for the Advancement of Teaching, 1994).

76. Lau and Kuan, *The Ethos of the Hong Kong Chinese*, p. 19.

77. Choi Po King, "Cultural Identity and Colonial Rule: The Hong Kong–China Connection," paper presented at the Chinese University of Hong Kong, Conference on Chinese Cultural Tradition and Contemporary Modern Education, November 7, 1988, p. 31.

78. Lau and Kuan, *The Ethos of the Hong Kong Chinese*, p. 1.

79. Lau, "Decolonization without Independence."

# 6

# Education in Hong Kong and China: Toward Convergence?

*Julian Y.M. Leung*

The most perplexing questions facing Hong Kong's educational future concern the potential for increasing integration between various parts of the educational systems of Hong Kong and the rest of China. Given the successful levels of cooperation and integration that the two economic systems have experienced, and the growing association of education with economic concerns such as human capital development, the question of educational integration is well posed. Moreover, the cultural foundations of education in Hong Kong already share a Confucian heritage with the rest of China. There are a number of examples of how such integration is already happening in language teaching, in political studies, in history, etc., and this is further amplified as academic exchange relationships become increasingly more pronounced. This chapter attempts to explore this issue by noting three pairs of forces at work during the transition: insulation and interdependence; decolonization and neo-colonization; and internationalization and indigenization.

### Insulation and Interdependence

The promulgation of the Basic Law at the National People's Congress in March 1990 signified Hong Kong's formal entry into a period of real transition. The Chinese government expects all parties to contribute toward a smooth transfer of sovereignty in 1997, including those whose major concern is with education in Hong Kong. Yet the concept of "one country, two systems" is by itself a source of ambivalence that will constantly affect the relationship between Hong Kong

The original version of this chapter appeared in *Education and Society in Hong Kong: Toward One Country and Two Systems*, ed. Gerard A. Postiglione (Armonk, NY: M.E. Sharpe, 1992).

and the rest of China. For instance, Chinese leaders like Deng Xiaoping have repeatedly stressed that Hong Kong should be governed by patriotic Hong Kong people who support the sovereignty of the PRC.[1] Yet Jiang Zemin, the Chinese Communist party general secretary, used the analogy "river water and well water should not mix," to indicate that the Chinese socialist system should not be subjected to subversive interference from Hong Kong, especially prodemocracy activities.[2] Thus one reading of these messages is that the two political systems should be kept insulated from each other. But how can one be patriotic if one's concern for the country's democratic development is considered a subversive activity? The application of the concept of "one country, two systems" in Hong Kong's educational transition has been met with ambivalence. Section six of the Basic Law stipulates that Hong Kong will keep all her unique educational features intact, including the existing structure of schooling, academic freedom, and language policy.[3] The underlying rationale, that education is merely the superstructure that rests on Hong Kong's economic foundation, defines education's function strictly in terms of its service to a capitalist economy. Educational changes in Hong Kong will be made by local educators in response to Hong Kong's economic changes. But does the preservation of status quo education in Hong Kong mean that the two educational systems should be insulated from each other as are the two political systems? Will the specific ideological and structural differences between education systems of Hong Kong and the PRC remain insulated from one another? How then can future academic exchanges and bilateral cooperation be increasingly deepened?

A closer examination of the two educational systems reveals that there are important similarities (Table 6.1). For example, both are highly centralized in administration and curriculum development. Both have an early differentiation of pupils and narrow specialization, with pronounced separation between the arts and sciences, with social science given low priority. Both have an overemphasis on higher education at the expense of primary schooling and preschooling. Above all, Hong Kong is basically a Chinese community having a strong cultural identity with mainland China. Indeed, mainland educators visiting Hong Kong have observed that Hong Kong preserves most of the Confucian traditions in education—such as obedience to the school authority, obedience to the enforced school regulations, and high esteem for success on examinations. Existing evidence indicates that a kind of benevolent interdependence between education in Hong Kong and China has developed and will be strengthened in the future. Historically, Hong Kong has been a center of cultural interchange between China and the West. Since the early nineteenth century Hong Kong has contributed to China's modernization, as evidenced by the production of "bicultural and bilingual middlemen."[4] It is seldom remembered that the University of Hong Kong was established in 1911 to serve China's modernization.

As Hong Kong's economy has become closely tied to the Chinese economy in recent years, the academic linkage between Hong Kong and the PRC has

Table 6.1

**A Comparison of the Educational Systems of the PRC and Hong Kong**

| | PRC | Hong Kong |
|---|---|---|
| Pupil population | 220 million | 1 million |
| Educational goals | Explicitly political—education is to serve proletarian politics, to produce faithful supporters of the Chinese road of socialism and modernization | Apolitical—all-round development of pupils and to fulfill manpower needs |
| Structure of school system | predominantly 6+6+4 | 6+5+2+3 |
| Ideological orientation | Socialist and paternalistic | colonial–capitalist and individualistic |
| Span of universal compulsory education | 9-year, partially implemented | 9-year, fully implemented |
| Curriculum control | highly centralized | highly centralized |
| Curriculum development | state-monopolized and controlled, dominated by academics | government-led but with greater degree of participation by principals and teachers |
| Curriculum uniformity | highly standardized syllabus and textbooks | uniform syllabus but allows diversities in textbooks |
| Curriculum arrangement | highly academic and compartmentalized; lacks diversity | academically oriented but recently vocationalized and diversified |
| Degree of differentiation | streaming after 16+, strong orientation toward science | streaming after 16+, strong academic orientation |
| Medium of instruction | Chinese for Han-Chinese | 90 percent English (in policy, but less in practice) |

correspondingly become closer. There is a growing number of mainland Chinese students being enrolled for higher degree studies in Hong Kong's tertiary institutions. Correspondingly, mainland Chinese tertiary institutions recruit hundreds of Hong Kong students every year, particularly in the fields of medicine, Chinese literature, law, and engineering. Other forms of academic linkages are flourishing. Examples include a part-time diploma in Chinese law, which is jointly offered by Shu Yan College and the People's University in Beijing. Also, the

Biotechnology Institution of the Chinese University of Hong Kong developed specific cooperation with Shanghai counterparts to disseminate biotechnical innovations in Hong Kong and internationally. There are many other examples. Hong Kong has already tapped the talent of mainland Chinese professionals, many of whom arrive in Hong Kong as legal immigrants and are absorbed by local industries as mid-level technicians or even engineers although their academic qualifications may not be formally recognized. They also form the backbone of Putonghua teachers in Hong Kong. A mini "Silicon Valley" has been set up in Shenzhen with a powerful Hong Kong electronics group to further research and development for Hong Kong. Chinese institutions of higher education are eager to sell their research results to Hong Kong industries. The newly established University of Science and Technology of Hong Kong will undoubtedly see joint research and development with Chinese institutions as one of its major tasks.

In the light of rapid expansion of higher education in Hong Kong and the brain drain, the Hong Kong Education Commission has advocated that short-term contracts be offered to mainland Chinese scholars.[5] At the same time, the PRC actively uses Hong Kong as a workshop for learning Western management skills. Through different foundations set up by patriotic Hong Kong industrialists, numerous training courses have been organized for Chinese bankers, international traders, hotel managers, and mayors. The Beijing-Hong Kong Academic Exchange Centre is working to promote technology transfer between Hong Kong and mainland Chinese higher institutions. The State Education Commission sends secondary school principals and teacher trainers to the University of Hong Kong for short- and long-term training, primarily because in addition to its proximity, Hong Kong best demonstrates how a Chinese community adopts Western educational philosophies and practices. Moreover, as W.O. Lee has described, educational development in Hong Kong is a "model of excellence" in terms of its contribution to economic development.[6]

To insulate Hong Kong and mainland China is economically impossible, as Hong Kong's economy is already strongly integrated with that of China. Political insulation just implies minimal commitment to mainland Chinese politics so that Hong Kong can survive in a better way. In the field of education it is expected that a kind of educational interdependence, mutually beneficial and complimentary for both Hong Kong and the PRC, will develop throughout the transition period. On the other hand, it is hoped that the Hong Kong educational system will maintain its uniqueness and independence.

## Decolonization and Neo-colonization

The literature on colonial education abounds with eulogistic, apologetic, or accusative discussions on the the nature and impact of colonial education. Among the stereotyped accusations of colonial legacies are the creation of: (a) a privileged,

Westernized elite divorced from the aspiration of the indigenous majority, especially the rural masses; (b) citizens unsure of their real identity or caught between two cultures; (c) an unchangeable administrative bureaucracy; (d) a belief system hostile to the indigenous culture, such as a Eurocentric, academic curriculum that overlooks manual work and the mother tongue; (e) a racially segregated schooling system based on "divide and rule"; and, (f) a "culture of silence" with low political aspirations.[7] It is common to find Hong Kong educators attributing educational problems such as juvenile deliquency and underinvestment in preschool education to the evils of "colonial education" often without any in-depth analysis.

Watson identifies three distinct features of British colonialism in education.[8] First, the British played the role of the "reluctant colonizers" who adopted a "laissez-faire" educational policy and tolerated indigenous education. Second, there was no common colonial educational policy due to the regionalization of policymaking in London. The strength of the personality of individual governors decided educational policy in the colonies. Third, Britain was prepared to hand over power to the colonized people after World War II. Thompson adds that the British educational mission is to train leaders during colonial rule and make the unequal equal during decolonization.[9] Local researchers who study the development of education in Hong Kong since 1840 share a similar viewpoint. Ng Lun Ngai Ha asserts that educational development in Hong Kong is not an uncritical transfer of content and system from the metropolitan country. The underlying forces of change that shaped Hong Kong's educational development were the social composition and attitude of the local Chinese community, the political conditions in China, and Britain's changing policy toward the Chinese government.[10]

Decolonization is a collective and individual adventure that involves both structural and cultural changes. Indeed, after the chief Chinese UN delegate announced that Hong Kong should not be categorized as a colony in 1973, the Hong Kong government had undertaken measures to decolonize Hong Kong. For example, Chinese was made a parallel official language with English and Hong Kong inhabitants were deprived of the right of abode in Britain. The urge for civic education in the early 1980s could be interpreted as a "conscientization" process to equip the young people of Hong Kong for their responsibilities as citizens of the future Special Administrative Region. The Hong Kong government has encouraged the use of Chinese (Cantonese) as a medium of instruction in schools by subsidizing the publication of Chinese textbooks and appointing additional Chinese language teachers. Examination rules have been revised to allow pupils to take subject examinations in Chinese at all levels without any indication of the use of language mode in the certificates. All these can be counted as decolonization or "domestication" measures to encourage a smooth integration with the mother culture when Hong Kong returns to China in 1997.

However, other educational policies can be interpreted as measures of neo-colonialism. For example, in 1988 it was argued that the existing 6+5+2+3 British model of schooling should be replaced by a 6+6+4 model in line with the dominant world trend and particularly with the mainland Chinese system. In June 1988, the Education Commission Report No. 3 reinforced the existing model of education. Accordingly, the Chinese University has to take students from a two-year matriculation course and abandon the four-year university structure. A local scholar cited this decision as a British conspiracy imposing an outdated British model of education on the future Hong Kong SAR for the purpose of extending British influence until 2047.[11] Similarly, the Hong Kong Education Commission's decision in May 1990 to introduce streaming of primary school graduates according to their language proficiency in Chinese and English could be seen as a major setback on the promotion of "mother-tongue" education because 20–30 percent of all pupils, those capable of following an English-medium secondary schooling, will become the future elite.

The decolonization-neo-colonization dichotomy can become a bone of contention during the transition period. Transition toward 1997 will not be trouble-free. In a time when the Sino-British relationship becomes strained, the Chinese government perceives every British action as conspiratorial, as exemplified by her attacks on the Right of Abode issue and the Bill of Rights. In April 1990, the Hong Kong government announced the proposal to remove the textbook approval system, which originated in 1930 to ensure that school textbooks are not subjected to Communist influence. This could be interpreted as a government decision to relax its political control over education and a step toward democratization. However, the suggestion was attacked in a leftist newspaper as a way of weakening the authority of the future SAR government.[12]

Ironically, it is the Basic Law that has guaranteed the continuation of the educational system and practices erected by the British colonial regime. It legitimizes the continued postcolonial influence of the British on the educational system's policies as well as the intellectual life of the educated. Moreover, the general public opts to support the colonial legacies. Parental choice of English-medium education, rather than government decree, is the greatest barrier to full-scale implementation of Chinese-medium education. Parental sentiment has led the teachers of one excellent Chinese-medium school to vote to switch back to English-medium instruction.[13]

In general, what teachers worry about is that after 1997 they may be compelled to switch to educational practices along the mainland Chinese model. Any measure to decolonize existing practices will be received with panic. After the June 4 crackdown of the pro-democracy movement, there is less likelihood that local Chinese inhabitants will become extremely nationalistic and anti-British as their predecessors had been in the 1920s and 1960s. The postcolonial impact of Britain on Hong Kong's educational system and policies as well as the international outlook of the local inhabitants will definitely persist, although such a phenomenon is labeled by Altbach and Kelly as a sympton of neo-colonialism.[14]

**Internationalization and Indigenization**

A number of forces have acted to both facilitate and stifle the international influence on Hong Kong's educational development. For example, due to the colonial status of Hong Kong, international organizations such as the World Bank and UNESCO, which have traditionally played a role in shaping education in developing societies, have had a negligible impact on educational developments in Hong Kong. Nevertheless, while Hong Kong's educational system has been most heavily influenced by that of the United Kingdom, it has also developed an expansive international character. The educational community is composed of an increasing number of those who have attended universities in Canada, the United States, Australia, and even Japan, although the leadership in the government Education Department is still a product of predominantly British-style education. Most of Hong Kong's elite schools are strongly influenced by the British system. This includes the University of Hong Kong, which favors recruitment from the United Kingdom and the Commonwealth for its overseas staffing. All this has contributed to the insular character of much of Hong Kong elite education. Only the reality of China's staunch Communist-dominated system on Hong Kong's border has prevented a strong reaction against the British-dominated character of much of Hong Kong education.

Heavy doses of overseas investment and technology transfer in Hong Kong have created opportunities to deepen the influence of Americans, Japanese, Australians, and continental Europeans. Aside from having their own international secondary schools in Hong Kong, these countries sponsor many Hong Kong students for overseas study, and when they return to Hong Kong they are often recruited by the respective national firms. However, the influence of these groups on the structure and content of the Hong Kong educational system remains minimal.

Neverthless, there have been new efforts to internationalize education. The severe brain drain has seriously crippled the localization of tertiary teachers and administrators. A large amount of recruitment is likely to be international, ending up with many posts being filled by foreign-passport holders. A large expatriate-staffed tertiary education sector may come to be viewed as contradictory to the expectation of Hong Kong people administering Hong Kong. At the same time, the increasing number of expatriates, including returned emigrants, in Hong Kong has created a growing demand for international schooling. Those lining up for emigration also put their children in international schools as preparation. The Sino-British Land Commission has set aside an area for the development of a school which is hoped to be the first of many that will internationalize education in Hong Kong. This sixth-form international school, the Lo Po Chun United World College, would draw students from overseas, as well as offer international qualifications to local pupils. The school would be independently operated, and would offer the international baccalaureate diploma.[15]

Opposite the internationalization pole of the dichotomy is indigenization. This force pulls Hong Kong in the direction of its inherent character as a unique Chinese society. Indigenous forces, as part of the culture and identity that Hong Kong has built up over several decades, have acted to anchor the educational system. Such forces not only moderate the forces of internationalization, but also temper the influence of contemporary mainland culture. If decoupled from the United Kingdom and from traditional Chinese culture, the Hong Kong indigenous educational power base may quickly disintegrate. Therefore, after 1997 it is likely that there will be a growing tension between internationally sponsored and Chinese-sponsored education. This could potentially lead, at the very least, to a controversy-bound transition process, or even to a crisis of Western education in Hong Kong.

## An Uncertain Future

The capacity of Hong Kong education to adapt to the transition will be greatly determined by the degree to which it justifies its existence within the "one country, two systems" framework. Three questions remain: First, will Hong Kong's economy continue to prosper so that its educational superstructure will still be considered as contributory to growth? Second, will the internationalization and democratization of Hong Kong's schooling system be tolerated by the Chinese government? Third, will the Chinese government pressure the Hong Kong educational system to inculcate "patriotism" to prepare patriotic Chinese inhabitants to administer the Hong Kong Special Administrative Region?

## Notes

1. Deng Xiaoping, "Maintain the Prosperity and Stability of Hong Kong," *The Birth of the Basic Law* (Hong Kong: Wen Wei Publishing Co., 1990), p. 185.
2. *People's Daily*, January 21, 1990.
3. *Basic Law of the Hong Kong Special Administrative Region of the People's Republic of China*, February 1990.
4. K.C. Fok, *Lecture Notes on Hong Kong History* (Hong Kong: The Commercial Press, 1990).
5. R. Fan, "Opportunities and Challenges of the Experience of Higher Education," *Wah Kiu Yat Pao*, May 14, 1990.
6. W. O. Lee, "Pressure for Educational Excellence in China: Implications for Education in Hong Kong," in *Education and Society in Hong Kong: Toward One Country and Two Systems*, ed. Gerard A. Postiglione (Armonk, NY: M.E. Sharpe, 1992).
7. M. Carnoy, *Education as Cultural Imperialism* (New York: David McKay, 1984); P. Freire, *Pedagogy of the Oppressed* (London: Penguin, 1971); P.G. Altbach and G.P. Kelly, *Educational Colonialism* (New York: Longman, 1978).
8. K. Watson, "Colonialism and Educational Development," in *Education in the Third World*, ed. K. Watson (London: Croom Helm, 1982).
9. A.R.Thompson, *Education and Development in Africa* (London: Macmillan, 1981).

10. L.N.H. Ng, *Interactions of East and West: Development of Public Education in Early Hong Kong* (Hong Kong: Chinese University Press, 1984).

11. Ming K. Chan, "Full Scale Restoration of British Education," *The British Sunset in Hong Kong* (Hong Kong Economic Journal, 1989), pp. 42–52.

12. "The Textbook Approval System Shound Not Be Removed," *Wen Wei Pao*, April 11, 1990.

13. *Ming Pao Daily News*, June 19, 1990.

14. Altbach and Kelly, *Education and Colonialism*.

15. "Site Set Aside for Unique International College," *South China Morning Post*, April 1990.

7

# Hong Kong in an International Migration System

*Ronald Skeldon*

## Hong Kong: A Spatially Mobile Society

The roots of Hong Kong's emigration go a long way into the past. Hong Kong was first occupied by the British in January 1841, when the population of the island was only a few thousand, probably between five and six thousand. By October of that year, the numbers had more than doubled, and almost four years later, in mid-1845, the population was estimated to have reached 23,817, of whom only 957 were non-Chinese.[1] Hong Kong as an urban center is thus fairly recent in historical terms. It was a creation of colonialism, and its population has been, throughout its history, heavily and often primarily migrant.

While the territory controlled by British administration expanded to incorporate fairly substantial village populations, particularly in the New Territories after the lease was signed in 1898, migration to and from China has been an integral part of Hong Kong's development. Only about 6 or 7 percent of the Chinese land population of Hong Kong in 1901 either considered Hong Kong to be their home or were residents of the villages within the territory. In 1931, about one-third of the Chinese population, or 270,478 persons, had been born in the territory; all the others were migrants from China, mainly the adjacent parts of Guangdong province. By 1991, the year of the most recent census, almost 60 percent of the total population was Hong Kong-born; that is, still over one-third had come from other places. Place of birth does not imply origin and, in 1981, when a question on origin was asked in the census, only 124,279 people, or 2.4

The original version of this chapter appeared in *Reluctant Exiles? Migration from Hong Kong and the New Overseas Chinese*, ed. Ronald Skeldon (Armonk, NY: M.E. Sharpe, 1994) percent of the total population, claimed their place of origin to be Hong Kong. This was at a time when some 2,854,422 people, or 57 percent of the total, had been born in the territory. To try to put the importance of migration in Hong Kong's development into context, let us use Singapore as a comparison. Just over three-quarters of Singapore's total permanent resident and non-resident population combined were born in Singapore. Hong Kong is very much the product of migration and may therefore have a substantial population that has only superficial roots in the territory.[2]

Until the disruptions of the Second World War, the migration from China, and principally from Guangdong Province, was rarely a simple move from China to Hong Kong. There was much migration back and forth across the border, with laborers returning to their villages after completing a job and much seasonal, weekly, and daily movement. During the late 1930s, for example, it has been estimated that around eight thousand people a day moved backward and forward across the border.[3] Although there was a trend toward a stabilization of the Chinese population in Hong Kong by the late 1930s, with more of the migrants bringing their families with them, these short-term migrants were still primarily male job-seekers. Most had left wives and children in China, or, if single, would return home to marry. The population of Hong Kong was, as a result, strongly masculine, with 184 males for every 100 females in 1911, a ratio of 185:100 in 1921 and of 135:100 in 1931.[4] Hong Kong's population was thus highly mobile, with people moving easily between the city and their homelands in China.

The Sino-Japanese War, which began in 1937, brought hundreds of thousands of refugees—some 750,000 up to 1941—virtually doubling Hong Kong's population to 1,639,337 by March 1941. The fall of the city to the Japanese at the end of that year reversed the flow, and the population was reduced to around 650,000 by May 1945. Within six months of the Japanese surrender in August 1945, numbers were again back over one million, and they continued to increase with the influx of people fleeing from the fighting between the Guomindang (Kuomintang) and communist armies. The flow of refugees continued after the establishment of the People's Republic of China in October 1949, and Hong Kong's population passed the two million mark in 1950. Some of these people eventually returned to their homes in China, but the addition of some one and a quarter million refugees to the population not only overstrained the territory's capability to deal with the rapid influx but was the foundation of the "refugee mentality."[5] There is then a substantial proportion of Hong Kong's population either with direct experience of flight or whose parents had such experiences and who may be prepared to move again as Hong Kong approaches 1997. The numbers of those with refugee experience—in today's climate they would probably be classified as "economic refugees"—increased in 1962 when many entered Hong Kong fleeing from the chaos engendered by the Great Leap Forward which had resulted in the widespread famine of 1959–61.

The cross-border movement that typified the period before the Second World

War period continued, with fluctuations, right through the Maoist period in China and has accelerated as we come to the present. During the mid-1950s, annual two-way cross-border movements exceeded three million, and by the early 1990s such annual two-way moves were in excess of thirty million, or about five per year for every resident of Hong Kong. During the Maoist period, two-way cross-border movement was limited primarily to Hong Kong residents returning for visits and, while they still dominate the flows, increasingly there are visitors from China. Some 1.7 million residents of China visited Hong Kong during 1994, up from 299,000 in 1991.[6]

The last great wave of migration to affect Hong Kong to date occurred during the late 1970s, after the economic reforms in China were initiated and people found it easier to move internally again. Between 1977 and 1982, almost half a million migrants entered Hong Kong from China, and Hong Kong's population had virtually reached five million by 1981. Since then, numbers of immigrants have been controlled through cooperation between British and Chinese authorities to around 27,000 a year, mainly dependants of people already in Hong Kong. The 1991 census results showed that the population had reached 5.67 million and had grown at an average rate of only 0.6 percent between 1986 and 1991, confirming that immigration was indeed under control, although low fertility and emigration were also important factors accounting for the low growth. In 1992, it was estimated that about 95,000 Hong Kong residents had a spouse living in China, 150,000 Hong Kong residents had children living in China, and the total number of children living in China with one or both parents resident in Hong Kong was in the region of 310,000.[7]

Hong Kong, with its tradition of immigration, might thus be expected to have a population more susceptible to further migration than an area with a long-established and fairly stable population. That said, however, there are relatively few urban centers in East and Southeast Asia which have had long-established and stable urban populations, and this is surely one factor in the rapidity in the acceleration of migration within and from this region that has occurred over the last twenty-five years, a trend that will be examined in more detail below.

## A Tradition of Emigration: The "Old" Overseas Chinese

The transient nature of the population of Hong Kong and its close relationship with China are reinforced by the colony's role as a transshipment point for migrants going overseas. From the middle of the nineteenth century until the Second World War, Hong Kong was one of the major ports from which Chinese laborers left for North America, Australasia, and Southeast Asia. Using harbormasters' reports, Elizabeth Sinn has shown that over six million Chinese left Hong Kong between 1868 and 1939.[8] This figure is certainly a substantial underestimate: it is known that, in order to avoid dues and to increase their own earnings, ship's captains did not declare all their passengers and overloaded their ships beyond legal capacity. These figures would also include numbers of non-

Chinese, even though the majority were undoubtedly Chinese. Also, the harbormasters' reports showed that about eight million Chinese returned over the same period, and, although there were other important ports involved in the export of Chinese labor, notably Xiamen (Amoy) and Shantou (Swatow), it is highly unlikely that more labor returned to Hong Kong than left in the first place. Again, many laborers undoubtedly made several trips; hence, these figures do not refer to numbers of individuals. A more reliable estimate of numbers, although again based upon "person departures" rather than on individuals, is that between 1876 and 1898, 1,349,705 persons left Hong Kong for foreign ports compared with 1,042,285 from Xiamen and 359,458 from Shantou. It can safely be concluded that the number passing through Hong Kong on their way to overseas destinations was in the millions between the mid-nineteenth and mid-twentieth centuries.

The exact number of Chinese participating in these movements will tax the ingenuity of historians for some time to come. What is important in the context of the present discussion is that Hong Kong, almost from its inception, has been oriented overseas. It has been a link between its hinterland in Guangdong and the wider world. Clearly, while the majority of those going overseas through Hong Kong in the nineteenth and early twentieth centuries came from Guangdong province rather than from Hong Kong itself, given the fluidity of movement between Hong Kong and China referred to earlier, no clear distinction can meaningfully be made between separate Hong Kong and Guangdong populations.

The second important point to be drawn from the historical experience that is relevant to an assessment of the present situation is the importance of the policies of overseas countries in affecting the flows. From the open pioneering societies of the 1850s to the 1870s, Australia, Canada, New Zealand, and the United States restricted, and eventually virtually excluded, migration from Asian countries from the 1880s.[9] Emigration through Hong Kong intensified but changed increasingly from these English-speaking settler societies to destinations in Southeast Asia. With global recession and rising nationalism in the 1930s, opportunities in these destinations too became gradually restricted. After a quasi-stability returned to the Asian region following the Second World War and the establishment of the People's Republic of China, there were few countries in the world willing to accept migrants from China. Also, China itself did not facilitate the emigration of its citizens; the 1950s and 1960s formed, in effect, a curious lull in the international movement of the Chinese, a lull that was to represent a break between what can be termed the "old" overseas Chinese and the "new" overseas Chinese migration.

## A Transition in Emigration

The "old" overseas Chinese were typified by the movements of unskilled laborers, overwhelmingly male, who saw themselves as sojourners. The new overseas

Chinese are typified by movements of the highly skilled—men, women, and families—many of whom are key players in regional and global economic networks. Yet that break was not absolute; there was a period of transition. During the later stages of migration to the Nanyang, there was increasing participation of women. In fact, the British government in Singapore restricted Chinese male migration from 1930 while encouraging female migration from China.[10] A case can be made for the main transition from the "old" to the "new" pattern occurring with the type of migration which existed from Hong Kong during the 1950s and 1960s. However, as will become clear below, there are also continuities with the "old" pattern in the present international migration from East Asia.

There was some migration of skilled labor from Hong Kong on three-year contracts during the 1950s to destinations such as British North Borneo, Brunei, and Sarawak. Numbers ranged between 1,500 and 2,100 per annum.[11] However, the major flow was to Britain, although there was also some migration to the United States. The British Nationality Acts of 1914 and 1948 had guaranteed freedom of access to the United Kingdom for Commonwealth citizens, and this legislation, together with a post-war demand for Chinese food, laid the basis for a significant population flow from Hong Kong throughout the 1950s and 1960s. Estimates put the emigrant flow at between fifty and sixty thousand over this period, small in terms of the scale of what had gone before and what would follow, but significant nevertheless.[12]

What makes the emigration from Hong Kong at that time interesting in terms of migration theory is that it cannot be related to the labor-surplus nature of the economy. Unemployment in the urban areas was undoubtedly high throughout the 1950s. Detailed and regular assessments of employment and unemployment do not become available for Hong Kong until 1975, but fairly reliable estimates for 1954 put the overall unemployment rate for the working population at 12 percent, with about 15 percent of immigrants out of work at that time.[13] Yet the emigration occurred not from the labor-surplus urban economy—where the hawker economy became the safety valve—but from the villages of the New Territories. The roots of this migration go back well before the Second World War when villagers were recruited to serve as deckhands or cooks on British ships. Recruitment intensified during the war, and in the immediate post-war period some jumped ship or were demobilized in British ports. So the seeds were laid for the establishment of the Chinese restaurant business in Britain and the beginning of a clear chain migration from the New Territories of Hong Kong—a story that had been well told elsewhere.[14] Most of these migrants, like their predecessors, were poorly educated but, unlike their predecessors, there followed a migration of women and children as families settled in Britain to participate in this unique economic niche.

## The Policy Changes of the 1960s: The Emergence of the "New" Pattern

The emigration from the New Territories villages was essentially over by the late 1960s. The Commonwealth Immigrants Acts of 1962 and, more significantly, of 1968 restricted immigration into the United Kingdom. The boom in the Chinese restaurant business was over. The increasing restrictions on movement to Britain and the decline in demand for Hong Kong Chinese workers coincided with the most significant changes that have affected the international migration systems over the last fifty years: the end of the major restrictions on non-European immigration in the main settler destination countries of Australia, Canada, the United States, and New Zealand.

Canada effectively removed racial discrimination as a major feature of its policy in its Immigration Regulations tabled in January 1962. The main reason for the change was not parliamentary or public demand but because some senior officials realized that Canada "could not operate effectively within the United Nations, or in the multiracial Commonwealth, with the millstone of a racially discriminatory immigration policy round her neck."[15] The United States was the next country to sweep away its national origin discriminatory policies with its Immigration and Nationality Act of 1 October 1965.[16] Although this did not become effective until 1 July 1968, pressure had been building up since the end of the Second World War to modify the national origins system. In fact, the Exclusion Act was repealed as early as 1943 but was replaced by a quota which allowed only 105 Chinese to be admitted annually, although this was gradually modified over subsequent years. For example, in 1946, Chinese wives of American citizens were exempted from quotas and, in 1952, Congress approved the Immigration and Nationality (McCarran-Walter) Act, which allowed a larger number of Asians, including those from Hong Kong, to move to the United States. Australia abandoned its "white Australia" policy in 1973, shortly after the accession of the Labor Government led by Gough Whitlam ended twenty-three years of Liberal-National Country Party rule.[17] In 1978, New Zealand was the last of the settler countries to abandon racial restrictions, from which year "neither considerations of assimilation and racial harmony nor consequent limitations upon the entry of Asians or others have appeared in any official statements of policy," although it was not for another nine years that there was full implementation of a policy that finally ended the preference for "traditional source countries."[18]

Thus, in all these countries, within about twenty years, immigration policies based upon national origin were swept away, and the new policies in all these countries came to be based more on the quality or skills of the immigrants. Canada and Australia developed their points systems and the United States its system of preferences, which came to favor Asians and set the scene for the migration of the "new" overseas Chinese, amongst others. Hence, in a period of about fifteen years, the legal basis that essentially controlled the volume of international migration to North America and Australasia was totally changed, and the recent migration from Hong Kong must be seen in this light.

## Recent Migration from Hong Kong: The Period from the Late 1960s to the Mid-1980s

Any discussion of migration from Hong Kong sooner or later must confront the issue of data. There are no official records kept of emigration, and government estimates of the total volume of emigration, made since the 1980s, are compiled from several sources.[19] One way of assessing the movement out of Hong Kong is to examine the annual figures for immigrants to the principal destination countries (table 7.1). These again are problematic as they only list those who "land" or are accepted as "settlers" and give no idea of return migration. However, they do give a fairly reliable idea of the volume and direction of emigration from Hong Kong. There are two different sets of figures: those based upon "place of birth Hong Kong" and those based upon "place of last permanent residence Hong Kong." Given the significant proportion of Hong Kong's population that was born in China but has lived in Hong Kong for many years, I have elected to use the place of last permanent residence figures. These may indeed include people of non-Chinese descent, but, given that they make up such a small proportion of the total population, about 5 percent in 1991,[20] this distortion is preferable relative to the underestimation of migration from Hong Kong that would result if the place of birth figures were to be used. For example, in 1990, 9,393 people born in Hong Kong were admitted to the United States compared with 14,367 admitted whose last place of permanent residence was Hong Kong. In 1990–91, the number of settler arrivals in Australia whose place of birth was Hong Kong was 13,541 compared with 16,747 whose last place of residence was Hong Kong. The figure for settler arrivals in Canada in 1989 whose place of birth was Hong Kong was 15,694 compared with 19,908 whose last place of permanent residence was Hong Kong. Hence, birthplace statistics are likely to underestimate the "real" migration from Hong Kong by at least one-quarter.

Information on emigration from Hong Kong from the 1960s using last place of permanent residence is given in table 7.1. In 1970, the main destination was the United States and, given the fairly rigid nature of the policy up to the new Immigration Act of 1990, based as it was on a worldwide limit of 270,000 plus a series of preferences for those not subject to limitation, the numbers have not fluctuated greatly since then. Ten to twelve thousand people have left Hong Kong annually for the United States over the last two decades. As mentioned earlier, the United States had begun to relax its restrictions upon the entry of Asians from the early 1950s, and 34,764 immigrants whose last place of permanent residence was Hong Kong had entered during the decade of the 1960s compared with some 9,657 during the decade of the 1950s.

Table 7.1

**Immigrants to Major Destinations Whose Last Place of Previous Residence was Hong Kong, 1960–1993**

| | Australia | Canada | United States |
|---|---|---|---|
| 1960 | — | 1,146 | |
| 1961 | n.a. | 710 | |
| 1962 | n.a. | 426 | |
| 1963 | n.a. | 1,008 | |
| 1964 | n.a. | 2,490 | |
| 1965 | n.a. | 4,155 | 75,007 |
| 1966 | n.a. | 3,710 | |
| 1967 | n.a. | 5,767 | |
| 1968 | n.a. | 7,594 | |
| 1969 | n.a. | 7,306 | |
| 1970 | n.a. | 4,509 | 9,720 |
| 1971 | n.a. | 5,009 | 7,960 |
| 1972 | 715 | 6,297 | 10,916 |
| 1973 | 734 | 14,661 | 10,300 |
| 1974 | 1,130 | 12,704 | 10,700 |
| 1975 | 1,593 | 11,132 | 12,547 |
| 1976 | 1,302 | 10,725 | 16,950* |
| 1977 | 1,633 | 6,371 | 12,272 |
| 1978 | 2,313 | 4,740 | 11,145 |
| 1979 | 1,836 | 5,966 | 16,838 |
| 1980 | 2,822 | 6,309 | n.a. |
| 1981 | 1,960 | 6,451 | n.a. |
| 1982 | 2,414 | 6,542 | 11,908 |
| 1983 | 2,756 | 6,710 | 12,525 |
| 1984 | 3,691 | 7,696 | 12,290 |
| 1985 | 5,136 | 7,380 | 10,975 |
| 1986 | 4,912 | 5,893 | 9,930 |
| 1987 | 5,140 | 16,170 | 8,785 |
| 1988 | 7,942 | 23,281 | 11,817 |
| 1989 | 9,998 | 19,994 | 12,236 |
| 1990 | 11,538 | 28,825 | 12,853 |
| 1991 | 16,747 | 22,340 | 15,564 |
| 1992 | 15,656 | 38,841 | 16,741 |
| 1993 | 8,111 | 36,510 | 14,010 |

*Sources:*

Australia: Department of Immigration and Ethnic Affairs, Australian Immigration, Canberra, *Consolidated Statistics*, No. 13, 1982; Department of Immigration, Local Government and Ethnic Affairs, Canberra, *Statistical Note 36: Asian Immigration*, 1988; Bureau of Immigration Research, *Immigration Update*, several issues.

Canada: Employment and Immigration Canada, Ottawa, *Annual Immigration Statistics*.

United States: U.S. Department of Justice, Washington, D.C., *Statistical Yearbooks of the Immigration and Naturalization Service*.

*Notes:*

1. Australia: settler arrivals for the financial year 1 July–30 June, with 1992 referring to settler arrivals 1991–92, etc.

2. Canada: landed immigrants in calendar year.

3. United States: immigrants admitted in fiscal year, 1 July–30 June from 1970 to 1975 and from 1 October–30 September from 1977 to 1989. The 1989, 1990, 1991, and 1992 figures exclude the intake under the Immigration Reform and Control Act (IRCA), which allowed people who had been resident unlawfully since 1 January 1982 to become residents during these years. The data for 1980 and 1981 have been "lost" at source.

*Includes transition quarter June to September in realigned year.

In 1970, relatively few Hong Kong people were going to Canada or Australia. Even the unstable conditions in the colony in 1966 and 1967 did not appear to give rise to significant volumes of outmigration, even if polls did show that 60 percent of civil servants would have liked to emigrate if they could.[21] Certainly, the number of immigrants to Canada from Hong Kong doubled from 1966 to 1968, from 3,710 to 7,594, and this could have been at least partially due to perceived uncertainty after the 1967 riots, but it could equally have been due to changes in the immigration regulations in Canada in that same year. These changes allowed people to apply for landed immigrant status from within Canada, and even gave a right of appeal to those who were deemed unsuitable to be accepted as immigrants. Although it took two to three years for the impact of these changes to be reflected in the overall immigration numbers, Hong Kong people were among the earliest to take advantage of these changes, encouraged by the conditions in the territory. By 1970, "floods of visitors began to arrive in Canada with the obvious intention of staying, applying for landed immigrant status and, if refused, submitting an appeal to the Immigration Appeal Board."[22] In fact, numbers of landed immigrants from Hong Kong dropped in 1970 to 4,509, from 7,306 in 1969, but nothing can be made of this decline as it is likely that Hong Kong people were still going to Canada in some other capacity and staying on.

The apparent upsurge in immigration from Hong Kong between 1973 and 1976 was partially the result of the 1973 adjustment of status program—essentially an amnesty—which was implemented to regularize the status of all illegal overstayers in Canada. Over one-fifth of those regularized by 31 July 1974—5,619 persons—were from Hong Kong. Whether this was due to pressure to emigrate caused by the political uncertainties of the late 1960s or whether it was but part of the "well known illegal migration industry in Hong Kong" or a combination of both is unlikely ever to be made clear.[23] It does appear likely that the critical factors in this emigration from Hong Kong were generated in Canada and that the political uncertainty of the time was more secondary in nature but, as with the situation in the 1990s, it is virtually impossible to separate the factors one from the other. By the mid-1970s, the movement from Hong Kong had subsided; it did not rise again significantly until the second half of the 1980s in the wave of emigration that is the primary concern of this chapter.

## Recent Migration from Hong Kong: The Lead-up to 1997

Official estimates of emigration from Hong Kong put the number of leavers to all destinations through the early 1980s at about 20,000 per annum (table 7.2). In 1987, this increased to 30,000; in 1988, it increased to 45,800; then there was a decline to 42,000 in 1989; it then climbed to reach levels of over 60,000 from 1990. These figures, with, as we will see, the exception of 1992, probably reflect reasonably well the real volume of emigration. Nevertheless, the figures do have

Table 7.2

**Official Hong Kong Government Estimates of Emigration, 1980–1992**

| Year | Number of emigrants |
|---|---|
| 1980 | 22,400 |
| 1981 | 18,300 |
| 1982 | 20,300 |
| 1983 | 19,800 |
| 1984 | 22,400 |
| 1985 | 22,300 |
| 1986 | 19,000 |
| 1987 | 30,000 |
| 1988 | 45,800 |
| 1989 | 42,000 |
| 1990 | 62,000 |
| 1991 | 60,000 |
| 1992 | 66,000 |

*Source:* Government Secretariat, Hong Kong.

to be treated with a great deal of caution. First, they exclude those going overseas on student visas. If these were included, another 20,000 or more could be added each year, just to the main destinations of Australia, Canada, the United Kingdom, and the United States, although the majority of these almost certainly return. Second, the figures exclude migrants to Taiwan and to mainland China. Information on movement to both of these destinations is sketchy, although in 1990 more than 7,500 persons were reputed to have moved to Taiwan, up from 4,896 in 1989 and 3,212 in 1988.[24] During the latter half of the 1980s, perhaps as many as 20,000 per annum moved back to mainland China. The majority of these would have been retirees going home to their villages in China, a flow that is, as yet, little appreciated.

The volume of movement out of Hong Kong is not important simply in terms of numbers of leavers but it is also significant in terms of number of arrivals at particular destination countries. Since 1987, Hong Kong has been the principal source area of immigrants to Canada, accounting for 15.4 percent of the total intake in 1992. In 1991–92, Hong Kong was also the principal source country for settler migration to Australia, having displaced the long-time dominant source of the United Kingdom in that year. Over the last five years Hong Kong has also emerged as the leading source for those approved permanent residence in New Zealand. Hence, for these three countries, Hong Kong and linkages with Hong Kong have suddenly become a major policy concern. The number of Hong Kong migrants to the United States still represents a relatively small proportion of the total immigration to that country.

In 1992, some 38,000 Hong Kong people moved to Canada, around 15,000 to Australia, between 15,000 and 16,000 to the United States, perhaps 3,000 or

Table 7.3

**Proportion of Total Population and of Emigrants to Principal and All Destinations Who Were Degree Holders, 1985–1991** (percentages)

| | Population distribution[a] | Canada | Australia | United States of America | All countries[b] |
|---|---|---|---|---|---|
| 1985 | 2.8 | 18.2 | 14.2 | 8.5 | 13.2 |
| 1986 | 3.0 | 14.3 | 13.4 | 9.2 | 11.8 |
| 1987 | 3.3 | 24.5 | 16.6 | 9.0 | 18.7 |
| 1988 | 3.5 | 17.4 | 14.5 | 11.1 | 15.0 |
| 1989 | 3.7 | 15.6 | 17.2 | 11.4 | 14.5 |
| 1990 | 4.0 | 12.8 | 24.2 | 9.3 | 14.5 |
| 1991 | 4.6 | 14.0 | 30.7 | 8.4 | 16.7 |

*Source:* Unpublished tabulations, Hong Kong government.

[a] Based on the yearly averages of general household survey quarterly figures, covering land-based, civilian, and non-institutional population only. The 1991 figure was based on the 1991 population census.

[b] Figures before the third quarter of 1989 cover seven major destination countries only; figures after the third quarter of 1989 cover twelve countries: Australia, Brazil, Canada, France, Germany, Mauritius, the Netherlands, New Zealand, Panama, Portugal, the United Kingdom, and the United States. Figures from 1990 onward include an estimate for Singapore.

4,000 to Singapore, some 3,000 to 3,500 to New Zealand, and perhaps 1,000 to the United Kingdom. Movement to other destinations is likely to have been in the low hundreds, although in 1992 more than a thousand people may have gone to South Africa. The total movement to settle, excluding Taiwan and mainland China, was, in 1992, probably between 75,000 and 80,000, considerably above the official government estimate of 66,000 for that year. Estimates for previous years do not appear to have been too far from the "real" flow as identified by landings at the destination. Just why the 1992 estimate was so far out is not clear. Total emigration, including movement to mainland China and Taiwan in 1992, was thus probably in excess of 100,000. How many have returned is, of course, a totally different matter, which will be addressed later. The figures are purely indicative rather than definitive and are more useful to identify trends than to establish absolute levels of movement.

Who, then, are those who are leaving Hong Kong for Australia, Canada, the United States, and New Zealand? They include some of the best educated, well trained, and highly skilled of Hong Kong's population. The emigrant profiles compiled from information on visa applicants show that, from 1987 to 1991, between 15 and 19 percent of all emigrants had attained degree level or higher in their education, compared with about 4 percent for the population as a whole (table 7.3).[25] Information on skill levels shows that, from 1987 to 1990, almost

Table 7.4

**Proportion of Total Population and of Emigrants to Principal and All Destinations Who Were in High-level Occupations, 1985–1991**
(percentages)

| | Population distribution[a] | Canada | Australia | United States of America | All countries[b] |
|---|---|---|---|---|---|
| 1985[c] | 5.0 | 15.8 | 22.6 | 9.1 | 14.0 |
| 1986[c] | 4.9 | 13.1 | 22.3 | 10.3 | 14.0 |
| 1987[c] | 5.1 | 30.7 | 26.2 | 11.6 | 24.6 |
| 1988[c] | 5.5 | 29.4 | 23.3 | 15.9 | 24.4 |
| 1989[c] | 5.7 | 26.7 | 27.5 | 16.3 | 23.4 |
| 1990[c] | 6.0 | 21.1 | 36.8 | 15.4 | 23.7 |
| 1990[d] | — | — | — | — | 34.0 |
| 1991[d] | 11.4 | 34.3 | 50.1 | 20.6 | 35.0 |

*Source:* Unpublished tabulations, Hong Kong government.

*Note:* From 1991 onward, the occupational classification is based on the new categorization adopted by the civil service which followed the International Standard Classification of Occupations (1988) recommended by the International Labour Organisation. The 1990 figure only for "all countries" has been recomputed using the "new" definition for comparative purposes.

[a] Based on the yearly averages of general household survey quarterly figures, covering land-based, civilian and non-institutional population only. The 1991 figure was based on the 1991 population census.

[b] Figures before the third quarter of 1989 cover seven major destination countries only; figures after the third quarter of 1989 cover twelve countries: Australia, Brazil, Canada, France, Germany, Mauritius, the Netherlands, New Zealand, Panama, Portugal, the United Kingdom, and the United States. Figures from 1990 onward include an estimate for Singapore.

[c] Using the "old" definition of "professional, technical, administrative and managerial" workers.

[d] Using the "new" definition of "managers, administrators, professionals and associate professional" workers.

one-quarter of the total number of emigrants, and around 44 percent of the emigrants of working age, could be classified as "professional, technical, administrative and managerial workers." This proportion was almost certainly an underestimate, and, in 1991, the government broadened the occupational classification to reveal that, in 1990, fully 66 percent of emigrants of working age and 34 percent of total emigrants could be considered "managers and administrators, professionals and associate professional" workers. The comparable figures for 1991 were 72 percent of working emigrants and 35 percent of total emigrants. The information on the skill levels of the flows to the three main destinations is available for the total emigrant populations only (table 7.4), not for the populations of working age. The figures in table 7.4 are discussed below.

Not only are the emigrants from Hong Kong educated and highly skilled, but many have considerable wealth. It is certainly the minority who are extremely wealthy, but the emigrants include large numbers who have substantial assets. Between one-third and one-quarter of Hong Kong migrants to Canada in recent years have gone under the business migration programs. These business migrants are made up of entrepreneurs, investors, and the self-employed, and the average Hong Kong investor household to Canada has been estimated to be worth around one and one half million Canadian dollars, with entrepreneur households worth around one million and the self-employed over C$400,000. This same source cites official Canadian estimates that, in 1992 alone, over five billion Canadian dollars flowed into Canada from Hong Kong.[26] Hong Kong has contributed just under half of those who have entered Canada under the investor program since its inception in 1986. About 13 percent of Hong Kong migrants to Australia in 1990–91 entered through the business program and, although there were no data available on the financial worth of Hong Kong migrants in particular, surveys have shown that the average business migrant to Australia transferred A$510,000.[27] Hong Kong people make up about one-third of the total. Almost 80 percent of the Hong Kong migrants who were approved for permanent residence between November 1987 and June 1992 did so under the business program.[28] The figures on wealth transferred clearly have to be treated with a great deal of care as capital must be mobile, and the transfer of fixed amounts to particular destinations is, to a large extent, notional. The true entrepreneur will be moving capital to places where it can realize the greatest return. However, unquestionably, the migrants from Hong Kong are an elite in terms of education, skills, and wealth.

## Of Brain Drains and Brain Gains

It has been the emigration of the "best and the brightest" that has captured so much popular as well as more academic attention. There have been two different, though clearly associated, aspects to this issue. On the one hand, Hong Kong is seen to be experiencing a brain drain that, in one reviewer's words, has "already sapped Hong Kong's dynamism"; on the other hand, the major destination countries are seen to be competing for these brains with the intention, according to one observer from the United States, "to get as many as possible of Hong Kong's people to its own shores, so that they will use their talents and energy to advance American rather than Australian or Canadian interests."[29] That is, Hong Kong is suffering a brain drain, while the destination countries are experiencing a brain gain. The case for the latter is much stronger than for the former. Yet, as I suggested in this chapter, it would be naive to assume that the migrants will "use their talents" for a specific and narrow nationalist interest.

Canada and Australia, in particular, have specifically set out to recruit the best possible migrants through their points system of selection. From the information on the characteristics of visa applicants to the various commissions in Hong Kong, we can see that Australia has most recently been attracting the most highly qualified migrants (see tables 7.3 and 7.4). In 1991, fully 30 percent of all Hong Kong emigrants to Australia were degree holders compared with 14 percent of Hong Kong emigrants to Canada, and just 8.4 percent of Hong Kong emigrants to the United States. Over half of the emigrants to Australia fell into the "managers, administrators, professional and associate professional" category compared with 34 percent of emigrants to Canada and 20 percent of emigrants to the United States. Part of the reason, of course, lies in the relative recency of the migration to Australia (see table 7.1). As migration evolves, there is an increasing demand for, and sponsorship of, family members as the initial skilled migrants "pull" family members through chain migration. This can be most clearly seen in the relative, but not absolute, decline in the importance of professionals in the flow to Canada between 1987 and 1990 (table 7.4). Part of the reason for Australia's success is because of its selection procedures. The change in the Immigration Act of the United States in 1990 virtually tripling the annual number of migrants in the high-level professional and skilled worker preference categories from 54,000 to 140,000 was made specifically to combat the obvious success of the Canadian and Australian programs in attracting the best possible immigrants and "gaining brains." The majority of these high-quality migrants come from the whole region of East and Southeast Asia and not just from Hong Kong, as will be seen in more detail below.

The business migration programs have been seen by some to have been so successful that they are threatening the very survival of Hong Kong and hence need to be modified to be less exploitative and more supportive of the territory in its run-up to 1997. The Canadians, in particular, have been sensitive to this issue,[30] and this leads to the other side of the equation: the brain drain of talent from Hong Kong and its impact. As the number of emigrants was seen to increase during the late 1980s, so too did public concern increase. A number of surveys of migration intentions were conducted amongst business and professional groups, and alarming conclusions were often drawn. For example, 66 percent of accountants had applied for foreign passports and 27 percent planned to emigrate; and 40 percent of civil engineers, 70 percent of government doctors, and 60 percent of lawyers planned to emigrate either before 1997 or within a few years of the surveys.[31] Questions on intention to migrate do have to be treated with a great deal of caution. They reflect not so much a real intention to move as a satisfaction, or dissatisfaction, with the local situation. These intentions are likely to change as fast as a situation changes, and Hong Kong is a fast-changing society. These surveys can perhaps be put in context when compared with a Gallup poll conducted in Britain during the winter of 1992–93 when 49 percent of those sampled said that they would like to settle abroad if they were free to do so.[32] Nobody, surely, seriously expects some twenty-six million people to emigrate from Britain—even if they could all find a country to take them. Similarly, the results of the Hong Kong surveys are likely to bear little relationship to the real pattern of emigration that will develop. Surveys of intention to migrate simply cannot be taken as serious indicators of future action.

The one fact that is clear from the studies of intentions to emigrate is, as one would expect, that the pressure to migrate is concentrated among the professional and wealthier groups in Hong Kong. The results of a random Hong Kong-wide survey of migration taken in mid-1991 revealed that only 5.6 percent of the respondents would "definitely migrate" before 1997.[33] This compares to results which have shown that close to one-half of respondents to surveys of professionals will migrate.[34] Hence, for the vast majority of people in Hong Kong, emigration is not seen as an option; their destiny is in Hong Kong, irrespective of the direction of the coming political changes.

## Passport and Right-of-Abode Schemes

The emigration or planned emigration of the professional groups is still seen as negative for Hong Kong and a brake on its development. In the viewpoint of some analysts it will erode the "functional core" of the labor force, particularly as Hong Kong moves toward a service economy.[35] Such was the official concern that Hong Kong was going to lose its skilled work force that the Hong Kong government encouraged the British government and several other foreign governments to provide passports or residence rights to Hong Kong people in order to allay their fears about the transfer of sovereignty in 1997. The logic of these schemes was that, if people knew they had a fall-back position and right of abode in another place, this would discourage them from emigrating now in search of foreign passports. These schemes were, in effect, *de facto* anti-migration policies. However, the whole issue was much more complex. It was associated with the very deep feeling that Britain had abandoned its responsibility to the Hong Kong people. Why had Britain not provided full British passports to those who had been born and raised on British territory? The British feared that, if such passports were provided to the 3.2 million who would be eligible, then Britain would be swamped with migrants, thus reversing the whole trend of immigration policy toward British Territories and Commonwealth countries of the previous twenty-five years. This was not seen by the Conservative Government of the time as being politically acceptable.

Such sentiments denied the reality of the migration patterns of Hong Kong in the late 1980s. Few Hong Kong people had linkages with Britain or with the previous Hong Kong migrants to Britain who had come from the New Territories villages. Few would want to go to Britain—a view substantiated by the somewhat lukewarm response to the British "right of abode" package when it was finally implemented. The final scheme was designed to give passports to 50,000 carefully selected heads of households, which, according to government statements, would grant rights to 225,000 individuals. The final number affected is likely to be considerably less as, given current low fertility, those highly qualified people selected for these passports are unlikely to have an average family size of 4.5. Only 65,000 families applied—far short of the 300,000 expected. The orientation of Hong Kong people was then, as it is now, oriented much more to North America and Australasia than to Europe. That is, they are oriented toward the higher-growth Pacific basin, in which Hong Kong itself is strategically based, rather than to the Atlantic basin in relation to which Hong Kong is on the periphery.

Apart from the British scheme, Singapore has made provision to grant permanent residence visas to 25,000 skilled workers and their families which can be deferred for five years in the first instance and deferred for another five years upon application. In addition, there is no limit on the number of Hong Kong professionals who wish to take up residence in Singapore. By mid-1993, residence visas had been allocated to some 37,000 principal applicants in these categories, although the number actually taking up the option was, according to Singaporean sources, around 5,000.

The United States made special provision in its 1990 Immigration Act both to increase the limit on preference immigration to bring it into line with the limits for separate foreign states and to create a separate category of visas that would be valid until January 2002. The latter includes a special allocation of visas for employees of large companies (defined as having an annual turnover of fifty million United States dollars per year and employing at least one hundred employees in the United States and at least fifty overseas) that amounted to 12,000 visas per year in the three years 1991 to 1993. While there has been widespread criticism of the British package, there has been little public examination of this American package. To July 1993, three months before the expiry of this American package, only 6,140 visas out of a possible 36,000 had been issued. Undeniably, the criteria pertaining to this package were high and the potential pool was limited but, as in the case of the British package, the whole atmosphere in Hong Kong at the time had been misinterpreted. Although emigration was high, there was no panic feeling of having to get out at any cost by seeking a foreign passport. The economic reality of stagnation in North America and Europe and a booming East Asia have been critical factors in the calculus of pragmatic Hong Kong people and in preventing the expected stampede.

Several other European countries have made special provision for employees working for their national companies, and there have been a host of minor legal and extra-legal passport-for-sale schemes designed to give residence rights to nervous Hong Kong people. With the possible exception of the British package, which has been seen as a grudging handout to Hong Kong, these schemes are as much concerned with the future competition for brains as they are with providing any benevolent safety net for Hong Kong residents. Apart from the possible exception of Singapore, these schemes are unlikely significantly to alter the major directions of current migration, and few people are likely to move to exotic destinations such as Tonga or Lesotho, which are among the more curious places which have been granting passports on one basis or another.

Plate 1. **Returning empty or returning full? Cathay Pacific 747 landing at Kai Tak** *(Photo by Ronald Skeldon)*

## The Brain Drain Reassessed

Let us leave the issue of passports and the question whether a "functional core" of the labor force can be identified, let alone eroded, to consider several other important aspects of the brain drain and brain gain. The first issue is that, in Hong Kong, the stock of persons with degrees and postgraduate levels of education and the stock of those who fall into the professional, technical, administrative, and managerial worker category have increased absolutely and relatively right through the period of recent emigration from 1987 to 1991 (table 7.5). For example, over the five-year period, those falling into the professional technical class increased by 25 percent and the number of degree holders increased by 30 percent. To be sure, these overall figures tell us nothing about the quality and experience of the personnel, but they at least caution against those who conclude that the functional core may be eroding or that Hong Kong's vitality is being sapped by emigration.

The second issue to be considered is that, just as emigration from Hong Kong

Table 7.5

**Stock of High-level Personnel in Hong Kong, 1987–1991**

| | Persons with degree or postgraduate educational attainments | | Persons in professional, administrative, and managerial occupations | | |
|---|---|---|---|---|---|
| | Number | Percentage of total population | Number | Percentage of total employed population | Percentage of total population |
| 1987 | 181,737 | 3.3 | 278,554 | 10.4 | 5.1 |
| 1988 | 193,211 | 3.5 | 300,401 | 11.0 | 5.5 |
| 1989 | 206,440 | 3.7 | 315,067 | 11.6 | 5.7 |
| 1990 | 223,160 | 4.0 | 335,986 | 12.4 | 6.1 |
| 1991 | 235,400 | 4.2 | 373,055 | 13.6 | 6.7 |

*Source:* Unpublished tabulations, Hong Kong government.

has accelerated since the mid-1980s, so too has immigration to Hong Kong (table 7.6). Legal immigration increased from around 50,000 in the mid-1980s to 95,425 in 1992. Those entering with employment visas increased from 15,261 in 1986 to 40,424 in 1992. While about two-thirds of the latter are domestic servants—who, parenthetically, contribute to the liberation of educated Hong Kong women into the labor force—the number of the highly skilled and professionals has also been increasing. For example, those entering as "other professionals and middle managers" increased from 2,612 in 1985 to 4,932 in 1992. Elsewhere, I have estimated that about one-third of skilled emigrants are being replaced by skilled immigrants.[36] This is not to say that the skills lost through emigration are matched by those imported. There is indeed a problem of a mismatch of skills in Hong Kong, but this is due more to the nature of the structural change in the economy in the switch away from industry and the move toward the very different demand of service activities than it is to problems caused simply by emigration. There is no evidence to suggest that the main reason for turnover, or personnel loss, in Hong Kong companies is due to emigration. Probably only just over one percent of staff turnover could be attributed to people leaving companies to emigrate from Hong Kong in 1990 even if that had increased markedly over the 1989 figure.[37]

The figures on immigration are likely to underestimate the volume of skill replacement in Hong Kong, which brings us to the third issue that must be considered: the return migration of those who previously emigrated. "Return migration" is not the most appropriate term as it may be a return movement without the intention of remaining; that is, it is simply a relocation within the network that has been established. The volume of these return movers is perhaps

Table 7.6

**Legal Immigration to Hong Kong, 1983–1992**

| | 1983 | 1984 | 1985 | 1986 | 1987 | 1988 | 1989 | 1990 | 1991 | 1992 |
|---|---|---|---|---|---|---|---|---|---|---|
| Legal entrants for residence from China | 26,701 | 27,475 | 27,285 | 27,111 | 27,268 | 28,137 | 27,263 | 27,976 | 26,782 | 28,367 |
| With employment visas | | | | | | | | | | |
| Technicians | 846 | 986 | 1,224 | 1,042 | 1,276 | 1,261 | 1,709 | 2,348 | 2,223 | 2,610 |
| Construction workers | 187 | 46 | 10 | 45 | 15 | 94 | 125 | 7 | 43 | 11 |
| Restaurant workers | 100 | 98 | 136 | 114 | 130 | 190 | 209 | 468 | 463 | 422 |
| Domestic workers | 7,456 | 6,499 | 8,454 | 8,845 | 11,792 | 14,735 | 18,870 | 22,145 | 26,083 | 28,091 |
| Other professionals and middle managers | 1,747 | 2,024 | 2,612 | 2,893 | 3,281 | 3,895 | 4,569 | 4,765 | 4,679 | 4,932 |
| Others* | 2,235 | 2,148 | 2,049 | 2,322 | 2,589 | 3,260 | 3,242 | 3,237 | 3,699 | 4,358 |
| Total | 12,571 | 11,801 | 14,485 | 15,261 | 19,083 | 23,435 | 28,724 | 32,970 | 37,190 | 40,424 |
| With residence visas | | | | | | | | | | |
| To join husband | 3,064 | 3,229 | 3,654 | 3,587 | 4,447 | 5,376 | 4,733 | 5,072 | 5,920 | 6,919 |
| To join wife | 146 | 141 | 140 | 126 | 541 | 577 | 472 | 558 | 740 | 651 |
| To join parents | 2,805 | 3,076 | 3,593 | 3,663 | 4,698 | 5,669 | 5,772 | 5,146 | 5,025 | 5,595 |
| To join son/daughter | 646 | 593 | 821 | 925 | 777 | 775 | 716 | 781 | 787 | 811 |
| Former resident | 624 | 494 | 504 | 320 | 302 | 136 | 90 | 96 | 59 | 87 |
| Right to land/right of abode | 2,740 | 3,351 | 4,709 | 5,195 | 7,057 | 7,795 | 8,197 | 8,657 | 10,088 | 12,505 |
| To join relatives, widows or widowers | 11 | 17 | 20 | 29 | 18 | 22 | 14 | 7 | 15 | 8 |
| To join relatives | 97 | 65 | 97 | 61 | 29 | 21 | 41 | 32 | 30 | 25 |
| Miscellaneous | 78 | 130 | 188 | 172 | 136 | 91 | 29 | 40 | 33 | 17 |
| Others | 9 | 2 | 6 | 7 | 2 | 10 | 12 | 0 | 8 | 16 |
| Total | 10,220 | 11,098 | 13,732 | 14,085 | 18,007 | 20,472 | 20,076 | 20,389 | 22,705 | 26,634 |
| Total | 49,492 | 50,374 | 55,502 | 56,457 | 64,358 | 72,044 | 76,063 | 81,335 | 86,677 | 95,425 |

*Source:* Unpublished tabulations, Immigration Department, Hong Kong government.

*Note:* The above statistics do not include: (a) British citizens/United Kingdom belongers; (b) dependants from Vietnam, Laos, and Cambodia; (c) persons from China; (d) persons from China via Macau unless the application was settled in Macau by 14 January 1979.

*Includes representatives of overseas companies and salesmen, trainees, sportsmen, and entertainers.

still the biggest unknown among all our uncertainties about immigration and emigration pertaining to Hong Kong. Government estimates suggest that 12 percent of those who emigrated between 1982 and 1992 have returned to Hong Kong, and numbers of returnees increased markedly between 1990 and 1992.[38] As the emigrants qualify for Australian and Canadian citizenship after two and three years respectively, and American citizenship after three to five years, we would expect them to return to Hong Kong's booming economy in increasing numbers. Some may, indeed, return on their new foreign passport and be recorded as "immigrants" but others, perhaps the majority, return on their Hong Kong passports or I.D. cards and will simply be recorded as returning Hong Kong residents. All the anecdotal evidence points to substantial numbers of returnees, but so far no reliable quantitative estimates are possible although some indication of the volume of circulation, including return movement, is given elsewhere.[39] Those who do return, as will be clear in the discussions, maintain ties with destination areas, often leaving family members there.

Perhaps the most useful data so far are from Australia, which allow the 1991 Hong Kong resident population in Australia to be compared with the immigration intake over approximately the same time period. The figures suggest that about 17 percent of the intake between 1986 and 1991 has "disappeared," through death, onmigration, or return migration. The most probable assumption is that the majority have returned to Hong Kong. This figure is somewhat higher than the estimates of around 12 percent return movement made by the Hong Kong government referred to above, although circulation from Australia may be higher than from other destinations. However, if we examine arrivals over the most recent eighteen-month period, in 1990–91, we find that turnover is much higher, perhaps one-third of all arrivals to Australia, showing that many are just "touching base" there before returning to Hong Kong. These data suggest that many are returning quickly to Hong Kong to continue to benefit from the booming economy rather than absenting themselves for the two years, in the case of Australia, to obtain a foreign passport.[40] This is further evidence of the pragmatism of the Hong Kong population. The returnees, together with those "emigrants-who-never-were"—the "astronauts" who landed in other countries but who returned virtually immediately leaving family members overseas—make any true assessment of the impact of emigration problematic indeed. As I argued earlier, it is not simply a question of associating manpower with a particular location. We have entered into an era of global networks through which individuals flow to take advantage of opportunities in several places, thereby reducing the risks inherent in basing oneself in any single place.

The fourth issue that must be considered in assessing the impact of migration from Hong Kong is the regional context.[41] Increasing emigration is not unique to Hong Kong but is a characteristic of much of the Asian region, and particularly of the Chinese peoples. The changes in immigration law referred to earlier in this chapter have completely transformed the international migration system. In the period from 1956 to 1960, Asia accounted for 7.8 percent of migrants to the United States and 2.7 percent of migrants to Canada. No figures are available for Australia for this period. By the early 1990s, Asians accounted for almost 40 percent of migration to the United States (excluding IRCA legalization),[42] 44 percent of migration to Canada, and almost half of migration to Australia. Apart from Hong Kong, mainland China and Taiwan have become significant sources for migration to all three destinations, and tiny Singapore has been a not unimportant source for Australia (tables 7.7, 7.8, and 7.9). Although it is not clear from the data, it is likely that ethnic Chinese have figured prominently in the movements from Malaysia and Vietnam, and also from the Philippines and Thailand. Migration from South Korea is also from an area of Confucian tradition. Hence, even though the migration from Hong Kong may, on a per capita basis, be much more important than from the other areas, it is nevertheless part of a regional pattern of movement, and particularly of a broader system of migration of the highly skilled.

This is not to say that there are no poor among East and Southeast Asian migrants—there have been and continue to be large numbers of relatively poor Asian migrants—but the migration out of the other three "little dragons" of South Korea, Taiwan, and Singapore has also been mainly of the highly educated, skilled, and professional groups. It has been estimated, for example, that South Korea lost 10 percent of its high-level manpower to the United States during the 1970s.[43] The number of graduate students leaving to continue their studies from Taiwan increased from around 2,000 per annum in the late 1960s and early 1970s to over 5,000 per annum in the mid-1980s, but only about one-quarter from any one year ever returned. In 1991–92, there were 35,550 students from Taiwan and 25,720 students from South Korea pursuing their studies in the United States, compared with 13,190 from Hong Kong. Taiwan and South Korea have been two of Asia's hypergrowth economies, and it is difficult to imagine them growing any faster if the educated and skilled leavers had stayed at home. Quite the reverse; it is likely that the skills learned overseas contributed to the growth of these economies once the migrants returned home. Between 20 and 30 percent of South Korean professionals were trained overseas, mainly in the United States but also in Japan. Hence, return movements are not limited to the Hong Kong case. The astronaut syndrome also applies to migrants from Taiwan, although there another aerodynamic concept is applied: the "parachute kids." These are children who are established in a big house in North America to attend school while the parents remain in Taiwan, returning only every few months to visit. A University of California at Los Angeles study has estimated that there are 40,000 parachute kids aged 8 to 18 years in the United States from Taiwan alone, with smaller numbers from Hong Kong and South Korea.[44]

Taking an even broader historical and geographical perspective, we know that between 1835 and 1938 more than 2.3 million people left Scotland—a very

Table 7.7

**Canada: Landed Immigrants by Country of Last Permanent Residence, Selected Asian Countries and Totals, 1980–1992**

| Region/country of last residence | 1980 | 1981 | 1982 | 1983 | 1984 | 1985 | 1986 | 1987 | 1988 | 1989 | 1990 | 1991 | 1992 (prelim-inary) |
|---|---|---|---|---|---|---|---|---|---|---|---|---|---|
| Afghanistan | 14 | 38 | 79 | 73 | 125 | 370 | 590 | 975 | 1,010 | 1,054 | 1,027 | 1,353 | 1,193 |
| Bangladesh | 76 | 73 | 58 | 78 | 84 | 94 | 449 | 473 | 454 | 337 | 534 | 1,063 | 1,591 |
| Cambodia | 3,265 | 1,337 | 1,378 | 1,542 | 1,727 | 1,803 | 1,745 | 1,612 | 1,543 | 2,041 | 766 | 424 | 337 |
| China | 4,936 | 6,551 | 3,572 | 2,217 | 2,214 | 1,883 | 1,902 | 2,625 | 2,778 | 4,430 | 7,989 | 13,915 | 10,420 |
| Hong Kong | 6,309 | 6,451 | 6,542 | 6,710 | 7,696 | 7,380 | 5,893 | 16,170 | 23,281 | 19,908 | 29,261 | 22,340 | 38,841 |
| India | 8,483 | 8,256 | 7,776 | 7,041 | 5,502 | 4,028 | 6,940 | 9,692 | 10,409 | 8,819 | 10,624 | 12,848 | 12,664 |
| Indonesia | 267 | 214 | 264 | 136 | 131 | 107 | 142 | 219 | 261 | 278 | 249 | 280 | 241 |
| Iran | 1,021 | 1,056 | 1,201 | 1,268 | 1,870 | 1,728 | 1,952 | 3,083 | 3,669 | 3,797 | 3,475 | 6,209 | 6,783 |
| Japan | 737 | 770 | 630 | 333 | 250 | 205 | 273 | 446 | 346 | 541 | 369 | 502 | 603 |
| Laos | 6,266 | 866 | 375 | 434 | 870 | 379 | 636 | 456 | 842 | 679 | 583 | 1,006 | 98 |
| Malaysia | 702 | 708 | 688 | 399 | 356 | 332 | 418 | 717 | 1,676 | 1,936 | 1,641 | 1,173 | 1,305 |
| Myanmar | 87 | 81 | 275 | 39 | 51 | 37 | 14 | 31 | 56 | 86 | 140 | 107 | 69 |
| Nepal | 10 | 6 | 7 | 1 | 2 | 5 | 12 | 8 | 14 | 4 | 20 | 34 | 28 |
| Pakistan | 881 | 731 | 868 | 836 | 611 | 479 | 643 | 991 | 1,242 | 2,007 | 2,114 | 2,883 | 3,822 |
| Philippines | 6,051 | 5,859 | 5,062 | 4,454 | 3,748 | 3,076 | 4,102 | 7,343 | 8,310 | 11,393 | 12,042 | 12,335 | 18,252 |
| Singapore | 290 | 389 | 435 | 241 | 176 | 166 | 220 | 489 | 1,141 | 1,634 | 1,077 | 807 | 616 |
| South Korea | 957 | 1,430 | 1,506 | 1,017 | 801 | 934 | 1,143 | 2,276 | 2,676 | 2,820 | 1,871 | 2,486 | 3,682 |
| Sri Lanka | 144 | 223 | 182 | 166 | 1,048 | 815 | 1,753 | 4,226 | 2,409 | 2,423 | 3,106 | 6,826 | 12,626 |
| Taiwan | 827 | 834 | 560 | 570 | 421 | 536 | 695 | 1,467 | 2,187 | 3,388 | 3,681 | 4,488 | 7,451 |
| Thailand | 396 | 123 | 201 | 128 | 125 | 73 | 86 | 118 | 154 | 194 | 181 | 262 | 229 |
| Vietnam | 25,541 | 8,251 | 5,935 | 6,451 | 10,950 | 10,404 | 6,622 | 5,668 | 6,196 | 9,425 | 9,081 | 8,963 | 7,674 |
| Total Asia | 71,602 | 48,834 | 41,624 | 36,906 | 41,896 | 38,597 | 41,600 | 67,327 | 81,136 | 93,213 | 90,798 | 101,140 | 123,525 |
| Total | 143,133 | 128,618 | 121,147 | 89,157 | 88,239 | 84,302 | 99,219 | 152,098 | 161,929 | 192,001 | 214,230 | 230,781 | 252,107 |

*Source:* Employment and Immigration Canada, *Annual Immigration Statistics*, Ottawa.

Table 7.8

**United States: Immigrants by Country or Region of Last Permanent Residence, Selected Asian Countries, 1982–1992**

| Region/country of last residence | 1982 | 1983 | 1984 | 1985 | 1986 | 1987 | 1988 | 1989* | 1990* | 1991* | 1992* |
|---|---|---|---|---|---|---|---|---|---|---|---|
| Afghanistan | 1,369 | 2,063 | 1,680 | 1,287 | 944 | 1,055 | 1,145 | 1,331 | 1,041 | 1,075 | 943 |
| Bangladesh | 524 | 654 | 737 | 1,017 | 1,521 | 1,536 | 1,253 | 2,068 | 3,439 | 6,247 | 3,035 |
| Cambodia | 11,750 | 14,830 | 6,045 | 5,754 | 4,502 | 3,979 | 2,612 | 1,728 | 1,668 | 830 | 766 |
| China | 15,919 | 14,335 | 14,425 | 15,578 | 16,458 | 18,589 | 21,924 | 20,672 | 20,879 | 23,121 | 29,461 |
| Hong Kong | 11,908 | 12,525 | 12,290 | 10,795 | 9,930 | 8,785 | 11,817 | 12,236 | 12,858 | 15,564 | 16,741 |
| India | 19,813 | 23,079 | 23,617 | 24,536 | 24,808 | 26,394 | 25,312 | 27,239 | 27,418 | 29,897 | 32,839 |
| Indonesia | 2,090 | 1,581 | 2,862 | 2,995 | 3,420 | 2,772 | 2,724 | 1,637 | 3,307 | 2,062 | 2,812 |
| Iran | 7,969 | 8,724 | 11,131 | 12,327 | 12,031 | 10,323 | 9,846 | 13,027 | 8,449 | 8,531 | 6,626 |
| Japan | 4,084 | 4,234 | 4,517 | 4,552 | 4,444 | 4,711 | 5,085 | 5,454 | 5,690 | 5,212 | 11,676 |
| Laos | 31,176 | 19,285 | 6,269 | 4,750 | 3,654 | 3,331 | 4,763 | 5,754 | 4,448 | 4,651 | 3,492 |
| Malaysia | 2,758 | 1,448 | 2,147 | 1,636 | 1,565 | 1,392 | 1,881 | 1,990 | 2,268 | 2,459 | 2,690 |
| Myanmar | 568 | 425 | 416 | 590 | 523 | 597 | 619 | 868 | 781 | 615 | 587 |
| Nepal | 81 | 108 | 76 | 58 | n.d. | n.d. | n.d. | n.d. | n.d. | n.d. | n.d. |
| Pakistan | 4,130 | 4,480 | 5,803 | 6,455 | 7,034 | 7,046 | 6,732 | 9,778 | 8,907 | 9,718 | 10,352 |
| Philippines | 43,600 | 40,397 | 46,985 | 53,137 | 61,492 | 58,315 | 61,017 | 59,129 | 62,819 | 60,729 | 61,692 |
| Singapore | 722 | 584 | 1,327 | 1,389 | 1,109 | 926 | 932 | 830 | 764 | 670 | 983 |
| South Korea | 30,697 | 31,449 | 32,537 | 34,791 | 35,164 | 35,397 | 34,151 | 31,604 | 28,720 | 20,808 | 18,374 |
| Sri Lanka | 406 | 377 | 694 | 435 | 457 | 503 | 563 | 655 | 694 | 908 | 880 |
| Taiwan | 12,099 | 19,018 | 14,684 | 17,517 | 15,931 | 14,080 | 12,376 | 14,705 | 16,344 | 15,067 | 17,905 |
| Thailand | 13,599 | 13,430 | 16,034 | 17,577 | 19,086 | 16,489 | 17,619 | 29,700 | 38,695 | 45,259 | 54,405 |
| Vietnam | 65,476 | 31,678 | 25,803 | 20,367 | 15,010 | 13,073 | 12,856 | 13,145 | 14,728 | 14,836 | 31,170 |
| Total Asia | 299,526 | 261,188 | 247,775 | 255,164 | 258,546 | 248,293 | 254,745 | 268,143 | 255,913 | 269,204 | 308,388 |
| Total | 594,131 | 599,763 | 543,903 | 570,009 | 601,708 | 601,516 | 643,025 | 612,110 | 656,111 | 704,005 | 774,635 |

*Source:* U.S. Department of Justice, *Statistical Yearbooks* of the Immigration and Naturalization Service, Washington, D.C.

*Excludes IRCA legalization (see note 40 to the text of this chapter). When this is included, the total intake is 1,090,924 in 1989, 1,536,483 in 1990, 1,827,167 in 1991, and 973,977 in 1992. The largest number of Asian immigrants legalized tend to come from India, Pakistan, the Philippines, and Bangladesh.

Table 7.9

**Australia: Settler Arrivals by Selected Country or Region of Last Permanent Residence (Asian Region), Financial Years 1980–81 to 1991–92**

| Region/country of last residence | 1980–81 | 1981–82 | 1982–83 | 1983–84 | 1984–85 | 1985–86 | 1986–87 | 1987–88 | 1988–89 | 1989–90 | 1990–91 | 1991–92 |
|---|---|---|---|---|---|---|---|---|---|---|---|---|
| Afghanistan | n.d. | n.d. | 24 | 31 | 87 | 97 | 121 | 92 | n.d. | n.d. | n.d. | n.d. |
| Bangladesh | n.d. | n.d. | 31 | 32 | 56 | 85 | 39 | 38 | n.d. | n.d. | n.d. | n.d. |
| Cambodia | n.d. | n.d. | 13 | 1 | 3 | 4 | 1 | 25 | n.d. | 10 | n.d. | n.d. |
| China | 799 | 843 | 375 | 369 | 1,439 | 1,663 | 1,041 | 1,014 | 1,570 | 1,005 | 1,128 | 1,525 |
| Hong Kong | 1,690 | 2,414 | 2,756 | 3,691 | 5,136 | 4,912 | 5,140 | 7,942 | 9,998 | 11,538 | 16,747 | 15,656 |
| India | 554 | 910 | 1,279 | 1,341 | 1,700 | 1,844 | 2,073 | 2,254 | 2,153 | 2,278 | 4,358 | 4,963 |
| Indonesia | 2,740 | 2,392 | 2,342 | 2,410 | 2,049 | 2,017 | 2,067 | 1,613 | 1,762 | 1,610 | 1,223 | 1,336 |
| Iran | n.d. | n.d. | n.d. | n.d. | n.d. | n.d. | n.d. | n.d. | n.d. | 406 | 573 | 325 |
| Japan | 505 | 301 | 331 | 327 | 286 | 358 | 479 | 873 | 840 | 710 | 634 | 577 |
| Laos | n.d. | n.d. | 7 | 1 | 3 | 3 | 13 | 13 | n.d. | n.d. | n.d. | n.d. |
| Malaysia | 7,783 | 7,835 | 5,153 | 4,503 | 4,762 | 3,652 | 5,025 | 7,295 | 8,812 | 8,073 | 6,211 | 3,158 |
| Myanmar | 77 | 79 | 64 | 73 | 98 | 76 | 156 | 184 | 150 | 100 | n.d. | n.d. |
| Nepal | n.d. | n.d. | 4 | 5 | 8 | 12 | 16 | 26 | n.d. | n.d. | n.d. | n.d. |
| Pakistan | 395 | 357 | 152 | 163 | 653 | 751 | 923 | 521 | 820 | 524 | 388 | 1,020 |
| Philippines | 3,123 | 3,704 | 3,998 | 3,650 | 3,520 | 4,337 | 6,431 | 10,745 | 9,288 | 6,233 | 6,451 | 5,893 |
| Singapore | 1,467 | 1,642 | 1,044 | 944 | 1,142 | 1,215 | 2,222 | 2,817 | 2,806 | 2,137 | 1,944 | 1,652 |
| South Korea | n.d. | n.d. | 569 | 564 | 636 | 1,201 | 1,510 | 1,756 | 1,627 | 1,338 | 948 | 1,174 |
| Sri Lanka | 452 | 557 | 343 | 1,281 | 2,158 | 1,400 | 2,310 | 2,314 | 2,204 | 1,761 | 2,858 | 2,325 |
| Taiwan | n.d. | n.d. | 176 | 233 | 344 | 575 | 987 | 1,320 | 1,884 | 2,889 | 3,261 | 2,946 |
| Thailand | 4,722 | 4,772 | 5,159 | 3,859 | 2,542 | 2,549 | 2,868 | 3,310 | 4,054 | 3,207 | 3,040 | 2,077 |
| Vietnam | n.d. | n.d. | 582 | 1,761 | 2,738 | 2,389 | 2,473 | 1,562 | 3,128 | 4,691 | 9,364 | 7,268 |
| Total Asia | 24,972 | 26,744 | 24,486 | 25,325 | 29,532 | 29,322 | 36,214 | 46,471 | 52,128 | 48,656 | 56,194 | 53,475 |
| Total | 111,190 | 118,700 | 93,177 | 69,808 | 78,087 | 92,410 | 113,309 | 143,490 | 145,316 | 121,227 | 121,688 | 107,391 |

*Sources:* Department of Immigration and Ethnic Affairs, Australian Immigration, 1982, *Consolidated Statistics*, No. 13, Canberra; Department of Immigration, Local Government and Ethnic Affairs, 1988, *Statistical Note 36: Asian Immigration*, Canberra; Bureau of Immigration Research, *Immigration Update*, December 1989–June 1992.

significant number if we take into consideration that the total population in 1901 was just under 4.5 million.[45] The Scottish emigrants, like their modern Asian counterparts, included large numbers of the elite, the "aristocracy of labor"; yet, during this period, Scotland became increasingly prosperous and emerged as a major industrial power.

The above discussion shows that, historically, as well as in the present, it is misleading, if not totally mistaken, to associate emigration necessarily with negative consequences for the development of the areas of origin. The truth is quite the reverse. The development of these areas brings about an increasing interchange of population that, while undeniably giving rise to some localized short-term bottlenecks, will ultimately be in the best interests of both origin and destination countries. This is a theme to which I will return in the conclusion of this chapter.

## The Future Trends in Migration

It is easy to make blythe predictions about the future course of migration but much less easy to make accurate assessments of what will actually happen. We cannot accurately predict the future. What we can do is to try to come to some educated guesstimates of likely trends, based upon what we know of the current situation. There are certain clear indications of what some of these may be.

First, as Hong Kong becomes more closely integrated into the economy of southern China, it is also becoming more closely linked with the pattern of migration both within and from China. The consequences of Hong Kong investment in China for increased migration to centers in the Pearl River Delta region from other parts of the country need not concern us here, but the linkages with emigration from China are becoming important. The migration from Hong Kong and from other Chinese areas of origin in Asia has involved primarily the educated and the highly skilled—those we have termed the "new" overseas Chinese as opposed to the "old" migration of laborers in the second half of the nineteenth and early part of the twentieth centuries. Yet there are continuities with the earlier pattern.

Over the last two to three years, the number of illegal immigrants from China—primarily from the province of Fujian and from particular districts within that province such as Changle county—have been increasing sharply. It now appears likely that over one hundred thousand Chinese were smuggled into the United States during 1992, a huge increase from relatively small numbers in the late 1980s. Increasing numbers are being transported by ship, although the majority are probably still moved by air.[46] It is becoming clear that a substantial part of this migration is being organized by, or at least brokered through, criminal organizations in Hong Kong. The cost of smuggling an individual from China to the United States appears to be in the region of thirty thousand United States dollars. Few will be able to pay this amount outright so, after a down payment, they will be expected to work off the balance upon arrival at the destination, which is usually New York.[47] This system parallels the credit-ticket system for the shipment of laborers during the last century. Most of the migrants are young males who are trying to make money in the United States before returning wealthy to China—an optimistic but somewhat unlikely outcome. The sojourner of the old overseas Chinese has returned, but now facilitated by elements of the new overseas Chinese. As China continues to open up, particularly in the southern provinces, this movement can but increase; it is a movement in which Hong Kong is a key catalyst and reflects the territory's return to China and its participation in regional flows. As in the case with migration in the past, it is becoming virtually impossible to separate Hong Kong emigration from migration from China.

Nevertheless, despite the provisos made above, the main area of local concern about the future trends must relate to what will happen to the emigration from Hong Kong itself. In 1992, more people left than at any other time in the recent past, with the government estimating that 66,000 people left the territory; my own estimates for that year, made earlier in this chapter, are considerably higher. The provisional estimate for 1993 is that around 60,000 will leave. If we accept all the difficulties with these estimates discussed earlier in this chapter and elsewhere, it is incumbent upon us to try to predict whether numbers are likely to increase, decrease, or remain more or less where they are in the lead-up to 1997. The two main forces that will affect the migration are clearly what will happen in China and what will happen to the international economy. The latter is perhaps less difficult to deal with than the former.

Southern China is the fastest economic growth area in the world today, and Hong Kong is very much part of this region. The economies of Australia, Canada, and the United States are still mired in extremely slow growth, averaging rates of growth of GDP per capita of 3.4 percent per annum each in the 1980s. Hong Kong averaged 7.1 percent growth over the same period.[48] Hong Kong is a labor-deficit economy, with unemployment at around 2 percent. Unemployment in both Canada and Australia exceeds 10 percent of the labor force, and in the United States it is around 7.5 percent. A survey of Hong Kong migrants to Canada in March 1991 showed that the majority experienced a drop in both income and rank in their first job after migration.[49] Hence, in terms of improving one's economic status, a migration from Hong Kong at present is unlikely to lead to immediate success. At a superficial level, the migration from Hong Kong thus appears somewhat paradoxical, with people moving from a high-growth, low-unemployment, low-tax area to low-growth, high-unemployment, and high-tax areas. However, the recurrent theme of this and the previous chapter relates to the migration system that is being created through the human networks of movement. Through these networks, people may flow to gain access to economic opportunities in various parts of the world. Risk, both economic and political, can be minimized through these networks which, over the long term, will provide better returns than a simple strategy to maximize short-term gain, which is again paradoxically seen as a Hong Kong characteristic. The current migration belies the trait, and short-term losses are balanced by perceived long-term gains in a risk-minimization strategy. The "astronaut" pattern is also an integral part of this strategy.

There is nevertheless evidence of some increase in visa wastage at present, although it is still very low—about 3 percent for Canada, for example. There is more evidence of people deferring their departure until the last possible moment, normally within twelve months of taking the medical examination. Also, in 1993, about one-quarter of business applicants granted interviews for migration to Canada were finding excuses not to turn up at the appointed time, thus deferring the whole process. Lastly, of course, there is the evidence of increasing return movement referred to earlier.

Australia has responded to the economic slowdown by markedly reducing the "target" for the annual intake of immigrants: from 126,000 in 1990–91 to 63,000 in 1993–94. The numbers going to Australia from Hong Kong have declined from 16,747 in 1990–91 to 15,656 in 1991–92, with the latest figures showing a 41.5 percent decline in the numbers from Hong Kong arriving during the last six months of 1992 compared with the last six months of 1991.[50] Canada has not reduced its annual target intake of 250,000 in the face of high unemployment. There have been fluctuations in the numbers of landed immigrants from Hong Kong between 1988 and 1992, but not too much can be read into these movements. Certainly, the high figure for 1990 reflects the increasing numbers who applied in the wake of the June 1989 events in Tiananmen Square, but the sharp increase in 1992 over 1991 was due more to dates of processing papers and numbers of immigration personnel allocated to the task of clearing the backlog of applications than to any increased pressure to migrate in Hong Kong. In mid-1993, substantial backlogs of applications are still being processed for Canada or are in the "queue" for the United States, and we can expect a steady movement to continue over the next two years. There is no such backlog for Australia, and the numbers moving to that country can be expected to be markedly down in the short term. This is more a response by Hong Kong people to the poor economic situation in Australia than to the reduction in target immigrant population. The highly qualified Hong Kong applicants are likely to be little affected by the change in target numbers, which will reduce those at the lower end of the skill spectrum. However, potential migrants from Hong Kong are very well informed and, given the economic slowdown in Australia, applications are down from a high of 14,029 in 1989–90 to 3,238 in 1992–93 (table 7.10). This decline of 77 percent may be explained by the high number of applications received after the Tiananmen Square incident in June 1989, but there was also an 86 percent decline in applications from people from Taiwan over the same period. Taiwan is much less affected by events in mainland China than Hong Kong, yet the pattern of migration is similar. This again suggests that Hong

Table 7.10

**Total Number of Applications Received at the Australian Commission in Hong Kong, 1986–1993**

| Year | Hong Kong | Taiwan | Macau | Total |
|---|---|---|---|---|
| 1986–87 | 6,317 | 745 | 116 | 7,178 |
| 1987–88 | 8,178 | 794 | 93 | 9,065 |
| 1988–89 | 6,882 | 1,011 | 64 | 7,957 |
| 1989–90 | 14,029 | 1,568 | 220 | 15,817 |
| 1990–91 | 11,414 | 1,455 | 71 | 12,940 |
| 1991–92 | 5,980 | 813 | 71 | 6,864 |
| 1992–93 | 3,238 | 212 | 19 | 3,469 |

*Source:* Unpublished tables, Australian Consulate General, Hong Kong.

Kong is very much part of a regional system of migration, with Chinese peoples throughout that region responding in similar ways to global economic conditions.

Hence, if the economies of Hong Kong and southern China are to continue on a relatively steady growth trajectory, migration from Hong Kong is likely to slow down, although movement from southern China itself, much of it illegal, may increase. As 1997 approaches, we can perhaps expect certain sectors of the public service and allied institutions such as tertiary education to experience sharp outflows. The private business sector is unlikely to be affected significantly so that the "functional core" of Hong Kong, assuming that such an entity exists, will persist. Much of Hong Kong's manufacturing base has already been transferred to China, and, from an economic point of view, Hong Kong's transition to China has already been accomplished.

The steady economic growth trajectory is, however, not a guaranteed scenario. There are already signs of serious economic overheating in China and strains between a central administration and distant provinces pursuing their own goals and intents. If the economic development of China is to stall, or if there is a break-up of China into rich and poor regions, then there will almost certainly be population movements on an enormous scale, not just from Hong Kong—the elite of Hong Kong will be well placed to flow to the destinations chosen long before—but also from China.

This chapter is not about crystal-ball gazing where one person's scenario is as good as anyone else's. It is about how Hong Kong people have moved to key areas, often global cities, over the last five to six years. Individual motivation is placed within a global context of national immigration policies. The resulting networks that have been established, and continue to be established, by the new overseas Chinese are fundamental linkages in the creation of any "new world order" in the post–Cold War era.[51]

## Conclusion

By the time this assessment appears in print, many of the conditions may have changed, rendering any conclusion obsolete. Over the last five years, we have seen dramatic shifts. From an area of major public and official concern between 1988 and 1990, migration has, by 1993, become virtually a non-event as far as public opinion and policy are concerned. Paradoxically, the information provided in these chapters has clearly shown that the numbers of people leaving Hong Kong up to 1992 did not decrease: in fact, more people left in 1992 than at any other time during the recent past. It has been the perception of the migration that has changed, and emigration has been overtaken in the public eye by the Patten proposals for electoral change.

The monthly magazine *Emigrant* began publication in August 1988 with its statement of purpose given as: "This magazine neither advocates nor discourages emigration. Its purpose is to offer information on the subject so that people can make their own choice." Its last month of publication was August 1991, with a cover story about migrants returning to Hong Kong. In true Hong Kong style, a commercial response to a market demand had been met rapidly and had faded just as quickly as the demand was satisfied. The surge and ebb of general interest were reflected at government level too. On 4 May 1988, the Hong Kong government announced in the Legislative Council that a special task force was to be formed consisting of a Principal Assistant Secretary supported by two Assistant Secretaries and a Senior Statistician to examine the whole issue of emigration and the brain drain. The task force was set up to collect information on something that, until then, few knew anything about, but also, and perhaps more importantly, to give the impression that the government was doing something about an issue that the public felt was a major threat to Hong Kong. Once the data-gathering system was in place, the number of senior officers was reduced, and the role of the task force was subsumed into "normal" government activities with the dissolution of the Administrative Services and Information Branch in August 1989 and the transfer of its functions to the Director of Administration, Chief Secretary's Office. There, emigration continued to have a fairly high profile for another year, until in mid-1990 its functions were transferred to become part of the duties of the Security Branch. Apart from an annual press release, its activities appear to have gone on largely unnoticed by the public since then. As I observed above, the high tide of emigration in 1992 seems to have been missed both by the government and by the general public, which again illustrates the sharp difference between reality and the perception of that reality.

As I have made clear, emigration is almost certain to slow down, at least over the next two years, assuming the continued economic growth of southern China. However, all could change if increasing regionalism in China and a realization of rising disparities between rich and poor lead to violence and economic chaos. Then, very large numbers indeed will leave Hong Kong, facilitated by the prepa-

Plate 2. **The politicization of the Hong Kong Chinese: Campaigning in Trinity-Spadina, Toronto, in the Canadian general election, October 1993** *(Photo by J.H. Galloway)*

rations that Hong Kong people have been able to make over the last six years in terms of obtaining foreign passports or residence rights overseas, or in terms of establishing family members at potential destinations. The phase of emigration from Hong Kong, as from many parts of Asia, over the last twenty-five years has been predicated primarily by the needs of destination countries. This is likely to continue, although increasing tensions, both internally and between countries, in the Asian region itself could mean that the next phase of emigration is predicated mainly by conditions in the sending rather than the receiving areas. This is the case in Western Europe in the post–Cold War period as migrants move from Eastern Europe, Africa, and the Middle East despite growing attempts to slow the flows. Growing national sentiment could also occur in Asia. The networks to facilitate flows of elites out of Hong Kong and other major Asian cities are already well established, and future volumes of emigration could be very substantial indeed.

I have argued elsewhere that the emigration from Hong Kong is likely to be positive rather than negative for both the future of Hong Kong and for the destination countries, as well as for most of the migrants.[52] If the migrants to Canada can be taken in any way as "typical," the majority of them appear to have taken a drop in salary or in status, although the majority also thought positively about their move to Canada, with almost one-quarter viewing it as "excellent."[53] Hong Kong gains from becoming established as a center of a network of international communities, which have been described in this book. Through these networks, Hong Kong people and companies gain access to niches in very different areas and at very different stages in the business cycle. Through these networks, too, Hong Kong may seek international support if attempts are made to change the system in an adverse way after 1997. Chinese authorities have been sensitive to any attempt, as they would perceive it, to internationalize the Hong Kong issue in terms of involving anyone but British or Chinese officials in Hong Kong affairs, yet the migration out of Hong Kong, as well as into Hong Kong, has truly internationalized the city, economically, socially, culturally, and politically. The new overseas Chinese from Hong Kong and from China itself are going to be a force that can but increase in influence on the world stage as we move into the twenty-first century.

From the point of view of destination countries, it should be obvious that the gain of large numbers of highly educated, innovative, and skilled migrants with capital can but be beneficial for their economies and societies. Even if some of these migrants spend much of their time in their places of origin, the net benefit is still likely to be positive for the destination countries. As we have seen in the specific chapters, Hong Kong migrants appear to make fewer demands upon welfare systems than the native-born in either Canada or Australia. Data from these two countries also show that there is no evidence that immigration increases unemployment;[54] quite the reverse—immigrants spend more on housing and food, stimulating demand and increasing production and employment, and immigrants make a positive contribution to capital accumulation in Canada.[55]

Despite the clear results of the studies that have generated these research findings, there is often the perception that migrants can be a drain on destination economies. There are migrants whose command of English and educational skills are limited and who make demands upon social services and on the supply of urban infrastructure. The Hong Kong migrants and the Chinese in general would not appear to fall into this category. Unfortunately, perceptions of some migrants may influence policy that must apply to all. In situations of persistent high unemployment in developed countries, is it realistic to assume that immigration will continue at present levels? European nations have already tightened restrictions, and there is a vigorous debate whether immigration is, in fact, desirable.[56] Australia alone of the settler societies, as we have seen, has already cut back its intake significantly. It may be that countries will come to depend more on temporary, skilled migration precisely of the kind exhibited by an important segment of the Hong Kong migrants—the "astronauts." The implications of such a policy shift for national development and citizenship await future investigation.

My conclusion that emigration from Hong Kong is good for the city has been seen as "optimistic."[57] I see the migration as neither optimistic nor pessimistic but as essential for any future development. The existence of the migration to date certainly does not preclude a pessimistic scenario if things should take a turn for the worse in China. The key point is counterfactual; if the emigration had not taken place, then Hong Kong would be in a much weaker situation today as it would be more isolated internationally.

The future of migration from Hong Kong will ultimately depend upon the direction taken by China, particularly after the death of Deng Xiaoping. Even if the present trend toward economic reform continues, we should not expect emigration to cease. It will continue, albeit perhaps on a reduced level, as one expects the free interchange of labor in a capitalist system. *Hong Kong 21*, a visionary report put out by a leading Hong Kong business and professional group, calls for priority action to reduce barriers to the movement of people.[58] As Hong Kong's population growth slows because of the persistent low fertility, there will be an increasing demand for labor at all skill levels. This is a situation that is also affecting Japan and the other three "little dragons" of Asia where there has been a migration "turnaround" from emigration under conditions of surplus labor to immigration under conditions of labor shortage.[59] While there will certainly be fluctuations in the volume of migration under the steady growth scenario, particularly around 1997, as many people in "sensitive" government occupations or those in areas that might be seen as "critical" of the region—in universities, for example—choose to leave. These should, nevertheless, be relatively minor fluctuations in a long-term shift from the trend toward emigration over the 1980s to a trend toward increasing immigration in the 1990s as Hong Kong's population ages and its economy moves toward a regional service center. Even within this trend toward increasing immigration, there will always be those who will leave, as occurs from any open city around the world. However, if the situation in China were to deteriorate markedly, then, as stressed above, the outflows from Hong Kong *and* China would be substantial.

## Notes

1. A summary of the early population figures is given in Endacott, G. B. (1973), *A History of Hong Kong*, rev. ed. Hong Kong: Oxford University Press. 1973, p. 65.

2. The figures in this paragraph are from the population censuses of Hong Kong, first taken in 1841, and then at regular five-year or ten-year intervals, depending upon circumstances, from 1881. The most recent data are from the 1991 Hong Kong population census. The data for Singapore are in Lau Kak En (1992), *Singapore Census of Population 1990: Demographic Characteristics*. Singapore: Department of Statistics.

3. Gillingham, P. (1983), *At the Peak: Hong Kong between the Wars*. Hong Kong: Macmillan, p. 10.

4. A useful summary of changing demographic characteristics in Hong Kong up to 1971 can be found in Economic and Social Commission for Asia and the Pacific (ESCAP) (1974), *Population of Hong Kong*. Bangkok: United Nations ESCAP, Country Monograph Series No. 1.

5. See Endacott, *A History of Hong Kong*, p. 289 and p. 310; also Davis, S. G. (1949), *Hong Kong in its Geographical Setting*. London: Collins, pp. 92–95.

6. The figures on cross-border movement are provided in the various annual reports issued by the Hong Kong government, of which *Hong Kong 1993* is currently the latest.

7. These data come from the Supplementary Enquiry via the General Household Survey, April to June 1991, "Hong Kong Residents in China," Census and Statistics Department, n.d.

8. The information in this paragraph comes from Sinn, Elizabeth (1995), "Emigration from Hong Kong before 1941: General Trends," and "Emigration from Hong Kong before 1941: Organization and Impact. In *Emigration from Hong Kong: Tendencies and Impacts*, ed. Ronald Skeldon. Hong Kong: The Chinese University Press, pp. 11–34 and 35–50. The data for the period 1876 to 1898 is from Chen Hansheng, *Materials on the History of the Emigration of Chinese Labourers* (Beijing: Zhonghua Shuju, 1981–85) (in Chinese), cited in Dr. Sinn's work.

9. Much has been written on the topic of exclusion policies in North America and Australasia. The classic study is perhaps still Price, C. A. (1974), *The Great White Walls Are Built: Restrictive Immigration to North America and Australasia 1836–1988*. Canberra: Australian National University Press. For a more recent account, see Daniels, R. (1988), *Asian American: Chinese and Japanese in the United States since 1850*. Seattle: University of Washington Press; and for a useful introductory summary, see Kitano, H. H. L. and R. Daniels (1987), *Asian Americans: Emerging Minorities*. Englewood Cliffs, NJ: Prentice Hall.

10. See Tan, T. T.-W. (1986), *Your Chinese Roots: The Overseas Chinese Story*. Singapore: Times Books International.

11. The information on these minor labor movements is contained in the Annual Reports for the 1950s published by the Hong Kong government.

12. See Watson, J. L. (1977). "The Chinese: Hong Kong Villagers in the British Catering Trade." In *Between Two Cultures: Migrants and Minorities in Britain*, ed. J. L. Watson. Oxford: Blackwell, pp. 181–213; and Freeberne, M. (1981), "Chinese Succeed in the UK." *The Geographical Magazine* 53(11), pp. 706–11. For a comprehensive analysis of British immigration policy and immigration to Britain in general, see Holmes, C. (1988), *John Bull's Island: Immigration and British Society, 1871–1971*. London: Macmillan.

13. Szczepanik, E. (1958), *The Economic Growth of Hong Kong*. London: Oxford University Press, p. 31.

14. See Baker, Hugh D.R. (1994), "Branches All Over: The Hong Kong Chinese in the United Kingdom." In *Reluctant Exiles? Migration from Hong Kong and the New Overseas Chinese*, ed. Ronald Skeldon. Armonk, NY: M.E. Sharpe, pp. 291–307; Watson, J. L. (1975), *Emigration and the Chinese Lineage: The Mans in Hong Kong and London*. Berkeley: University of California Press; and Watson, J.L. (1977), "The Chinese: Hong Kong Villagers in the British Catering Trade." In *Between Two Cultures: Migrants and Minorities in Britain*, ed. J. L. Watson. Oxford: Blackwell, pp. 181–213.

15. The most succinct discussion of Canadian immigration will be found in Hawkins, F. (1989), *Critical Years in Immigration: Canada and Australia Compared*. Kingston: McGill-Queen's University Press. The quotation is from p. 39.

16. For changes to American law, see Kitano and Daniels, *Asian Americans*; Bernard, W. S. (1982), A History of U.S. Immigration Policy. In *Immigration: Dimensions of Ethnicity*, ed. R. A. Easterlin et al. Cambridge, MA: Belknap/Harvard; amd Jones, M. A. (1992), *American Immigration*, 2nd ed. Chicago: University of Chicago Press.

17. Hawkins, *Critical Years in Immigration*, is the best source.

18. New Zealand's changing policy is described in Trlin, A. D. (1986), "New Zealand's Immigration Policy in the Early 1980s." In *New Zealand and International Migration: A Digest and Bibliography, No. 1*, ed. A. D. Trlin and P. Spoonley. Palmerston

North: Massey University, Department of Sociology, pp. 1–21; and Trlin, A. D. (1992), "Change and Continuity: New Zealand's Immigration Policy in the Late 1980s." In *New Zealand and International Migration: A Digest and Bibliography No. 2*, ed. A. D. Trlin and P. Spoonley. Palmerston North: Massey University, Department of Sociology pp. 1–28. The quotation is from Trlin, "New Zealand's Immigration Policy in the Early 1980s," p. 19.

19. These are discussed in Skeldon, R. (1991), "Emigration, Immigration, and Fertility Decline: Demographic Integration or Disintegration?" In *The Other Hong Kong Report 1991*, ed. Y. -W. Sung and M. -K Kwan. Hong Kong: The Chinese University Press, pp. 233-58.

20. Hong Kong Census and Statistics Department (1991), *Hong Kong 1991 Population Census: Summary Results*. Hong Kong: Government Printer. The 5 percent cited refers to place of birth data. No information on ethnic origin was included in the 1991 census. Another indicator is usual language used in the home. Only 3.2 percent of the population 5 years of age or older used languages other than a Chinese language.

21. Cited in Wong Siu-lun (1992), "Emigration and Stability in Hong Kong." *Asian Survey* 10, p. 921.

22. Hawkins, F. (1989), *Critical Years in Immigration: Canada and Australia Compared*. Kingston: McGill-Queen's University Press, pp. 45–46.

23. The data on the adjustment of status program and the statement about the illegal migration in Hong Kong are from Hawkins, *Critical Years in Immigration*, p. 49.

24. Mr. Wang Yuan-jen, Director of the Bureau of Entry and Exit, quoted in the *South China Morning Post*, 19 November 1991.

25. The information on the emigrant profile is based on unpublished data provided by the Security Branch, Hong Kong government. See also Lary, Diana and Luk, Bernard (1994), "Hong Kong Immigrants in Toronto." In *Reluctant Exiles? Migration from Hong Kong and the New Overseas Chinese*, ed. Ronald Skeldon. Armonk, NY: M.E. Sharpe, pp. 139–62.

26. Data made available by the Canadian Commission, Hong Kong, and published in Henders, S. and D. Pittis (1993), "Hong Kong Capital Flows into Canada." *Canada and Hong Kong Update* 10, pp. 1–6.

27. Keys Young, M. S. J. (1990), *Expectations and Experiences: A Survey of Business Migrants*. Canberra: Australian Government Publishing Service.

28. Ho, Elsie S. and Farmer, Ruth (1994), "The Hong Kong Chinese in Auckland." In *Reluctant Exiles? Migration from Hong Kong and the New Overseas Chinese*, ed. Ronald Skeldon. Armonk, NY: M.E. Sharpe, pp. 215–32.

29. The first quotation appeared in a review of Gerald Segal's book, *The Fate of Hong Kong*, by Alexander Nicoll, which appeared in the *Financial Times* on 11 March 1993; the second quotation is from McGurn, W. (1992), *Perfidious Albion: The Abandonment of Hong Kong*. Washington: Ethics and Public Policy Center, p. 7.

30. See, for example, the assessment in Nash, (1993), "Hong Kong's Business Future: The Impact of Canadian and Australian Business Migration Programs." In *Pacific Asia in the Twenty-first Century: Geographical and Developmental Perspectives*, ed. Yue-Man Yeung. Hong Kong: The Chinese University Press, pp. 309–39.

31. The surveys are summarized in Kwong, P. C. K. (1990), "Emigration and Manpower Shortage." In *The Other Hong Kong Report 1990*, ed. R. Y. C. Wong and J. Y. S. Cheng. Hong Kong: The Chinese University Press, pp. 297–337. See also Nash, "Hong Kong's Business Future."

32. The results of a survey run for the *Daily Telegraph* newspaper in early 1993 and summarized in Hong Kong in the *South China Morning Post* on 23 February 1993.

33. The results of a survey taken as part of the project "Emigration from Hong Kong:

Tendencies and Impacts," sponsored by the Hong Kong University and Polytechnic Grants Committee, on which the author is a co-researcher. The results are published in Skeldon, Ronald, ed. (1995), *Emigration from Hong Kong*. Hong Kong: The Chinese University Press.

34. See, for example, Lam, J. T. M. and J. C. Y. Lee (1991), *The Political Culture of the Voters in Hong Kong: A Study of the Professional Constituencies of the Legislative Council in Hong Kong*. City Polytechnic of Hong Kong, Department of Public and Social Administration; also Kwong, "Emigration and Manpower Shortage."

35. This idea is developed in Kwong, P. C. K., P. W. Liu, and S. Tang (1989), *Functional Core of the Labour Force: Towards the Retention of Key Personnel in Hong Kong*. Hong Kong: The Chinese University of Hong Kong, Department of Economics. (Mimeo)

36. The whole issue of immigration and emigration is considered in Skeldon, "Emigration, Immigration, and Fertility Decline: Demographic Integration or Disintegration?"

37. Tang, S. F. Y. and H. K. L. Choi (n.d.), *Emigration from Hong Kong: 1991 Organizational Survey*. Hong Kong Institute of Personnel Management.

38. Hong Kong government, Security Branch, press release, 4 March 1993.

39. See also Kee Pookong and Skeldon, Ronald (1994), "The Migration and Settlement of Hong Kong Chinese in Australia." In *Reluctant Exiles? Migration from Hong Kong and the New Overseas Chinese*, ed. Ronald Skeldon. Armonk, NY: M.E. Sharpe, pp. 183–96; Ho, Elsie S. and Farmer, Ruth, "The Hong Kong Chinese in Auckland"; and Y. Sharma, "Brain Gain as Recession Hits Western Countries," *Business Times* (Hong Kong), 1 April 1991.

40. See Kee Pookong and Skeldon, Ronald, "The Migration and Settlement of Hong Kong Chinese in Australia."

41. Much fuller discussion of the regional context will be found in Skeldon, R. (1992), "International Migration within and from the East and Southeast Asian Region: A Review Essay." *Asian and Pacific Migration Journal* 1, pp. 19–63; and Skeldon, R. (1992), "International Migration and the ESCAP Region: A Policy-Oriented Approach." *Asia-Pacific Population Journal* 7, pp. 3–22.

42. IRCA refers to the Immigration Reform and Control Act of 1986, which allowed two groups of illegal migrants in the United States to take up legal permanent residence. This applied to those who had been illegally resident since 1 January 1982 and to those who had been seasonal agricultural workers in the United States between May 1985 and May 1986 for at least ninety days. The act mainly benefited Mexicans and other Latin Americans and relatively few East and Southeast Asians appear under this category. Because the IRCA numbers do not refer to a flow within a particular time period, I have excluded them from the calculations and in the data presented in table 7.8.

43. The information on South Korea in this section is mainly from Kuznets, P. W. (1987), Koreans in America: Recent Migration from South Korea to the United States. In *The Economics of Mass Migration in the Twentieth Century*, ed. S. Klein. New York: Paragon, pp. 41–69; and on Taiwan from Hsieh, K.-C. et al. (1989), *An Investigation of the Current Situation and Problems of Emigration*. Taipei: Development Review Council (in Chinese). The figures on the numbers of students are from Institute of International Education (IIE) (1992), *Open Doors 1991/92. Report on International Educational Exchange*. New York.

44. Results of this study were cited in a report in the *International Herald Tribune*, 25 June 1993. See also the age data presented by Ho, Elsie S. and Farmer, Ruth, "The Hong Kong Chinese in Auckland."

45. Devine, T. M. (1992). "Introduction: The Paradox of Scottish Emigration." In *Scottish Emigration and Scottish Society*, ed. T. M. Devine. Edinburgh: John Donald.

46. This issue receives much fuller treatment in Skeldon, R. (1994), "East Asian

Migration and the New World Order." In *Population Migration and the Changing World Order*, ed. W. Gould and A. Findlay. London: Belhaven.

47. The conditions under which many of these people work are described in Kwong, Peter (1994), "New York is Not Hong Kong: The Little Hong Kong that Never Was." In *Reluctant Exiles? Migration from Hong Kong and the New Overseas Chinese*, ed. Ronald Skeldon. Armonk, NY: M.E. Sharpe, pp. 256–68.

48. Figures from World Bank (1992), *World Development Report*. New York: Oxford University Press.

49. Employment and Immigration Canada (1991), *Hong Kong Immigrants in Canada*. Published in collaboration with the Hong Kong Institute of Personnel Management and Alberta Career Development and Employment.

50. Bureau of Immigration Research (1993), *Immigration Update, December Quarter 1992*. Canberra: Australian Government Publishing Service.

51. This theme is developed in Skeldon, "East Asian Migration and the New World Order."

52. Skeldon, R. (1990–91), "Emigration and the Future of Hong Kong." *Pacific Affairs* 63(4), pp. 500–23.

53. See Lary, Diana and Luk, Bernard, "Hong Kong Immigration in Toronto," and Employment and Immigration Canada, *Hong Kong Immigrants in Canada*.

54. These issues are discussed for Australia in Wooden, M. et al. (1990), *Australian Immigration: A Survey of the Issues*. Canberra: Australian Government Publishing Service (Bureau of Immigration Research); and Murphy, P. A. et al. (1990), *Impact of Immigration on Urban Infrastructure*. Canberra: Australian Government Publishing Service (Bureau of Immigration Research). For Canada, they are discussed in Hersak, G. and D. Thomas (1988), *Recent Canadian Developments Arising from International Migration*. Ottawa-Hull: Employment and Immigration Canada; and Employment and Immigration in Canada (1989), *Immigrant Asset Performance* (research abstract). Ottawa-Hull: Ministry of Supply and Services.

55. See the summary of a research project on this topic in Employment and Immigration Canada, 1989, *Business Immigration Program: Immigration Regulations, Guidelines and Procedures*.

56. See Coleman, D. A. (1992), "Does Europe Need Immigrants? Population and Workforce Projections." *International Migration Review* 26, pp. 413–61; and Salt, J. (1992), "The Future of International Labor Migration." *International Migration Review* 26, pp. 1077–1111.

57. Segal, G. (1993). *The Fate of Hong Kong*. London: Simon and Schuster, p. 64.

58. *Hong Kong 21: A Ten Year Vision and Agenda for Hong Kong's Economy*, Business and Professionals Federation of Hong Kong, 1993, pp. 45–46.

59. This was the theme of the papers presented at the international seminar "Turning Points in International Labour Migration" sponsored by the International Labour Office, the Korea Labor Institute and the United Nations University in Seoul, 6–7 April 1993. The paper on Hong Kong is published as Skeldon, R. (1994), "Turning Points in Labor Migration: The Case of Hong Kong." *Asian and Pacific Migration Journal* 3, pp. 1–26.

# 8

# New York Is Not Hong Kong: The Little Hong Kong That Never Was

*Peter Kwong*

After the passage of the United States Immigration Act in 1965, many Hong Kong immigrants escaped the economic and political uncertainties of Hong Kong and found refuge in New York's Chinatown. They brought skills and know-how acquired in Hong Kong's industrial society to "develop" the Chinese community in America. By the mid-1970s, New York's Chinatown had grown into a thriving economic entity that promised to become a little "Hong Kong." It never happened. The capital influx from Hong Kong was diverted into speculative investment which undermined the very prosperity it had earlier created. Without increased productivity, profits were maintained through raw exploitation. Workers labored under sweatshop conditions for long hours, for low wages, and without benefits. Although New York's Chinatown continues to attract immigrants, it has now become the dumping ground for the desperate undocumented. Fewer Hong Kong residents are coming now as the opportunities for upward mobility that the Chinatown community once offered to the new immigrants have disappeared. The influence of Hong Kong may now be more as a facilitator of undocumented migration from China rather than as a source of migration. Hong Kong-based criminal societies play a major organizational role in the current wave of undocumented migration from southern China to the United States, and mainly New York.

The failure of the Hong Kong community in New York directly contradicts the scholars who promote the virtues of "ethnic enclaves" as a new alternative for immigrants. They argue that strong family ties and ethnic solidarity within these enclaves permit immigrants to save and start their own small businesses.

The original version of this chapter appeared in *Reluctant Exiles? Migration from Hong Kong and the New Overseas Chinese*, ed. Ronald Skeldon (Armonk, NY: M.E. Sharpe, 1994).

Map 1. **New York's Chinatown**

As a result, the residents in the enclave are able to join the American middle class without assimilation.[1]

The New York Chinatown experience indicates that sustained economic growth within the enclave is necessary in order to provide immigrants with continued opportunities. In turn, this requires supportive external conditions. Since the mid-1970s, New York City has been an unfriendly environment for small businesses. The situation became worse in the 1980s and was characterized by unchecked real estate speculation, deteriorating transportation systems, crumbling social services, decaying housing stock, and the indifference of local law enforcement officers to organized crime. Such conditions were not conducive to planned capital investment. Without investment, there could be no growth to elevate the community economy to a higher level of productivity and wealth.

Hong Kong is a "paradise of free enterprise," because the colonial government has tried in every possible way to build a stable and amicable economic environment to attract investors. The current American conditions, on the other hand, have lacked planning and restrictions, providing an atmosphere of "free enterprise," that is, giving the capital side all the leverage and thereby imposing what is called "market discipline." At the same time, the government has initiated no policies and allocated no funding to encourage business investment. Working conditions in Chinatown are reminiscent of the nineteenth-century Dickensian exploitative system. Ironically, the American "laissez faire" system of the 1980s has hastened its economic decline, whereas Hong Kong's paternalistic governmental policies have produced a more advanced economy.

## The Arrival of Hong Kong Residents

Before the mid-1960s, New York's Chinatown had a small, "pre-capitalistic" economy mainly consisting of small restaurants, gift shops, and dry goods stores. At its peak, the community encompassed only a six-block area, with a population not exceeding fifteen thousand. Most of the residents were male and of rural origin, which could be narrowed down to the Pearl River delta region of Guangdong Province. By the 1960s, New York's Chinatown was an aging, dilapidated, bachelor community (though the sex ratio improved somewhat after the Second World War with the War Brides Act and the Alien Fiancées Act, which permitted those Chinatown residents who were in the services to bring their wives and fiancées to New York). The privileged few who had families with children tended to move into more integrated areas beyond their Lower East Side neighborhood. Chinatown was on the verge of disappearing as the older bachelors passed on.

The 1965 Immigration Act reversed the decline of New York's Chinatown. Relatives of old-time residents were able to migrate to the United States through the provisions for family reunification. American citizens of Chinese descent were able to bring not only their spouses but also direct relatives, grown chil-

New York . . .

is not Hong Kong . . .

nor is Toronto . . .

Plate 3. **Three global cities** *(Photos by Ronald Skeldon)*

dren, and siblings to the United States. As a result of the passing of the new law, the population of Chinatown quickly multiplied.

The newcomers, being relatives of the old-time residents, were most likely to come from Guangdong Province. However, until 1979, when the United States and the People's Republic of China finally established diplomatic relations, the Cantonese relatives of Chinatown residents eligible to enter the United States had to go through Hong Kong, and the vast majority had been residents of that territory. These people migrated again to the United States for economic or political reasons, avoiding political instability in Hong Kong such as the 1966 and 1967 riots (which were at least partially due to the Cultural Revolution in China), and particularly from the early 1980s, after the commencement of negotiations between Great Britain and China which eventually led to the British government agreeing to return the colony to China in 1997. Chinatown was thus replenished with Hong Kong residents of Guangdong origin who had urban experience and exposure to Western systems and values.

## The Modernization of Chinatown

The first observable impact of the 1965 Immigration Act was the reduction of sexual imbalance in the community and its gradual transformation from a bachelor to a family community. The influence of women gave the community a new spark of life and a large ready and available female labor force. As Chinatown's population grew, the women were eager to obtain employment in order to supplement the family income.

As it happened, opportunities opened up in the garment industry. New York was historically the center of the American garment industry, but it had experienced a serious decline by the 1960s because of the competition and the loss of its older workers of European origin. The industry adjusted by exporting its production overseas, while at the same time looking for cheap and reliable labor in the city to replace the aging European laborers. It found Chinese men and women who had worked in Hong Kong factories.

Beginning from the 1950s, Hong Kong had developed into an export-oriented light-industry and manufacturing center, particularly in the garment and textile trades.[2] Many of the New York Chinatown residents had already worked in the garment industry in Hong Kong as seamstresses, pressers, foremen, or contractors. In fact, they had often worked for the same kind of large American manufacturers that were subcontracting both in Hong Kong and in New York.

The conditions in Chinatown were ideal for the American garment industry. Not only would this solve the labor shortage, but garment manufacturers could leave factory management to the Chinese contractors, who already had experience in the industry. They knew the operations and could handle the language problem when working out the wage scale or dealing with the union. It is not surprising that large manufacturers encouraged Chinese to get into the industry by helping them to set up factories. Since the mid-1960s, 90 percent of the garment factories that employ Chinese women have been owned by the Chinese. In the 1960s, there were eight Chinese factories, in 1974 there were 209, and in 1984 there were 500. By that time, 20,000 Chinese women had joined the garment workforce,[3] and almost every family in Chinatown had a member employed in the industry. It became the foundation of the new Chinatown economy.

The large number of garment factories boosted the local restaurant business. Hong Kong-style fast-food operations, well suited to an industrial economy, were transferred to New York. Hundreds of small restaurants were established simply to service the busy working women who no longer had time to cook for their families. Competition led to an improvement in the quality and variety of Chinese cuisine, propelling the industry into servicing a more sophisticated New York professional class. Chinatown expanded into the tourist trade modeled on the example of Hong Kong. The restaurant and garment industries became the twin pillars of the Chinatown family economy, with husbands often working for restaurants and wives working in garment factories. As these jobs grew, more opportunities opened up and more immigrants were encouraged to come.

As this new immigrant community grew, the need for bilingual services grew as well. Opportunities were opening up for Hong Kong professionals who had a command of the English language. Bilingual bank officials, accountants, journalists, and social workers educated and trained in Hong Kong could fit straight into Chinatown's growing economy. As a multi-class community took root, more Hong Kong residents were attracted, leading to more expansion and more investment. By 1980, the population of Chinatown had grown to 150,000, its parameters encompassing a significant part of the Lower East Side.

The new Hong Kong exiles, having come from a more developed economy, literally modernized the Chinatown community. By the mid-1970s, New York City had become the most desirable destination for Hong Kong immigrants, according to a Hong Kong immigration survey.[4] Their heavy presence was attested by the fact that the spoken dialect in the community shifted from Taishan (which was originally the provenance of the majority of the Chinatown community) to "Hong Kong," a much more urban version of the Cantonese dialect.

Chinatown was developing into a "little Hong Kong," attracting more and more capital investment and industrial know-how. In time, it was expected to grow and prosper just like another "little dragon," right on the tip of Manhattan Island. Chinatown is what sociologists like Alejandro Portes call an "ethnic enclave," a new option for immigrants to succeed in America without assimilation. Unlike the inner-city ghettos or the European immigrant slums earlier in the century, these enclaves provide jobs right within the community —jobs that pay higher wages than the larger American labor market for people who do not speak English and possess no marketable skills.[5] Through the cooperative efforts of the co-ethnics, many enclave residents are able to accumulate enough capital to start their own small businesses. According to the "enclave theory," sociologists believe that places like Little Havana in Miami and New York's Chinatown are the new type of economic phenomenon in the American economy.[6]

## From Dragon into Snake

The growth of New York's Chinatown economy did not continue. The capital investment needed to develop Chinatown into the next economic stage never materialized. The influx of capital was diverted to speculative ventures, and particularly into real estate. This was a direct result of the belief that Chinatown would continue to attract immigrants and that the value of land in the area would continue to increase unabated. When the United States normalized relations with the People's Republic of China in 1979, that country became entitled to up to 20,000 places in the Eastern Hemisphere allocation, which effectively increased the immigration from Chinese areas, which had been essentially Hong Kong and Taiwan, from 20,600 to 40,600 a year. The assumption by speculators was that there would be many more Chinese coming to seek business and living quarters. An investor in Chinatown real estate could easily double the investment in a few years.

Real estate speculation in Chinatown was, in part, proceeding along with the American speculative trend of the 1980s. Investment in Chinatown real estate could hardly be regarded as risky considering the general rise of real estate value in Manhattan. Poorer neighborhoods were being "gentrified" through the conversion of tenement buildings into high-rise condominiums. Chinatown, with its prime location near Wall Street and South Street Seaport—the two most valuable commercial and office districts in the city—was high on the investment lists of Hong Kong's migrant developers.

The value of Chinatown real estate was thought to be even more impervious to downward trends, because Hong Kong capital was "refugee" capital, which was simply being exported out of the colony to avoid local instability. In the case of this kind of capital, the sole objective of the investors was to position themselves in the Chinatown real estate market. This long-term view accepted a lower rate of return than would commonly be expected of ordinary American capital.

A wild speculative fever ensued. Even those who had originally made their money in industry started converting their profits into real estate speculation. The prices of buildings leaped out of proportion to the rental income. According to a study carried out in 1986 by the Real Estate Board of New York, the annual rent per square foot for retail space on Canal Street at that time was US$275; that is, higher than rents on Madison Avenue above Forty-second Street ($255), higher than the most desirable parts of the Upper West Side, and far higher than on Wall Street, where the rents were around $175 per square foot.[7] Landlords eventually realized that they had to increase rents, or even better to transform

Chinatown into a high-rent district. Starting from the mid-1980s, real estate interests tried slowly to replace resident apartments and factory space with condominiums, boutique storefronts, and office space. This undermined the very foundations of the Chinatown economy, yet New York City had no effective control over this kind of gentrification process.

Further economic growth would have required profits being reinvested in the community. Improving productivity would have meant acquiring advanced technology or diversifying into more capital-intensive industries for higher returns. This did not happen in Chinatown. Businesses let their machinery, equipment, and facilities deteriorate. They had no long-term strategy other than acquiring the cheapest labor force possible. There was no shared interest among manufacturers, the Chinese contractors, and Chinese workers.

The "industrial district" models in Italy, where owners, management, and workers cooperate to improve products and secure a market share are quite different.[8] Firms in the Emilia-Romagna region of Italy, for instance, have "formed industrial networks: strategic alliances, buyer-supplier partnerships, joint ventures." They go for the "upmarket," where consumers are willing to pay high prices for quality products.[9] The businesses are profitable because they escape competition from low-cost producers. At the same time, the workers enjoy stable and high wages. Some of the Hong Kong garment manufacturers have followed the Italian model. Others, in the 1960s, moved away from the labor-intensive garment industries into more sophisticated electronic industries, making higher profits and creating more job opportunities for the economy.

Investors are willing to commit to planned growth if they feel optimistic about the economic environment; and even more so if they are given favorable conditions by the public sector. In Hong Kong, the colonial government provided such conditions. It has always been assumed that Hong Kong's success came from its free-market economy. However, it was aided by the colonial government, whose civil servants greatly facilitated industrial planning and the development of local industry.

Since the 1950s, the Hong Kong government has invested heavily in the construction of roads, ports, railways, tunnels, and a subway system. It responded quickly to the needs of multinational companies planning to set up operations in Hong Kong. It used public funds to develop many areas as industrial estates and then made the land available to manufacturing firms. In the meantime, it helped local enterprises with export promotion and planning advice. From the early 1950s, the colonial government took responsibility for building public housing and instituted public health programs.[10] In the labor management area, the government instituted codes to regulate working hours and factory conditions. Above all, it instituted strict immigration control to prevent oversupply of labor, specifically from China. This helped the workers in the colony to maintain their wage level, while also keeping down the unemployment rate.

### The Dickensian Conditions of Chinatown

The government sector in America provides few such advantages for business investors. New York City, for instance, has adopted a post-industrial strategy of planned shrinkage of manufacturing. By encouraging growth in service and high-tech industries, it has made little effort to make manufacturers feel welcome.[11] Meanwhile, the existing conditions are inhospitable to small businesses: congested and crumbling transportation systems, high commercial taxes, no effective zoning protection for factory space, and the perceived indifference of the local police to street and organized crime. Small-business owners citywide see themselves as victims of these conditions and have little incentive to invest. They simply operate in such a way as to cut their costs to the minimum. They make profits by squeezing the workers.

Chinatown owners have adopted the same attitude. Those who work for Chinese bosses soon learn that all standard American labor practices are ignored. Waiters and shop clerks are expected to work six-day weeks, more than ten hours a day, with no compensation for overtime, no holidays, and no sick leave. They are paid below the minimum wage. Employees get no health and accident insurance. Restaurant owners are not concerned with maintaining a healthy and safe working environment. Air and grease filters in kitchens are rarely in working order, spouting harmful pollutants through the work space and into the street. Bathrooms in most restaurants are never properly cleaned. Emergency fire exits are regularly blocked to keep thieves from breaking in. Most restaurant owners do not train new workers in any way; these are simply expected to learn from the complaints of impatient patrons, the scolding of chefs and bosses, and the insults of disgruntled fellow waiters.

Such harsh labor practices are so firmly entrenched that even the garment workers in the community face similar outrageous conditions. Employers continue to ignore regulations regarding the forty-hour week, overtime pay, and health and safety provisions. Workers work by the piece-rate and rarely receive even the national minimum wage, let alone the union minimum.

The Chinese are driven by a grueling incentive system. Waiters work hard to get more tips; garment workers work faster to complete more pieces. These are jobs for the young, those with the energy to work furiously in order to earn more money. However, most workers suffer job-induced ailments after a few years. A seamstress must then request less strenuous tasks as a cutter at lower wages. A waiter will have to search for work in a less popular or a suburban restaurant, where the pace is not so fast—but at much lower wages. The prospect for an immigrant who remains in Chinatown as a worker is downward mobility.

Conditions in the factories continue to deteriorate. Individuals who have worked in Hong Kong testify that Hong Kong conditions are better, with a clean, well-lit, and well-ventilated work space and usually separate quarters for coffee and lunch breaks. The sewing machines in Hong Kong are up-to-date Japanese models which are fast and capable of a variety of functions. In Chinatown, machines are often thirty- or forty-year-old models that constantly break down. Wage levels in Hong Kong in the 1980s were about the same as in Chinatown, though the cost of living in Hong Kong was lower.[12] With the structural transformation of Hong Kong toward a primarily service economy from the second half of the 1980s, average living standards there improved markedly, and, in the 1990s, prices are comparable with or even higher than those of New York. Workers in Hong Kong have access to public housing and to public health facilities. The new arrivals in America, on the other hand, since they need to be close to Chinatown, are forced to settle into illegal makeshift apartments set up by greedy landlords. One-bedroom apartments are often rented to three families, converted cellars to dozens of people, while a "bed-space" in a crowded room rents for US$80 a month.

The unions have done little to improve the situation, even though most of the Chinese seamstresses are members of the International Ladies Garment Workers Union. The ILGWU is more concerned about collecting membership dues than enforcing wage agreements. It is more interested in appeasing the factory owners so that they do not decide to close down than in protecting the workers. The state labor department never intervenes, claiming that no one has complained. When someone did complain, the response was that the department did not have the resources to hire bilingual officers to check on violations because of budget cuts. Currently, hundreds of workers are complaining that owners owe them back wages. Again, the labor department and the union are dragging their feet and abrogating their responsibilities.[13] The last resort is to send one's grievance to the National Labor Relations Board. Unfortunately, it is usually years before a case comes up for deliberation.

Since the mid-1980s, with the real estate speculative fever and the massive increase of immigrants from China, the situation in Chinatown has worsened. Some immigrants have arrived illegally, under a virtual bondage system requiring each to pay off thirty thousand United States dollars to the smugglers, known as snakeheads. Without legal status and recourse, these illegals live a hellish existence, willing to labor at almost any wage and under almost any conditions. A wage rate of US$1.50 per hour is quite common. The New York *Daily News* reported on 23 September 1990 that some illegal immigrants are even obliged to work for three years without pay, "to work off the fees" charged by the smugglers or face torture and beating. Their presence in Chinatown has dramatically reduced the already low wage scale and increased the instances of abuse by employers.

Chinatown exists as an extraterritorial entity outside American laws, where owners violate workers' rights at will. In addition, the tongs within Chinatown act as effective guarantors of owners' oppression of the working people.

## Other Hong Kong Imports: The Colonial Mentality and Organized Crime

The most unwelcome import from Hong Kong is organized crime. New York Chinatown has long had its own underworld organizations, the tongs, but the triad members from Hong Kong are more sophisticated; they are connected to international networks involved in drugs, illegal immigrant smuggling, and money laundering.[14]

This criminal element, too, arrived in New York to escape from political uncertainty in Hong Kong but, at the same time, its intention was to diversify its operations. By the mid-1970s, the Hong Kong element had taken control of the tongs. The newly transformed tongs continue their role as protectors of Chinatown's business elite and now particularly of those recently arrived Hong Kong business interests. Workers do not dare to object to abuses, tenants are reluctant to complain of landlords' violations, and small businesses victimized by extortions remain silent.

American authorities excuse their inaction by claiming that the Chinese are not willing to cooperate with the law enforcement. When Chinese citizens do cooperate, they risk their lives since the police are unwilling to provide full protection. In the meantime, American politicians interested in campaign donations willingly accept money from Hong Kong business and community leaders. Such casual contacts only enhance the power of these individuals in the community.

Today, organized crime elements originating in Hong Kong hide under the cover of the Chinatown community and provide 70 percent of the heroin supply on the east coast of the United States.[15] Although law enforcement agencies are now taking some action, their sole concern is to eliminate the drugs from American streets and not the criminals' terrorizing presence in the Chinese community.

Hong Kong immigrants originally came to New York for better opportunities but found themselves competing with immigrants from China, who were willing to work even longer hours and at even lower wages, after the late 1980s. Consequently, the rate of migration from Hong Kong has slowed down. It was the Hong Kong immigrants who built the foundation of the new Chinatown economic structure; now they have left it to the illegals and the desperate from mainland China and Malaysia. The illegals from China, who probably numbered more than 100,000 per annum in the early 1990s, require separate discussion, but large numbers, almost certainly the majority, head for New York.[16] Chinese have been leaving Malaysia in response to what they consider discriminatory ethnic policy toward them in favor of the Malays. The poor, and those without professional skills, cannot come in legally except on tourist visas. Most overstay and become "undocumented." Without legal status, they have to be content with manual jobs working for Chinese employers.

## An American Development in Microcosm

The difficulties of economic development in Chinatown reflect the larger problems of the American economy. Modern corporations, attempting to maintain profitability through decentralization of their production processes, have moved their factories to southern states or third world countries so as to be more responsive to varied market conditions and to avoid organized labor.

For those factories which still remain in this country, the most effective way of cutting costs is to subcontract work to smaller operators, thus leaving to them the problems of acquisition of supplies, quality control, cost cutting, and labor relations. Even better, they subcontract work to immigrant communities where unregulated underground economies exist. Large corporations reap high profits by offering as little as possible to the subcontractors, while not having to take the blame for exploitation. After all, in Chinatown "it is only Chinese exploiting Chinese." Such underground economies exist in Vietnamese, Cuban, Dominican Republic, and Central American ethnic enclaves, as well as in Chinatowns.

The casualization of labor practices in New York's Chinatown is spreading throughout the American economy.[17] This type of "free-enterprise system" may be profitable for the capital in the short run, but it inevitably sows the seeds of its own destruction as a result of its lack of modernization. Exploitation of the immigrant communities only strips the United States of the technological advantages in international competition. The comparison between Hong Kong and New York's Chinatown clearly brings out this reality.

## Notes

1. Zhou, Min (1992), *Chinatown: The Socioeconomic Potential of an Urban Enclave.* Philadelphia: Temple University Press, pp. 1–17.
2. Vogel, E. F. (1991), *The Four Little Dragons: The Spread of Industrialization in East Asia.* Cambridge, MA.: Harvard University Press, pp. 70–72.
3. International Ladies Garment Workers Union, Local 23–25 (1983), *The Chinatown Garment Industry Study,* p. 1.
4. International Ladies Garment Workers Union, p. 45.
5. Portes, A. and R. Bach (1985), *Latin Journey: Cuban and Mexican Immigrants in the United States.* Berkeley, CA: University of California Press, p. 341.
6. Zhou, *Chinatown: The Socioeconomic Potential of an Urban Enclave*, p. 5.
7. See the article by Alberto Scardino, "Commercial Rents in Chinatown Soar as Hong Kong Exodus Grows," *The New York Times*, 24 December 1986; and the assessment in my book, Kwong, P. (1987), *The New Chinatown.* New York: Hill and Wang, pp. 50–53.
8. Petras, E. Mc. (1992). "Industrial Sweatshops or Industrial Districts: Restructuring Garment Manufacturing in Philadelphia and Valencia." Paper presented at the International Sociological Association meetings held in Los Angeles from 23 to 26 April 1992.
9. Reported by R. Fitch, "The New Worker Atop," *New York Newsday*, 21 February 1993, p. 35.
10. Vogel, *The Four Little Dragons*, pp. 69–72.

11. See R. Fitch's article in *New York Newsday*, 21 February 1993.

12. See P. Kwong and J. Lum, "Surviving in America: The Trials of Chinese Immigrant Women," *The Village Voice*, 31 October 1989, pp. 30–41.

13. Newsletter of the Chinese Staff and Workers Association, 1992, *CSWA: The Voice of Chinese American Workers* (New York), 3(2), pp. 1–2.

14. See P. Kwong and D. Miscevic, "The Year of the House: The New Heroin Warlords," *The Village Voice*, 17 July 1990, pp. 26–34.

15. Ibid.

16. For a preliminary study, see Skeldon, R. (1994), East Asian Migration and the New World Order. In *Population Migration and the Changing World Order*, ed. W. Gould and A. Findlay. London: Belhaven.

17. For a discussion of this issue for New York and other "global cities," see Sassen, S. (1991), *The Global City: New York, London, Tokyo*. Princeton: Princeton University Press.

# 9

# Economic Integration of Hong Kong and Guangdong in the 1990s

*Yun-wing Sung*

The inauguration of the People's Republic of China's Open-door Policy in 1978 has led to the rapid integration of Hong Kong with China, especially with Guangdong Province. As wages have risen rapidly in Hong Kong, its labor-intensive industries have moved to the mainland on a large scale. The synergy of China's cheap labor with Hong Kong's know-how and capital was the main factor behind China's spectacular export drive, as acknowledged in earlier chapters.

Economic statistics are more available on a national level. This is especially true of Hong Kong trade statistics, which are classified by country of origin or destination but not classified by province. China's trade statistics are disaggregated by province, but provincial trade statistics are much less detailed than national trade statistics. Whenever statistics are not available for Guangdong, this chapter will describe the integration of Hong Kong with China rather than with Guangdong. This is not a serious drawback, as Guangdong accounted for the bulk of trade and investment between Hong Kong and China, and Hong Kong–China links in trade and investment tend to reflect Hong Kong's trade and investment with Guangdong.

There is no doubt that the economies of mainland China and Hong Kong are highly integrated. The mainland is Hong Kong's foremost trading partner and vice versa. In 1991, China's exports to (imports from) Hong Kong accounted for 45 (42) percent of China's exports (imports), whereas Hong Kong's exports to (imports from) China accounted for 27 (38) percent of Hong Kong's exports (imports). Hong Kong and the mainland are the foremost investors in each other.

---

The original version of this chapter appeared in *The Hong Kong–Guangdong Link: Partnership in Flux*, ed. Reginald Yin-Wang Kwok and Alvin Y. So (Armonk, NY: M.E. Sharpe, 1995).

To understand China's statistics on foreign investment, it is necessary to distinguish between direct foreign investment and "other foreign investment," which includes foreign funds involved in processing/assembling operations, compensation trade, and leasing. "Other foreign investment" constitutes commercial credit, while direct foreign investment does not, since the Chinese partner theoretically controls the operation and usually pays for foreign machinery and technical assistance with labor services used in making goods for the foreign partner. In this chapter, the term "foreign investment" includes both direct foreign investment and "other foreign investment." In terms of contribution to capital formation, "other foreign investment" is relatively small because processing/assembling operations are labor-intensive rather than capital-intensive. From 1979 to 1990, the cumulative stock of "other foreign investment" was only 10.7 (14.6) percent of contracted (utilized) foreign investment in China. However, processing/assembling operations are very important in China's exports because they tend to be export-oriented. In 1990, exports from processing/assembling operations amounted to U.S. $25.4 billion or 40.9 percent of China's exports (Sung, 1991c: 23). In comparison, exports from enterprises with direct foreign investment amounted to only U.S. $7.8 billion or 12.6 percent of China's exports. In other words, foreign investment (both direct foreign investment and other foreign investment) accounted for 54 percent of China's exports in 1990, or for 64 percent of the *increase* in China's exports from 1978 to 1990. As Hong Kong's cumulative contracted investment in China from 1979 to 1990 amounted to U.S. $26 billion or 59 percent of the national total, the crucial role of Hong Kong in China's export drive is evident.

Hong Kong is also the pivot of China's economic links with the outside world, especially with Taiwan. In late 1987, Taiwan lifted its ban on travel to the mainland and also started to ease its restrictions on trade and investment with the mainland. Since then, Taiwan's trade with the People's Republic of China (PRC) and Taiwan's investment in the People's Republic have increased very rapidly. After Hong Kong, Taiwan has become the mainland's second most important economic partner, albeit a distant second. Taiwan still stipulates that all trade with China and all investment in China have to be conducted indirectly, most often through Hong Kong. The growth of trade and investment between the People's Republic and Taiwan has further strengthened the position of Hong Kong as China's middleman.

The economic ties of the mainland with Hong Kong and Taiwan have become especially important since the Tiananmen Incident of June 1989. Since Tiananmen, China has become more isolated, but China's economic links with Hong Kong and Taiwan have strengthened. Since June 1989, investment and tourism from developed countries have declined, but investment and tourism from Taiwan have increased sharply, and investment and tourism from Hong Kong rebounded rapidly in 1990 after sharp declines in the second half of 1989. Thanks to investment from Taiwan and Hong Kong, total contracted foreign investment in China grew from U.S. $6.2 billion in 1988 to U.S. $6.3 billion in 1989 and grew further to U.S. $6.9 billion in 1990. China's tourism earnings decreased from U.S. $2.2 billion in 1988 to U.S. $1.9 billion in 1989, but recovered to U.S. $2.2 billion in 1990 largely due to the continuing surge of tourists from Taiwan, Hong Kong, and Southeast Asia. In a nutshell, Hong Kong and Taiwan are essential to the success of China's Open-door Policy.

The nature of the economic ties between the mainland and Hong Kong and Taiwan is qualitatively different from China's ties with the developed countries. China's commodity trade with the latter is mostly interindustry trade, whereas its trade with Hong Kong and Taiwan includes substantial intraindustry trade. This is because China, in the aspect of development, is closer to Hong Kong and Taiwan than to the developed countries. Moreover, Hong Kong and Taiwan have invested heavily in outprocessing operations in China, giving rise to thriving intrafirm trade. Hong Kong and Taiwan have less of the advanced technology of the developed countries, but their medium-level technology may be more suited to China's level of development and could enhance China's bargaining power in acquiring technology from the developed countries. The investment from Hong Kong and Taiwan tends to be in export-oriented processing/assembling operations, whereas Japan and the United States tend to invest in import-substitution enterprises. The investment from Hong Kong and Taiwan is the most significant factor behind China's successful export drive.

After the Tiananmen Incident, the prestige and authority of Beijing and the Communist Party suffered severely. Meanwhile, Guangdong and Fujian have continued to gain in economic strength, thanks to their links with Hong Kong and Taiwan. China's economy has become increasingly regionalized and southeast China is emerging as a dynamic and distinct economic entity.

Hong Kong's ties with Guangdong are particularly strong. Table 9.1 shows the importance of Hong Kong's investment in Guangdong. From 1979 to 1990, contracted foreign investment in Guangdong amounted to U.S. $20 billion or 45 percent of the national total. Hong Kong's contracted investment in Guangdong amounted to U.S. $15 billion, accounting for 75 percent and 34 percent, reespectively, of total foreign investment in Guangdong and in China, or equal to 57 percent of Hong Kong's investment in China. However, statistics of contracted investment are likely to exaggerate Guangdong's share because many contracted investment projects in Guangdong in the early years of the Open-door Policy never materialized. Figures on utilized investment would be a better indicator of Guangdong's share. From 1979 to 1990, utilized foreign investment in Guangdong amounted to U.S. $8 billion or 37 percent of the national total. Utilized investment from Hong Kong in Guangdong amounted to U.S. $5 billion, accounting for 64 percent and 23 percent, respectively, of total foreign investment in Guangdong and in China, or equal to 40 percent of Hong Kong's utilized investment in China. Figures for the period 1985 to 1990 tell roughly the same story. We can conclude that while Hong Kong accounted for the bulk of foreign

Table 9.1

**Cumulative Foreign Investment in China and in Guangdong**
(in U.S. million dollars)

| | | National Total | In Guangdong | From Hong Kong | From Hong Kong in Guangdong |
|---|---|---|---|---|---|
| 1979–90 Foreign Investment | contracted | 45,245<br>(100) | 20,332<br>(44.9) | 26,480<br>(58.5) | 15,208<br>(33.6) |
| | utilized | 22,219<br>(100) | 8,132<br>(36.6) | 12,888<br>(58.0) | 5,180<br>(23.3) |
| 1985–90 Direct Foreign Investment | contracted | 33,454<br>(100) | 11,484<br>(34.3) | 18,415<br>(55.0) | 8,652<br>(25.9) |
| | utilized | 15,922<br>(100) | 5,307<br>(33.3) | 9,657<br>(60.7) | 4,239<br>(26.6) |

*Source:* Data for the national total, and for investment from Hong Kong, are obtained from the *Almanac of China's Foreign Relations and Trade* (1984–91); data for investment in Guangdong and for investment from Hong Kong in Guangdong are obtained from the *Guangdong Statistical Yearbook* (1983–91).

*Note:* Figures in parentheses represent percentage share of the national total.

investment in Guangdong, Guangdong accounted for less than half of Hong Kong's investment in China.

Hong Kong's trade with Guangdong is also very important. In 1990, Guangdong's exports amounted to U.S. $10,560 million or 19 percent of the national total, and Guangdong's exports to Hong Kong amounted to U.S. $8,543 million, accounting, respectively, for 81 percent of Guangdong's exports and 46 percent of China's exports to Hong Kong. These statistics were collected by China's Ministry of Foreign Economic Relations and Trade (MOFERT), and they grossly understated Guangdong's exports because the MOFERT included in its statistics only the processing fees of processing/assembling operations instead of the value of goods exported from such operations. Processing fees are usually only 10 percent of the value of goods exported, and exports from processing/assembling operations have been very important in Guangdong. China's Customs Statistics, which consistently value exports by the value of goods exported, would give a more accurate picture of Guangdong's exports. Unfortunately, China's Customs Statistics are not available in great detail at the provincial level. It is known, however, that the China's Customs Statistics for 1991 exports of goods made in Guangdong was U.S. $22,800 million[1] or 32 percent of the national total, whereas the corresponding MOFERT figure was only U.S. $13,548 million.

Hong Kong accounts for the bulk of investment in processing/assembling operations in Guangdong, and the overwhelming portion of the output of such operations is exported to Hong Kong. Guangdong's 1990 share of 46 percent in China's exports to Hong Kong calculated from MOFERT statistics is thus a gross underestimation. Exports of Guangdong goods to Hong Kong were also not published in China's Customs Statistics. However, Guangdong's 1990 exports to Hong Kong can reliably be estimated to be U.S. $16,697 million,[2] accounting for 86 percent and 27 percent, respectively, of Guangdong's and China's exports, or 73 percent of China's exports to Hong Kong. In a nutshell, Hong Kong accounted for the bulk of Guangdong's exports, and Guangdong also accounted for the bulk of China's exports to Hong Kong. Unfortunately, statistics on Guangdong's imports were less useful because they included only imports handled by provincial authorities, excluding the substantial imports handled by Beijing. Guangdong imports from Hong Kong in 1990 amounted to U.S. $4,116 million or 72 percent of Guangdong's imports.

The rest of this chapter is organized as follows. Section two discusses the degree of economic integration between China and Hong Kong. Section three covers trade and investment between Hong Kong and China. Section four evaluates the prospect of Hong Kong as a middleman for China. Section five analyzes the impact of China's opening up to Hong Kong manufacturing. Section six concludes the chapter.

## The Degree of Economic Integration Between Hong Kong and China

Economic integration means the lowering of barriers to economic interactions across countries or regions, thereby facilitating trade and investment. Economic integration can occur through institutional channels such as the establishment of a free trade area or granting mutual discriminatory preferences to the parties involved. It can also occur naturally without the establishment of a formal institution, as in the case of a fall in transportation costs as a result of technological advancement.

Despite intense trade and investment flows, there is an obvious lack of institutional integration between Hong Kong and China. The three important institutional barriers to economic integration often listed in textbooks are tariffs, controls on factor movements, and exchange risks. On these three counts, the barriers to economic integration between Hong Kong and China are still very high. Even though China will resume sovereignty over Hong Kong in 1997, it is specified in the Sino-British agreement on Hong Kong that Hong Kong will remain a separate customs territory and will continue to have its own currency. Migration from China to Hong Kong will be strictly controlled. It can be argued, therefore, that even after 1997 Hong Kong and the mainland will be less institutionally integrated than, say, Greece and Ireland, which are both members of the European Economic Community (EEC); there is complete freedom of movement of goods and factors between these two countries. Moreover, both countries are members of the European Monetary System and have pegged exchange rates. As

China is not a member of the GATT (General Agreement on Tariffs and Trade) and the Chinese currency is not convertible, Hong Kong is institutionally more closely integrated with most of the economies of the free world than it is with China.

Though economic theory concentrates on tariffs, controls on migration, and exchange integration, the effect of geographical and cultural distances may be even more important. Hong Kong is only a half-hour's train ride from China, and Taiwan is quite close to China in terms of geography. The importance of cultural affinity is quite evident; Guangdong has received the bulk of Hong Kong's investment in China; Taiwan's investment is similarly concentrated in Fujian.

Geographic and cultural proximity can enable businesses to evade the formal barriers to trade and investment. Tariffs can be evaded through smuggling, and there is rampant smuggling from Hong Kong to China. The movement of people from Hong Kong and Taiwan to China is relatively free, though movement in the other directions is highly controlled. However, illegal immigrants from the mainland are quite common in Hong Kong. Though the Chinese yuan is not convertible, the Hong Kong currency has circulated widely (and unofficially) in Guangdong, especially in the Shenzhen Special Economic Zone (SEZ). It has been estimated that the amount of Hong Kong dollars circulating in China amounts to HK $6,300 million (U.S. $808 million) or 16 percent of the total supply of the Hong Kong currency (*Hong Kong Economic Times,* 3–21–1991).

The foremost barrier to economic integration between Hong Kong and China is the command economy in China. It is inherently difficult for a command economy to benefit from international trade and investment, because a command economy is designed to insulate itself from the world market. A command economy tends to have an overvalued and inconvertible currency, which is a big obstacle to international economic integration. Moreover, it is extremely difficult for the planner of a command economy to know what goods should be exported or imported because the economy tends to have a highly distorted and arbitrary price system. East–West trade is characterized as "asymmetric integration" because it involves the interaction of two economic systems that are functionally very different. It is no accident that the partial marketization of the Chinese economy is the single most important factor in the promotion of economic integration between Hong Kong and the mainland, and this integration will inevitably be limited unless China can further marketize its economic system.

In the era before the Open-door Policy, the economic ties linking the mainland and Hong Kong were quite strong, but the relationship was asymmetric and one-sided. Hong Kong was open to China's export and investment, but China was closed to Hong Kong's export and investment. Large numbers of Hong Kong people were able to visit their relatives on the mainland, and remittances from Hong Kong residents to their mainland relatives were quite large, but mainland Chinese could not visit Hong Kong. In the 1960s, Hong Kong was the foremost market for the mainland. China's trade surplus with Hong Kong was around one-fifth of China's total exports, and China used the hard currency thus earned to finance its imports of grain, industrial raw materials, and capital goods from developed countries. With the inauguration of economic reforms and the Open-door Policy in the mainland in 1978, the economic relationship between the mainland and Hong Kong has become much more balanced and multifaceted.

China has tailored its Open-door Policy to build closer links with Hong Kong and Taiwan. In 1979, Guangdong and Fujian were given authority to operate Special Economic Zones that have autonomy in trade and investment. Guangdong operates three such zones: the Shenzhen and Zhuhai zones, which are adjacent to Hong Kong and Macao respectively, and the Shantou zone, which has close links to overseas Chinese populations, including a community in Hong Kong that originated in Shantou. Fujian operates the Xiamen Special Economic Zone, which is across the strait to Taiwan and only a few miles from the two coastal islands controlled by Taiwan.

Hong Kong businesses receive no favorable concessions in China over other overseas businesses. In reality, due to geographical proximity and kinship links, Hong Kong businesses have a significant advantage. Hong Kong investors have been able to obtain favorable concessions from local authorities in Guangdong as a result of the kinship network. It is also easier for Hong Kong Chinese than it is for foreigners to visit the mainland, as visas are not required by Hong Kong Chinese. China is thus more open to Hong Kong than it is to other economies. Hong Kong, as a free economy, is open to the whole world including China. It should be noted, however, that, as a result of the fear of illegal immigrants from the mainland, Hong Kong's controls on visitors from the mainland are stricter than its controls on visitors from other places. In cooperation with Hong Kong, Beijing also imposes strict controls on visits to Hong Kong. Mainlanders often complain that it is easier for them to visit foreign countries than to visit Hong Kong. There are few restrictions against mainlanders entering Hong Kong on official passports, however, and it is estimated that more than sixty thousand mainland cadres are working in mainland companies in Hong Kong. Due to kinship links, a substantial number of mainlanders, especially those from Guangdong, have been able to settle in Hong Kong and some of them function as business representatives of local authorities or enterprises. Guangdong has concluded a special agreement with Hong Kong whereby the Guangdong government can issue special passes to its personnel, enabling them to enter Hong Kong without a visa or passport as long as their trips last no more than seven days. Such passes have greatly facilitated the integration of Hong Kong and Guangdong.

### Trade and Investment Between Hong Kong and China

As a large fraction of China's trade is conducted via Hong Kong in the form of entrepôt trade, the statistics on China's trade by country are very misleading. In trade statistics, exports are classified by country of destination whereas imports are classified by country of origin. For example, in United States–China trade, both countries regard their exports to each other through Hong Kong as exports to Hong Kong. Both countries thus understate their exports to each other. Imports are not understated because they are traced to the country of origin. Both countries thus overstated the bilateral trade deficits or understated the surpluses. In 1990, according to statistics published by the United States, it had a deficit of U.S. $11.5 billion in its trade with China, whereas China claimed a deficit of U.S. $1.4 billion in its trade with the United States!

While the value of Hong Kong's reexports of Chinese goods can be obtained from *Hong Kong Trade Statistics,* the value of Hong Kong's imports from China for reexport is unknown because the importer usually cannot ascertain whether a certain import is destined for reexport at the time of importation. To obtain the value of Hong Kong's imports from China for reexport, we have to subtract an estimated reexport markup (usually obtained from sample surveys) from the value of Hong Kong's reexports of Chinese goods.

To obtain the value of China's indirect exports via Hong Kong from the value of Hong Kong's imports from China for reexport, we have to subtract from the latter the cost of transporting and insuring the goods between China and Hong Kong, which is equal to the difference between the cost, insurance, and freight (c.i.f.) price of Hong Kong's imports and the free-on-board (f.o.b.) price of China's exports.

While the difference between the c.i.f. and f.o.b. prices are usually quite small (a few percentage points of the value of the goods traded), the reexport markup, which is earned by the Hong Kong middleman, is very substantial. The reexport markup includes profits and the cost of transportation, storage, insurance, packaging, and minor processing that is not substantial enough to confer country of origin. The reexport markup for Chinese goods is estimated to be 25 percent, whereas that for non-Chinese goods is 15 percent. The reexport markup for Chinese goods is much higher because a lot of Chinese goods are packaged or processed in Hong Kong before exportation (Sung, 1991e: 480–82).

In this, all statistics on China's trade by region include the direct trade as well as the indirect trade via Hong Kong. The reexport margin is netted out of indirect exports because exports should be reported on an f.o.b. basis. However, the reexport margin is not netted out of indirect imports because imports should be reported on a c.i.f. basis. The procedure used in this chapter should give the best estimates of trade with China.

Using the above procedure, the true United States–China trade balance can easily be calculated. In 1990, 62 percent of China's exports to the United States were reexported through Hong Kong, whereas the corresponding percentage for the United States was 20 percent. The United States' deficit should be U.S. $10.3 billion whereas China's surplus was U.S. $7 billion. The difference between the two figures largely represents Hong Kong's reexport markup.

The high reexport markup for Chinese goods implies that Hong Kong earns a lot from reexporting Chinese goods, and Hong Kong would lose heavily if the United States were to revoke China's most-favored-nation (MFN) status. In 1990, 62 percent of China's exports to the United States went through Hong Kong in the form of reexports. If China loses its MFN status, China's exports to the United States will decline substantially, and Hong Kong will lose considerably in the reexport margin as well as in the profits of its investment in China. Though China's loss of exports would be substantial, most of these exports would be from processing/assembling operations that have a low value-added margin and a high import content. The wages (processing fees) that China earns from such operations are usually no more than 10 percent of the value of the exports. This implies that Hong Kong's loss is likely to be as large as that of China in absolute terms if China loses its MFN status (Sung, 1991d: 15.6–15.9).

### *China's Commodity Trade with Hong Kong*

In analyzing China's trade with Hong Kong, we must distinguish between China's trade with third countries via Hong Kong, and China's trade with Hong Kong itself (Table 9.2). For China's exports, we distinguish between China's goods retained in Hong Kong for internal use and those reexported via Hong Kong. For China's imports, we distinguish between China's imports of Hong Kong goods and imports of third-country goods via Hong Kong.

To estimate China's exports to Hong Kong for internal use, we first subtract the value of Hong Kong's imports of Chinese goods for reexport from the value of Hong Kong's total imports from China to calculate the value of Hong Kong's retained imports (that is, imports retained for internal use) from China. Then we form the ratio of Hong Kong's retained imports from China to Hong Kong's total imports from China. In 1990, the ratio was 16 percent, showing that the bulk of China's exports to Hong Kong was reexported. Lastly, we multiply China's exports to Hong Kong (obtained from China Customs Statistics) by this ratio.

China's statistics of imports from Hong Kong are highly misleading. China's imports from Hong Kong in 1990 amounted to U.S. $14 billion according to China Customs Statistics, while Hong Kong's trade statistics show that Hong Kong's domestic exports (that is, exports of Hong Kong goods) to China amounted to only U.S. $6 billion, though there was another U.S. $14 billion of third-country goods reexported. It appears that China included as imports from Hong Kong some but not all of Hong Kong's reexports. Overinvoicing of imports on the Chinese side would explain part of the discrepancy. We would expect significant overinvoicing of imports in China, as it is a classic means of evading foreign-exchange control. Since China's statistics on its imports from Hong Kong are inaccurate, we take China's imports from Hong Kong to be Hong Kong's domestic exports to China. Time lags and differences between f.o.b. (free on board) and c.i.f. (cost, insurance, and freight) prices are ignored.

Due to the geographical proximity of the mainland and Hong Kong, such differences should be quite minor.

Table 9.2 shows China's trade with Hong Kong. As mentioned previously, in the pre-1978 era, China had a large trade surplus with Hong Kong and most of China's exports were consumed in Hong Kong. China's imports from Hong Kong were negligible. China–Hong Kong trade was transformed in the reform era. Of China's exports to Hong Kong, the reexported portion grew rapidly and exceeded the retained portion by 1986. The share in total Chinese exports of Chinese goods reexported through Hong Kong rose from 6 percent in 1977 to 40 percent in 1991. China's imports from Hong Kong also grew rapidly: From 1977 to 1991, imports via Hong Kong and imports that were of Hong Kong origin grew 517 times and 996 times respectively. The share of indirect imports in China's total imports rose from 0.5 percent in 1977 to 31 percent in 1991. Hong Kong reemerged as a major entrepôt for China, and China also become a major market for Hong Kong products. Domestic exports from Hong Kong to China have grown from negligible amounts to U.S. $7,001 million in 1991. In 1984, Hong Kong became the third largest supplier of goods to China after Japan and the United States. Part of the reason for the rapid growth of Hong Kong's domestic exports is due to Hong Kong investment in processing/assembling operations in China. Hong Kong firms supply such operations with the required raw materials and components, parts of which are made in Hong Kong.

The share of the Chinese market in Hong Kong's domestic exports had risen rapidly. China became the second largest market for Hong Kong's domestic exports in 1984, with a market share of 8.2 percent, surpassing that of the United Kingdom (7.6 percent), but still much lower than that of the United States (44 percent). In 1991, China's share rose to 24 percent, while the United States' share dropped to 27 percent. China surpassed the latter to become the largest market for Hong Kong products in 1992. It should be remembered, however, that the bulk of Hong Kong's domestic exports to China consisted of semimanufactures that were further processed in China for export, and that the United States was China's foremost market. If we exclude the cross-flow of semimanufactures between Hong Kong and China and just look at the export of finished goods, the United States would still be by far Hong Kong's foremost market.

Hong Kong was the largest final market (that is, excluding Chinese exports via Hong Kong) for Chinese exports in the late 1960s and early 1970s, but the Hong Kong market was overtaken by the Japanese and United States markets in 1973 and 1987 respectively. The Hong Kong market still accounted for 5 percent of China's exports in 1991, however.

China's exports retained in Hong Kong have been stagnating since 1987, and their share of China's total exports has declined sharply. China has been unable to capture the higher end of Hong Kong's market, which was dominated by Japan. Given the increasing affluence of Hong Kong and the Japanese dominance in vehicles, capital goods, and quality consumer durables and consumer

Table 9.2

**China–Hong Kong Trade (in U.S. million dollars)**

| | China's exports to Hong Kong | | | China's imports from Hong Kong | | |
|---|---|---|---|---|---|---|
| | Total | Retained in Hong Kong | Reexported elsewhere | Total | Hong Kong goods | Hong Kong reexports |
| 1931–38 Average | 87 (31.5) | 16 (6.3) | 70 (25.2) | 87 (21.3) | 9 (2.1) | 79 (19.2) |
| 1950 | 137 (24.8) | — | — | 221 (37.8) | — | — |
| 1951 | 151 (20.0) | — | — | 281 (23.4) | — | — |
| 1952 | 145 (17.6) | — | — | 91 (8.1) | — | — |
| 1955 | 157 (11.1) | — | — | 32 (1.8) | — | — |
| 1960 | 207 (11.2) | — | — | 21 (1.1) | 2 (0.1) | 19 (1.0) |
| 1965 | 487* (20.5) | 399* (16.8) | 88* (3.7) | 13 (0.6) | 3 (0.2) | 10 (0.5) |
| 1970 | 467 (20.7) | 376 (16.6) | 91 (4.0) | 11 (0.5) | 5 (0.21) | 6 (0.2) |
| 1975 | 1,378 (19.0) | 1,096 (15.1) | 282 (3.9) | 33 (0.5) | 6 (0.08) | 28 (0.4) |
| 1977 | 1,734 (22.8) | 1,306 (17.2) | 428 (5.6) | 44 (0.6) | 7 (0.09) | 38 (0.5) |

| | | | | | | |
|---|---|---|---|---|---|---|
| 1979 | 3,044<br>(22.3) | 2,139<br>(15.7) | 905<br>(6.6) | 383<br>(2.5) | 121<br>(0.8) | 263<br>(1.7) |
| 1981 | 5,293<br>(24.1) | 3,465<br>(15.7) | 1,828<br>(8.3) | 1,961<br>(8.9) | 523<br>(2.4) | 1,438<br>(6.5) |
| 1983 | 5,818<br>(26.2) | 3,680<br>(16.6) | 2,139<br>(9.6) | 2,531<br>(11.8) | 856<br>(4.0) | 1,675<br>(7.8) |
| 1984 | 6,689<br>(25.6) | 3,979<br>(15.3) | 2,709<br>(10.4) | 5,033<br>(18.4) | 1,443<br>(5.3) | 3,590<br>(13.1) |
| 1985 | 7,168<br>(26.2) | 3,746<br>(13.7) | 3,422<br>(12.5) | 7,857<br>(18.6) | 1,950<br>(4.6) | 5,907<br>(14.0) |
| 1986 | 9,778<br>(31.6) | 4,734<br>(15.3) | 5,045<br>(16.3) | 7,550<br>(17.6) | 2,310<br>(5.4) | 5,241<br>(12.2) |
| 1987 | 13,762<br>(34.8) | 5,710<br>(14.4) | 8,052<br>(20.4) | 11,290<br>(26.1) | 3,574<br>(8.3) | 7,716<br>(17.9) |
| 1988 | 18,269<br>(38.4) | 5,579<br>(11.8) | 12,690<br>(26.7) | 17,030<br>(30.8) | 4,874<br>(8.8) | 12,157<br>(22.4) |
| 1989 | 21,916<br>(41.7) | 4,599<br>(8.8) | 17,323<br>(32.9) | 18,816<br>(31.8) | 5,548<br>(9.4) | 13,268<br>(22.4) |
| 1990 | 26,650<br>(42.9) | 4,361<br>(7.1) | 22,287<br>(35.9) | 20,305<br>(38.1) | 6,086<br>(11.4) | 14,219<br>(26.6) |
| 1991 | 32,137<br>(44.7) | 3,687<br>(5.1) | 28,450<br>(39.6) | 26,631<br>(41.7) | 6,975<br>(10.9) | 19,656<br>(30.8) |

*Sources:* Hong Kong data for 1931–38 from Tom (1957); 1948 and after, from *Hong Kong Trade Statistics* (1960–91); 1966 and after, from *Review of Overseas Trade* (1966–91). Chinese data for 1931–48 from *Yearbook of International Trade Statistics*, various issues; 1950–79, from *Statistical Yearbook of China* (1981); 1981 and after, from *China Customs Statistics* (1982–92).

*Note:* Figures in parentheses represent percentage share of China's total exports (imports).

* Export figures are for the year 1966.

Table 9.3

**China's Trade by Region in 1990** (in U.S. million dollars)

| | Total Trade | | Exports | | Imports | |
|---|---|---|---|---|---|---|
| | Value | Rank | Value | Rank | Value | Rank |
| U.S. | 20,142<br>(17.5) | 1 | 13,554<br>(21.8) | 1 | 6,588<br>(12.3) | 2 |
| Japan | 18,230<br>(15.8) | 2 | 10,642<br>(17.1) | 2 | 7,588<br>(14.2) | 1 |
| Hong Kong | 10,447<br>(9.1) | 3 | 4,361<br>(7.1) | 3 | 6,086<br>(11.4) | 3 |
| Germany | 6,732<br>(5.8) | 4 | 4,048<br>(6.5) | 4 | 2,684<br>(5.0) | 5 |
| Taiwan | 5,666<br>(4.9) | 5 | 932<br>(1.5) | — | 4,734<br>(8.9) | 4 |
| USSR | 4,379<br>(3.8) | 6 | 2,239<br>(3.6) | 6 | 2,140<br>(4.0) | 6 |
| South Korea | 3,652<br>(3.2) | 7 | 2,099<br>(3.4) | 7 | 1,553<br>(2.9) | 8 |
| Singapore | 3,231<br>(2.8) | 8 | 2,373<br>(3.8) | 5 | 858<br>(1.6) | — |
| France | 2,897<br>(2.5) | — | 1,234<br>(2.0) | — | 1,663<br>(3.1) | 7 |

*Source:* Data on China's direct trade are obtained from *China's Customs Statistics* (1982–92), and data on China's indirect trade via Hong Kong are obtained from the Census and Statistics Department of Hong Kong.

*Note:* China's indirect trade with other countries via Hong Kong is excluded from the Hong Kong figures and included in the figures of other countries. Data for Taiwan are taken from Sung (1992: 39) and include direct trade as well as the indirect trade via Hong Kong. Figures in parentheses represent percentage share of China's total trade/exports/imports.

goods, the future of Chinese products in Hong Kong is not very bright (Sung, 1991a: 119–22). The exports of Hong Kong goods to China has exceeded China's exports retained in Hong Kong since 1989, and Hong Kong has had a surplus in its direct trade with China from 1989 onward.

### *China's Trade by Country and Region*

Given the estimates of China's trade with Hong Kong, we can form an accurate picture of China's trade by country and region in Table 9.3. China's trading activities with third countries via Hong Kong are distributed to their final destinations or initial sources. China's trading partners in 1990, in order of importance, were the United States, Japan, Hong Kong, Germany, Taiwan, USSR, and South Korea. In order of importance, China's major markets were the United

States, Japan, Hong Kong, West Germany, Singapore, USSR, and South Korea, and China's major suppliers were Japan, the United States, Hong Kong, Taiwan, West Germany, USSR, France, and South Korea. China regards Hong Kong as both its largest market and its supplier because in Chinese statistics China's trade with third countries via Hong Kong is regarded as trade with Hong Kong. It should be noted that, in the first half of 1991, Taiwan surpassed both Hong Kong and the United States to become the mainland's second largest supplier after Japan (Sung, 1992: 22–24).

### *China's Trade with Third Countries Through Hong Kong*

Since the inauguration of the Open-door Policy, China has established numerous direct links with the rest of the world, including diplomatic, commercial, and transportation links. Paradoxically, the middleman role of Hong Kong is becoming more prominent, and an increasing share of China's commodity trade is handled through Hong Kong. To explain this paradox, it is worthwhile to construct a theory of intermediation. The theory has strong predictions for entrepôt trade and services trade.

In explaining entrepôt trade, it is important to distinguish transshipment from entrepôt trade. Transshipment means that goods are consigned directly from the exporting country to a buyer in the importing country, though the goods are transported via an entrepôt and may be stored there for onward shipment. Transshipped goods are not regarded as part of the trade of the entrepôt and they do not clear customs because they represent only goods in transit.

Unlike transshipment, entrepôt trade is part of the trade of the entrepôt. Imports for reexport are consigned to a buyer in the entrepôt and the buyer takes legal possession of the goods after clearing customs. These imports may then be processed before being reexported as long as the processing is not substantial enough to confer country of origin.

The usual explanation of entrepôt trade in terms of transportation cost is faulty because it ignores the importance of transaction costs. It is useful to distinguish processed reexports from pure reexports. *Processed reexports* are those that have been physically treated (packaged, sorted, and so on), whereas *pure reexports* have not been changed in any physical way.

Pure reexports are difficult to account for theoretically because reexports involve higher costs than transshipment (other things being equal) owing to two factors: one, reexports have to clear the customs of an entrepôt twice, whereas transshipped goods do not have to clear the customs of the entrepôt at all, so fewer delays and lower storage costs for transshipment are involved; and, two, transshipped goods are insured and financed just once, whereas reexports have to be insured and financed twice—first when they are imported into the entrepôt, and second when they are reexported. While transportation costs determine transshipment, pure reexports are determined by both transportation costs and transaction costs, and processed reexports involve processing costs as well.

Since China's adoption of an Open-door Policy in 1978, it has been easier to trade directly with China. The transaction cost of establishing a direct trade link has gone down and this should lead to a rise in direct trade relative to indirect trade. However, China started to decentralize its foreign trade system in 1979, replacing vertical channels of command with horizontal links. The number of trading partners and trade links multiplied rapidly, creating a huge demand for intermediation. Before 1979, establishing trade links with ten state trading corporations would have ensured a complete coverage of China trade. By 1984, however, the number of trading corporations increased to more than one thousand. It is very costly for an individual firm to establish trade links with the mushrooming number of Chinese trading corporations, intermediation has emerged as a more economical way to facilitate the process, and this demand for intermediation has been channeled to Hong Kong due to its comparative advantage in trading. China's foreign trade decentralization came in four waves: 1979, 1984, 1988, and 1991. The share of China's trade through Hong Kong jumped after each wave of decentralization (Table 9.2).

The market composition of China's indirect trade via Hong Kong and the change over time of these markets in dependency on Hong Kong's entrepôt trade confirm the overwhelming importance of trade decentralization on intermediation (Sung, 1991a: 141–43). Countries with a long history of trading with China have found it worthwhile to pay the fixed cost of establishing trade links, and they are less dependent on Hong Kong than are the new entrants. Political recognition and trade pacts also lower dependency on Hong Kong. However, the decentralization of China's trading system in 1979 and 1984 increased the dependency of both old China hands and new entrants on Hong Kong's entrepôt trade. For instance, the dependence of Canada and the United States on Hong Kong for China's exports decreased in the early 1970s as they established political and commercial links with China, but this trend was reversed in 1979. Starting from 1984, the dependence of all of China's major markets (Japan, United States, Singapore, West Germany, United Kingdom, Canada, and Australia) on Hong Kong for China's exports increased substantially. Similarly, starting from 1979, all of China's major suppliers (Japan, United States, West Germany, United Kingdom, France, Italy, and Singapore) became more dependent on Hong Kong for their exports to China.

### *China's Service Trade with Hong Kong*

Trade in services between the mainland and Hong Kong is extremely important. Conceptually, the reexport margin that Hong Kong earns through entrepôt trade in fact represents the export of services. Such services are embodied in the goods sold, however, and are usually recorded in trade statistics as export of goods rather than export of services.

For tourist services, Hong Kong visitors accounted for 66 percent of tourist arrivals as well as tourist expenditure in China in 1990. Hong Kong also exports transportation services, trading services, construction services, financial services, and business services to China. However, besides the data on entrepôt trade and tourism, only some data are available for shipping, trading, and financial services. Reliable data are lacking for the other categories. Hong Kong's export of financial services to China will be discussed in the section below on investment. Though Hong Kong's export of construction services and business services to China is very important, there are very little data to go by. Hong Kong is the foremost base for China consultancy services. According to *Intertrade* (10–1984: 2), half of the foreign law firms in Hong Kong provide legal advice on China's trade.

Hong Kong is also the foremost gateway for foreigners touring China. Many foreigners also join package tours of China that are organized in Hong Kong. Though China has established more and more direct air links with other countries since 1978, the percentage of foreign tourists leaving (visiting) China via Hong Kong increased from 40 (34) percent in 1982 to 55 (44) percent in 1987. Again this paradox can be explained by the theory of intermediation, as China decentralized part of the authority to organize China tours from the China Travel Service to provincial and local authorities in the early 1980s. Taiwan lifted its ban on travel to the mainland in 1987, and this of course led to another jump in the number of foreigners visiting China via Hong Kong.

In commodity trade, Hong Kong is an important entrepôt as well as a center of transshipment for China. The value of transshipped goods is not available since they do not go through customs, but their weight is known. In 1990, transshipment of goods to (from) China weighed as much as 9 (13) percent of China's imports from (exports to) Hong Kong. If we assume that the value of transhipment to (from) China per ton is the same as China's imports from (exports to) Hong Kong, transshipment of goods to (from) China via Hong Kong would amount to 3.6 (6) percent of China's imports (exports) by value in 1990. Hong Kong trading firms also perform an important brokerage role for China's direct trade, amounting to U.S. $15 billion or 7 percent of China's total trade in 1988 (Hong Kong Trade Development Council, 1988). Lacking data from after 1988, we make the simple assumption that Hong Kong brokers involved in China's direct trade continued to account for 7 percent of China's trade after 1988. The shares of China's exports consumed, reexported, transshipped, and intermediated by Hong Kong were 7 percent, 36 percent, 6 percent, and 7 percent, respectively, in 1990. The total of the four categories was 56 percent. Though there is likely to be some overlap in the last two categories, we can safely conclude that Hong Kong plays an important role in over half of China's exports. On the import side, the shares of China's imports produced, reexported, transshipped, and intermediated by Hong Kong were 11 percent, 27 percent, 4 percent, and 7 percent, respectively, in 1990. The total of the four categories was 49 percent. We can thus conclude that Hong Kong plays an important role in close to half of China's imports.

It should be noted that China's export of services to Hong Kong has increased rapidly in recent years. China's construction firms are active in construction projects in Hong Kong. A large number of mainland Chinese are working in Hong Kong, including manufacturing workers imported to relieve the labor shortage in Hong Kong, and engineers working in mainland-owned factories in Hong Kong. Hong Kong residents have also traveled to China for medical treatment because the price of health care is lower in the mainland.

### *Investment Between Hong Kong and China*

Table 9.4 shows China's inward foreign investment by source. The large share of Hong Kong in China's direct foreign investment conceals the important middleman role of Hong Kong. In China's statistics, investment from Hong Kong includes the investment of the subsidiaries of foreign companies incorporated in Hong Kong. Many multinational companies like to test the Chinese investment environment through investments from their Hong Kong subsidiaries because Hong Kong has the required expertise. If such investment is successful, then the parent company will also invest in China.

The United States and Japan have been significant investors in China. The investment of both countries has decreased appreciably, however, since the Tiananmen Incident. Moreover, the investment of the two countries in China is minuscule compared with their total overseas investment. For instance, Japan's cumulative investment in China was only 29 percent of its investment in Hong Kong and only 0.9 percent of its total overseas investment by June 1990. China had openly complained about the lack of Japanese investment in China and Japanese stinginess in technology transfer. Japan's strategy has been to invest in Hong Kong, since Japanese business regards Hong Kong as the future capital of an industrialized southern China. Similarly, cumulative investment in China by the United States was only 37 percent of its investment in Hong Kong and only 0.57 percent of its total overseas investment by the end of 1990.

#### *Hong Kong's Investment in China*

Hong Kong's investment in China is very diversified, ranging from small-scale labor-intensive operations to large-scale infrastructural projects. Though manufacturing in Hong Kong is not as sophisticated as that in South Korea and Taiwan, Hong Kong has considerable expertise in service industries including construction, hotels, and financial services.

The share of Hong Kong in China's external loans was small in the early 1980s, but the share rose from 0.6 percent in 1983 to 9.4 percent in 1989. Hong Kong's share was low partly because Hong Kong does not extend official loans to China. However, China-backed companies registered in Hong Kong began to raise funds in Hong Kong's stock market through share placements in 1987

Table 9.4

**Foreign Investment in China by Source, 1979–90** (contracted investment U.S. million dollars)

| | 1979–84 | 1985 | 1986 | 1987 | 1988 | 1989 | 1990 | Total share | Cumulative percentage |
|---|---|---|---|---|---|---|---|---|---|
| National Total | 11,791 | 6,333 | 3,330 | 4,319 | 6,191 | 6,294 | 6,986 | 45,244 | 100 |
| Hong Kong | 6,495 | 4,134 | 1,449 | 2,466 | 4,033 | 3,645 | 4,258 | 26,480 | 58.5 |
| United States | 1,025 | 1,152 | 541 | 361 | 384 | 646 | 366 | 4,476 | 9.9 |
| Japan | 1,158 | 471 | 283 | 386 | 371 | 515 | 478 | 3,662 | 8.1 |
| Taiwan | — | — | — | 100* | 420 | 480 | 1,000 | 2,000 | 4.4 |
| Singapore | 117 | 77 | 141 | 80 | 137 | 148 | 107 | 805 | 1.8 |
| Canada | 66 | 9 | 91 | 34 | 40 | 49 | 21 | 309 | 0.7 |
| Australia | 91 | 14 | 32 | 47 | 17 | 84 | 18 | 303 | 0.7 |
| South Korea** | — | 0.1 | 1.8 | 6.0 | 5.4 | 14.5 | 57 | 81 | 0.2 |

*Sources:* Data for Taiwan are obtained from press releases of the Xinhua News Agency. Data for South Korea are obtained from the Korean Overseas Trade Association. Data for other economies are obtained from the *Almanac of China's Foreign Relations and Trade* (1984–91).

*Cumulative total up until 1987.

**Direct investment in China approved by the South Korean Government. Data are obtained from the Korean Overseas Trade Association.

(*South China Morning Post,* 6–18–1987). Due to the differences in accounting systems and company law, it is more difficult for Chinese firms registered in China to raise funds in the Hong Kong stock market. However, many firms in Guangdong are amending their accounting systems to prepare for listing in the Hong Kong stock market.

Hong Kong is the center for raising 80 percent of China's syndicated loans. Loan syndication is an important middleman function performed by Hong Kong. The share of China's external loans (syndicated loans and other loans) syndicated in Hong Kong rose from 6 percent in the period 1979 to 1982 to 31 percent in 1987 and then declined to 14 percent in 1989. Such changes can be explained by the theory of intermediation. The rapid jump of the share of China's loans syndicated in Hong Kong in 1987 was related to the 1986 decentralization of the power to raise foreign loans to selected provincial governments and enterprises. The rapid decline in the share of China's loans syndicated in Hong Kong since 1988 was related to the 1988 recentralization of the power to borrow foreign loans as part of the retrenchment program. Decentralization had a decisive impact on intermediation in the commodity trade and tourist trade, as well as in financial services.

### *China's Investment in Hong Kong*

China's investment in Hong Kong is likely to exceed Hong Kong's investment in China. According to Chinese statistics, Hong Kong's contracted investment in China from 1978 to 90 amounted to U.S. $26.5 billion. However, Hong Kong's utilized investment in China was only around 49 percent of contracted investment. Hong Kong's utilized investment in China from 1978 to 1990 is thus estimated to be around U.S. $13 billion. This is likely to be a gross overestimate, however, as it includes the investment of the subsidiaries of Taiwanese companies and multinational companies in Hong Kong. In fact, mainland companies have also invested in China through their Hong Kong subsidiaries in order to qualify for the concessions granted to overseas investors. From anecdotal evidence, it is known that Hong Kong investors often overstate the value of their investment in China with the connivance of local officials. For example, Hong Kong manufacturers tend to put a high value on the outdated machinery that they move to China. It is well known that government officials in command economies tend to exaggerate economic achievement, resulting in such phenomena as the "success indicator problem."

China's cumulative investment in Hong Kong was estimated to be around U.S. $10 billion, but this is likely to be an underestimate as there is an incentive for China's local authorities and enterprises to establish unofficial subsidiaries in Hong Kong to evade controls on foreign trade as well as foreign-exchange controls. China's investment in Hong Kong is thus likely to exceed Hong Kong's investment in China.

There are no accurate statistics on Guangdong's investment in Hong Kong.

From anecdoctal evidence, however, it is known that many firms backed by Guangdong's provincial government or local authorities are very active in Hong Kong.

China's investment in Hong Kong is very diversified, covering nearly all sectors of the Hong Kong economy, namely banking, insurance, entrepôt trade, shipping, aviation, real estate, and manufacturing. China's investment strengthens the ties between Hong Kong and China and enhances the position of Hong Kong as the gateway to China.

## The Prospect of Hong Kong as a Middleman for the Mainland

The role of Hong Kong as a middlemen for China is important both in commodity trade and services trade, including tourist services and financial services. A middleman creates opportunities for trade and investment by lowering transaction costs. An efficient middleman thus enhances the degree of economic integration between different economies. Due to the many rigidities of China's economy and political barriers, the efficiency of Hong Kong as a middleman is crucial for its economic interactions with the world, especially for transactions with Taiwan and South Korea.

The Tiananmen Incident has paradoxically speeded up the reform and decentralization of China's foreign trade, and such reforms have enhanced the middleman role of Hong Kong. After the cutting off of soft loans following the Tiananmen Incident, China was under great pressure to expand its exports to pay off its foreign debt. China devalued the renminbi against the United States dollar in December 1989 and in November 1990 by 21 percent and 9.6 percent respectively. China further decentralized its external sector in early 1991. Provincial governments and export enterprises were allowed to retain 80 percent of their foreign-exchange earnings, and subsidies on exports were abolished. The number of commodities that required licensing for export decreased from 185 categories to roughly 90 categories. China's exports continued to grow at double-digit rates from 1989 to 1991. As expected, the further decentralization of China's trade enhanced the middleman role of Hong Kong. The share of China's exports (imports) reexported via Hong Kong jumped from 36 (27) percent in 1990 to 40 (31) percent in 1991 (Table 9.2, page 187).

As China is likely to further decentralize its foreign trade and investment, the prospect of Hong Kong as a middleman is very bright. There are significant economies of scale and economies of agglomeration in trading activity and it is very difficult for other cities such as Singapore or Shanghai to compete with Hong Kong, because Hong Kong is the established center for China's trade. The existence of economies of scale in intermediation would enhance the demand for the middleman, as small firms will not be able to trade efficiently.

Traders tend to agglomerate in a city, suggesting that there are significant external economies involved. This implies that once a city acquires a comparative advantage in trade, the advantage feeds upon itself, and more trading firms will come to the city, making it even more efficient in trade (Sung, 1991a: 28–42).

Though the greater part of Hong Kong's entrepôt trade is China-related, the non-China component of Hong Kong's entrepôt trade is also thriving, growing faster than world trade. This implies that an increasing share of the trade among market economies is handled through Hong Kong in the form of entrepôt trade, confirming our theory on the efficiency of large trading centers.

Empirical analysis also indicates that Hong Kong's entrepôt trade is much more capital- and skill-intensive than Hong Kong's wholesale trade, retail trade, and exports manufacture. The skills required for international trade include a good knowledge of English, familiarity with modern business practices, the ability to work in different cultural and legal environments, and proficiency with complex contractual forms. The supporting industries of international trade, namely, shipping, air transport, communications, finance, insurance, and business services, are also capital- or skill-intensive. As Hong Kong has a long-run labor shortage due to declining fertility rates and an aging demographic structure, the factor requirements of entrepôt trade are consistent with Hong Kong's changing factor endowments and dynamic comparative advantage.

It should be noted that economies of agglomeration and economies of scale characterize most economic activities, including agriculture, manufacturing, transportation, trading, business services, and financial services. As business activities agglomerate, land prices and wages start to rise, putting a drag on the tendency to agglomerate. Agriculture will be the first activity to move out of the city because it is land-intensive. Manufacturing will be the second activity to relocate, and a lot of Hong Kong manufacturing firms are moving their land-intensive and labor-intensive processes to China. Transportation will be the next activity to be affected, as ports and airports are also land-intensive. The high cost of Hong Kong's new airport is a testimony to the difficulty of building a big airport in land-scarce Hong Kong. The new Hong Kong airport will be twenty times as expensive as the Huangtian airport in Shenzhen, which will also have two runways when it is fully developed. Were it not for political barriers, it would be more rational to put Hong Kong's new airport in Shenzhen. China's customs administration is not noted for its efficiency, however, and it would be risky for Hong Kong to put its new airport in Shenzhen unless China thoroughly reforms and modernizes its administration. The completion of such reforms cannot realistically be expected in the near future. But when such reforms are completed, and when Hong Kong's new airport also gets congested, it will be rational for Hong Kong to divert a substantial portion of its air traffic to Shenzhen.

Trading, business services, and financial services will be least affected by rising land prices and wages, because such activities are neither land-intensive nor labor-intensive. It should be noted that New York and London long ago lost their comparative advantage in manufacturing, but their positions as centers of trading, business, and finance remain formidable.

In the long run, China is likely to overcome its transportation bottlenecks and acquire modern trading skills. China may even clean up its bureaucracy. But China will still rely on Hong Kong for trade and financial and business services because of the economies of scale and of agglomeration in such activities.

The Chinese themselves are establishing many trading companies in Hong Kong, showing that they recognize the established efficiency of Hong Kong in trading. Some Hong Kong traders fear competition from Chinese trading companies in Hong Kong. The situation is not a zero-sum game, however, because of economies of agglomeration; the arrival of Chinese trading companies further enhances the position of Hong Kong as a trading center.

It is often alleged that if South Korea and Taiwan were to establish direct commercial links with the mainland, the role of Hong Kong as a middleman in China's trade would decline. This view is mistaken, being supported neither by theory nor by empirical evidence.

The combined indirect trade of Taiwan and South Korea with the mainland via Hong Kong was only 13 percent of China's indirect trade via Hong Kong in 1990. As mentioned before, though most countries have direct commercial and diplomatic relations with China, they have became more dependent on Hong Kong for their trade with China since 1979.

Canada, the United States, and Indonesia established direct commercial or diplomatic relations with China only in the 1970s or 1980s, and their experiences again confirm the efficiency of Hong Kong in intermediation. In these four countries, the establishment of direct commercial or diplomatic relations led to a sharp decline in their dependence on Hong Kong, but their dependence on Hong Kong rose again as China decentralized its trading system. For example, in the case of China's exports to the United States, the share of indirect exports via Hong Kong fell sharply from 100 percent in 1970 to 15 percent in 1975. However, the share rose in 1979 with the decentralization of China's trade, and it increased to over 62 percent in 1990. In the case of China's exports to Canada, the share of indirect exports via Hong Kong also fell sharply to as low as 7 percent in 1975, but it also rose in 1979, and increased to 59 percent in 1990. In the case of China's exports to Indonesia, the share of indirect exports via Hong Kong fell to a low of 50 percent in 1988, but it rose slowly thereafter.

### Hong Kong–Guangdong Link

The impacts of China's opening on Hong Kong's trade and services have been described in some detail. China's opening also has significant impacts on Hong Kong's manufacturing, as Hong Kong manufacturers have relocated the more labor-intensive part of their production processes into Guangdong on a large scale.

The moving of labor-intensive processes to China has been described negatively in some quarters as the "hollowing out" of Hong Kong manufacturing. This description is misleading in some ways. What has happened is a division of labor between Hong Kong and the Pearl River Delta, with Hong Kong concentrating on the skill-intensive processes (product design, sourcing, production management, quality control, technical support, and marketing) while the labor-intensive and land-intensive processes have moved to the Pearl River Delta. The division of labor is beneficial: labor shortage and inflationary pressures in Hong Kong have been alleviated; labor upgrading and employment opportunities in the delta have been introduced.

Though the availability of cheap labor in China has led to high profits in Hong Kong manufacturing, manufacturing investment in Hong Kong in the 1980s was quite modest in light of the colony's past experience. The uncertainty generated by the 1997 issue and the Tiananmen Incident had depressing effects on manufacturing investment in Hong Kong (Sung, 1991b: 10–14). Despite modest manufacturing investment, manufacturing labor productivity had grown at an average annual rate of close to 10 percent in the 1980s. This rate of growth was higher than the historical average in Hong Kong manufacturing and also higher than the rates achieved in the 1980s in Singapore (5.3 percent), South Korea (4.9 percent), and Taiwan (4.8 percent) (Sung, 1991b: 22). The relocation of low-productivity and labor-intensive processes to China has boosted the growth of manufacturing labor productivity in Hong Kong. The latter's manufacturing has remained very competitive due to high rates of growth in labor productivity and moderates rates of growth in wages.

The proximity of Guangdong has enabled many of the ancillary services of Hong Kong's relocated industries to be performed in Hong Kong. The linkages of the manufacturing sector with other sectors have thus been preserved. Demand for ancillary services has increased tremendously due to the expansion of the scale of production after relocation. As mentioned before, China's opening and the decentralization of China's trade and finance have increased the demand for Hong Kong's trading, financial, business, and transportation services, and the industrialization of Guangdong has led to a further increase in the demand for these services. The relocation of Hong Kong industries to Guangdong has accelerated the transformation of Hong Kong into a commercial, financial, and service center. Relocation has increased the demand for services and facilitated the expansion of services by releasing scarce labor for the use of services industries.

The infusion of Hong Kong know-how and capital into Guangdong has led to the economic takeoff of Guangdong. In the reform era (1978 to 1990), Guangdong's real per capita gross domestic product (GDP) has grown at an average annual rate of 11 percent per year, a performance exceeding that of the East Asian Newly Industrializing Economies (NIEs) at the time of their economic takeoff. In his tour of Guangdong in January 1991, Deng Xiaoping affirmed Guangdong's leading status in China's opening and economic reform.

Guangdong is trying to vie with Thailand for the title of "fifth little dragon." It should be noted that, in 1991, approvals of foreign investment in Thailand dropped by close to 60 percent while contracted foreign capital in Guangdong jumped by 83 percent. After Deng's tour and Thailand's political disturbances in 1992, Thailand's investment environment deteriorated further while the pace of foreign investment continued to accelerate in Guangdong.

In short, Hong Kong has become the economic capital of an industrialized Guangdong. The region, often called "greater Hong Kong," has a vast development potential. Guangdong alone has a population of 63 million, which is equal to the combined population of South Korea and Taiwan.

## The Future of "Greater Hong Kong"

It is clear that China's Economic Reform, especially reform of the external sector, has permitted the synergy whereby Hong Kong's and Taiwan's know-how and capital have combined with Guangdong's labor into a potent force with which to penetrate the world market. The role of Hong Kong is particularly important, not only as financier, investor, consumer, supplier, middleman, and technical consultant, but also as a catalyst in China's Economic Reform and trade liberalization.

Of course, China's export expansion may run into demand-side constraints, and its trade friction with the United States may be a harbinger of an all-out trade war. Trade and investment is not a zero-sum game, however. China can ease trade frictions by liberalizing its imports. Moreover, the U.S. trade deficit with China is partly a statistical artifact. Hong Kong and Taiwan are giving up their labor-intensive industries, making way for the expansion of China's exports. China's Open-door Policy has facilitated the industrial restructuring of the Asian NIEs, since they can move their labor-intensive industries to China.

There have been a number of proposals for promoting the integration of the mainland, Hong Kong, and Taiwan through institutional arrangements such as the formation of a free trade area, or the use of unilateral tariff preferences. Most of these proposals are utopian and counterproductive. The reality is that there are very real political differences dividing the mainland and Taiwan, and such differences are not going to disappear overnight. Moreover, the foremost barrier to economic integration between China and any other economy is the command economy in China, not tariffs or exchange risks. It is not fruitful to concentrate on tariff preferences unless China can further marketize its economy, and that further reform and marketization of the Chinese economy will inevitably be a lengthy process.

Though Hong Kong is irrevocably integrated with the mainland, it must be remembered that Hong Kong can function as the bridge linking the mainland and the world only because Hong Kong is also irrevocably integrated with the world economy. An inward-looking bloc involving Hong Kong and the mainland would be detrimental to both.

Hong Kong is traditionally a free port, and the freedom of movement of goods and capital in Hong Kong is enshrined in the Sino-British agreement on the future of Hong Kong as well as in the Basic Law because all parties involved recognized that such freedom is essential to the future prosperity of Hong Kong. As the free-port status of Hong Kong is guaranteed by constitution and international agreement, the only way that the mainland and Hong Kong can form a trade bloc is for the mainland to abolish all its tariffs. This is obviously ludicrous and utopian.

Even a trading bloc comprising Hong Kong and Shenzhen is utopian. Shenzhen has built a "second line" managing the flow of goods and people between its Special Economic Zone and the rest of China, and Shenzhen has plans for becoming a free trade area. If Beijing allows Shenzhen to become a free trade area, trade between Hong Kong and Shenzhen would be similar to trade between Hong Kong and any other free trade area (between Hong Kong and Kaoshiung, for example). There are obstacles to the formation of a trade bloc. If Hong Kong and Shenzhen were to become a trade bloc such as a customs union, the two would have to bargain as a single entity in world trade and also agree on the sharing of textile quotas. A prerequisite for that is Shenzhen acquiring autonomy in external economic affairs. This implies that Beijing would have to relinquish control of Shenzhen's external economic affairs and China would have to enter the General Agreement on Tariffs and Trade (GATT) as the mainland minus Shenzhen, because the bargaining position of Shenzhen in world trade may differ from that of Beijing. Another problem is that the union would undermine Hong Kong's autonomy. Hong Kong's autonomy in external economic affairs is guaranteed by both the Sino-British agreement and the Basic Law, and Hong Kong is a member of the GATT. A trading bloc of Shenzhen and Hong Kong would give an institutional channel to Beijing to encroach on Hong Kong's autonomy and a say over the utilization of Hong Kong's textiles and clothing quotas.

In 1991, some Hong Kong businessmen lobbied for tariff preferences from the mainland. Such preferences, if granted, would be un-GATT-able and also detrimental to both the mainland and Hong Kong. Free competition has long been the source of strength and dynamism in the Hong Kong economy. Such preferences would entice Hong Kong businessmen to spend their energy on lobbying for favoritism instead of concentrating their resources on improving productivity. Moreover, there is no "free lunch," and Hong Kong's seeking of favoritism from the mainland would invite the mainland to ask for reciprocal favoritism from Hong Kong. Given Chinese sovereignty and Beijing's intervention-prone record, Hong Kong would have a hard time preserving the autonomy promised in the Basic Law. The seeking of favoritism from Beijing would further compromise Hong Kong's ability to manage its own affairs. It should be stressed that the erosion of Hong Kong's autonomy and dynamism would also be detrimental to China's long-term interests.

It is often not realized that tariff preferences and institutional arrangements may not be important for economic integration. That goal requires the lowering of transaction costs, and tariffs are often only a small part of transaction costs. Other factors, such as transportation costs, cultural affinity, foreign-exchange controls, and government regulations, may be much more important. The integration of "greater Hong Kong" will continue to be largely market-driven, though consultation to improve information flow and to coordinate policy, especially policies on transportation and infrastructure, will be useful. Bilateral discriminatory preferences are utopian and counterproductive, and unilateral discriminatory preferences are un-GATT-able and detrimental.

Some commentators speak of the tremendous economic potential of "greater China," including the mainland, Taiwan, and Hong Kong. It is more realistic, however, to confine the attention to "greater Hong Kong," as the successful synergy of foreign know-how and capital with China's resources is largely confined to Guangdong. A large part of the Chinese economy, especially the big state enterprises and heavy industries, is still mired in bureaucratic red tape and inefficiency. While China's economic reforms have achieved spectacular success in Guangdong, the national picture is less sanguine.

The dynamic growth of Guangdong is perhaps the brightest spot in China's Open-door Policy and Economic Reform. Though China's Economic Reform has run into many of the same problems of Eastern European reforms, the success of Guangdong has no Eastern European parallel, and the availability of kindred resources in Hong Kong and Taiwan is the obvious factor accounting for Guangdong's success. The dynamism of Guangdong may help China to pull through the long and tortuous process of economic reform.

The future prosperity of "greater Hong Kong" is by no means assured, however, and the Tiananmen Incident has severely tested the confidence of the Hong Kong community. Whether Beijing can honor its pledges to Hong Kong after 1997 is uncertain. The possibility of tensions heightening across the Taiwan Straits cannot be ignored, as the Taiwanese independence movement is becoming more assertive.

The paradox of the future of "greater Hong Kong" is that the political side of the picture looks gloomy but the economic side of the picture looks bright. While the future of "greater Hong Kong" is not assured, it must be stressed that "greater Hong Kong" has tremendous economic potential. The labor force of Guangdong is as large as the labor forces of the four Asian NIEs combined. The exports of "greater Hong Kong" have already led to a lot of trade friction between China and the United States. The world cannot afford to ignore the emergence of "greater Hong Kong."

## Notes

1. Information obtained from interview with Guangdong official.

2. The figure is estimated as follows. We add Guangdong's 1990 exports to Hong Kong of U.S.$8,543 million (obtained from MOFERT statistics) to Guangdong's 1990 processing/assembling exports to Hong Kong of U.S.$9,055 million (obtained from China's Customs Statistics). The latter figure was given by Guandong officials to the Hong Kong Trade Development Council. The sum of these two figures is U.S.$17,598

million. Then we have to substract from the total the processing fee of exports from processing/assembling operations to Hong Kong, because the processing fee is included in both figures. We know from MOFERT statistics that Guangdong's 1990 processing fee amounted to U.S. $990 million, and Hong Kong accounted for 93 percent of Guangdong's investment-related exports (exports from processing/assembling operations and enterprises with foreign investment). Guangdong's 1990 processing fee of exports to Hong Kong from processing/assembling operations was thus estimated to be U.S.$919 million (0.93 × U.S.$990 million). This gives the estimate of U.S.$16,679 million (U.S.$17,598 million – U.S.$919 million).

## References

*Almanac of China's Foreign Relations and Trade* (1984 to 1991), Hong Kong: China Resources Trade Consultancy Co., Ltd., various issues.

*China Customs Statistics* (1982 to 1992), Hong Kong: Economic Information and Agency, various issues.

*Guangdong Statistical Yearbook* (1983 to 1991), Beijing: China Statistical Publishing Company, various issues.

*Hong Kong Economic Times,* March 21, 1991.

Hong Kong Trade Development Council (1988), *Survey on Hong Kong Reexports: Summary Report,* November (mimeo).

*Hong Kong Trade Statistics* (1960 to 1991), Hong Kong: Census and Statistics Department, various issues.

*Intertrade,* October 1984.

*Review of Overseas Trade* (1966 to 1991), Hong Kong: Census and Statistics Department, various issues.

*South China Morning Post,* June 18, 1987.

*Statistical Yearbook of China* (1950 to 1979), Beijing: China Statistical Publishing Company.

Sung, Yun-wing (1991a), *The China–Hong Kong Connection: The Key to China's Open-Door Policy,* Cambridge: Cambridge University Press.

——— (1991b), "Competitiveness of Hong Kong Manufacturing Versus Its Major Competitors," paper presented to the *Symposium on Industrial Policy in Hong Kong: An Interdisciplinary Chapter,* organized by the Hong Kong Institute of Asia-Pacific Studies, Chinese University of Hong Kong in Hong Kong, July 12–13, 1991, photocopied.

——— (1991c), "Explaining China's Export Drive: The Only Success among Command Economies," Occasional Paper, Hong Kong Institute of Asia-Pacific Studies, Chinese University of Hong Kong.

——— (1991d), "Foreign Trade and Investment," in *China Review,* ed. Hsin-chi Kuan and Maurice Brosseau, Hong Kong: Chinese University of Hong Kong Press, pp. 15.1–15.22.

——— (1991e), "Hong Kong's Economic Value to China," in *The Other Hong Kong Report 1991,* ed. Sung Yun-wing and Ming-kwan Lee, Hong Kong: Chinese University Press, pp. 477–504.

——— (1992), "Non-institutional Economic Integration Via Cultural Affinity: The Case of Mainland China, Taiwan, and Hong Kong," Occasional Paper No. 13, Hong Kong Institute of Asia-Pacific Studies, Chinese University of Hong Kong, July.

Tom, C.F. (1957), *Entrepôt Trade and the Monetary Standards of Hong Kong, 1842–1942,* Chicago: University of Chicago Press.

*Yearbook of International Trade Statistics*, United Nations Statistical Office, various issues.

# 10

# Socioeconomic Center, Political Periphery: Hong Kong's Uncertain Transition Toward the Twenty-first Century

*Alvin Y. So and Reginald Y. Kwok*

The 1990s will prove to be a turning point in Chinese history. The Hong Kong–Guangdong integration process will have significance not just to Hong Kong and Guangdong, but also to other parts of mainland China, to Taiwan, and even to Korea.

As such, the Hong Kong–Guangdong integration process is bound to be highly controversial. In this volume, there are two sets of contradictory arguments with respect to the future of Hong Kong–Guangdong/mainland integration. Ming K. Chan, Xueqiang Xu, R. Y. Kwok, Lixun Li, Xiaopei Yan, Victor Sit, Yun-wing Sung, Greg Guldin, and Graham Johnson have presented an optimistic view on the economic integration process (see Kwok and So, 1995). On the other hand, Ian Scott and Ming-kwan Lee have presented a pessimistic view on the political linkages between Hong Kong and mainland China (Kwok and So, 1995). How then can we explain their differences in interpreting the Hong Kong–Guangdong/mainland China integration? Why do scholars who have been widely published in this field disagree with one another?

The explanation, we argue, is due to the complexity and the indeterminate nature of the integration process. The Hong Kong–Guangdong/mainland China integration is not just economically promising, it is at the same time politically destabilizing. This imbalance between the economy and the polity will have

The original version of this chapter appeared in *The Hong Kong–Guangdong Link: Partnership in Flux*, ed. Reginald Yin-Wang Kwok and Alvin Y. So (Armonk, NY: M.E. Sharpe, 1995).

profound implications on the future of the integration process.

In order to analyze this economic-political imbalance, we have adopted a center–periphery framework, as suggested by R. Y. Kwok and Roger Ames (see also Kwok and So, 1995; So, 1990). There are several key features of this center–periphery framework. First, center and periphery always coexist and are defined in relation to one another; a center is not a center unless it has a periphery under its control. Second, the center–periphery relationship is highly dynamic. Center always wants to exercise more exploitation on the periphery, while periphery always wants to resist such exploitation. Finally, center–periphery relations are highly complex. They are not confined to the economic sphere, but are extended to the political, social, and cultural spheres as well.

Using such a center–periphery framework, we argue that while Hong Kong has risen to be the socioeconomic center of Guangdong, it has become the political periphery of Beijing since the signing of the Joint Declaration between the British and Chinese governments in 1984.

**Hong Kong as the Socioeconomic Center of Guangdong**

Following the founding of the People's Republic of China in 1949, as Victor Sit points out, the border between Hong Kong and Guangdong was turned into an effective divide for two different ideologies and economic systems. Hong Kong, forced by the dwindling China market, turned to export-led industrialization and became one of the four "little dragons." The economy of Guangdong grew only slowly, under a new reign of socialist centralism and self-sufficiency.

After China adopted the Open-door Policy in 1978, however, the economy of Hong Kong and Guangdong experienced substantial restructuring and rapid integration into what Graham Johnson calls a "Pearl River Delta region" (Kwok and So, 1995).

On the one hand, Hong Kong is becoming the center of the Pearl River Delta economy. There is a massive northward shift to Guangdong of Hong Kong's labor-intensive, low-value-added manufacturing industries (like the garment, footwear, and plastics industries). Ming Chan points out that over 3 million Guangdong workers are currently employed in Hong Kong–owned and –managed enterprises in the delta. This figure is much larger than the total manufacturing work force in Hong Kong itself (estimated at about 0.74 million in 1991; see Kwok and So, 1995). This shift has released pressure on labor and land resources, which are both short in Hong Kong, and has allowed Hong Kong to concentrate its energy on economic diversification and structural transformation. As a result, the colony has upgraded itself to be the financier, investor, supplier, designer, promoter, exporter, middleman, and technical consultant of the Pearl River Delta economy. Yun-wing Sung asserts that Hong Kong has been the pivot of Guangdong's economic links with the world economy since the 1980s (Kwok and So, 1995).

On the other hand, Guangdong is turning into the periphery of the Pearl River Delta economy. Xueqiang Xu, et al., report that there is a division of labor in the delta economy through the pattern of "front shop, back factory" (*qiandian houchang*) (Kwok and So, 1995). Marketing, design, financing, and administration take place in the "front shop" in Hong Kong, while manufacturing and assembly are done in the "back factory" in Guangdong. As a result, Guangdong is dependent upon Hong Kong businessmen for capital, technology, machinery, and management; Guangdong becomes the supplier of labor, land, and raw intensive industries that have little in the way of high-tech components. In addition, Guangdong engages in cash-crop cultivation—such as vegetables, fruit, pigs, poultry, and fish—for the Hong Kong consumer.

Nevertheless, Guangdong is actively resisting the peripheralization of its economy. Since Guangdong is more economically advanced than other Chinese provinces, it is making use of its Hong Kong connections to turn other Chinese provinces into its periphery. Consequently, Xu et al. observed that there is a continuous migration from other provinces to provide cheap, docile labor to the Guangdong economy; that other provinces supplied raw materials and minerals to Guangdong; that other provinces became the domestic market of Guangdong light industries (Kwok and So, 1995). Due to these domestic linkages as well as to the external linkages with Hong Kong, Guangdong has experienced the highest growth rate of any Chinese province and a very rapid increase of income level, all of which serves to widen the gap between Guangdong and other mainland provinces. In this respect, although Guangdong stands on the economic periphery of Hong Kong, it has become an economic center to other provinces in mainland China (see Kwok and So, 1995; Kwok, 1992).

On the cultural front, Greg Guldin argues that a Pearl River Delta cultural area (the *Namyuet* culture) has gradually emerged in the last decade (Kwok and So, 1995). Since Hong Kong represents not only prosperity but also a sinified version of Western prosperity, the "south wind" that blows into Guangdong from Hong Kong thus brings with it a model of modernity that is adjusted for local tastes. From computer links to academic conferences to trade exhibitions, the Hong Kong cultural model has established itself firmly in the minds of Guangdong businessmen and women. Through videos, radio, television, newspapers, and magazines, Hong Kong ideas and lifestyles have found a ready and receptive audience across the Guangdong border. For example, Guangdong residents now spend their evenings glued to television showings of Hong Kong's soap operas, kungfu movies, and variety shows. The reunified Guangdong cultural area also witnesses linguistic changes (the spread of Hong Kong speech styles) and the comeback of opera in Guangdong.

In the Pearl River Delta, therefore, Hong Kong has emerged since 1978 as the center of Guangdong in both the economic and the cultural spheres. With Guangdong providing labor, raw materials, and investment opportunities, Hong Kong's economy is booming. With Guangdong residents aspiring to the Hong Kong cultural model, the Hong Kong people tend to look down on their Guangdong "country cousins." Nevertheless, Guangdong has not suffered from

Hong Kong's core domination. In fact, Guangdong's economy has a remarkable growth rate because it has used its Hong Kong connections to dominate other mainland provinces; and Guangdong's residents do not seem to mind Hong Kong arrogance because they are enjoying a more diversified lifestyle than before.

Consequently, economists, urban planners, economic geographers, and anthropologists tend to offer a highly optimistic view of the future: Hong Kong and Guangdong working harmoniously with one another toward a bright socioeconomic integration. Nevertheless, political scientists and political sociologists offer a different, pessimistic, picture of Hong Kong transition.

### Hong Kong as the Political Periphery of Beijing

In the political sphere, the integration process is between Hong Kong and Beijing, not between Hong Kong and Guangdong. In 1997, the sovereignty of Hong Kong will be resumed by the Beijing government of mainland China, not by the provincial Guangdong government. The negotiation talks and the Joint Declaration were conducted and signed by the London and Beijing governments; the people of Hong Kong had little control over these two crucial events that determined their future (Kwok and So, 1995; So, 1993). In this respect, although Hong Kong is the socioeconomic center of Guangdong province, it is merely at the political periphery of the central Beijing government.

Since the signing of the Joint Declaration in 1984, the Beijing government has been actively interfering in Hong Kong politics. Beijing successfully shelved the proposal to have a direct election in 1988, slowed down the democratic reforms through the drafting of the Basic Law, pressured the London government to reformulate its Ports and Airports Development Scheme, and heavy-handedly challenged the new Governor's democratic proposal (*South China Morning Post,* 12–23–92).

This being so, Ian Scott is concerned about the political future of Hong Kong. He points out that political legitimacy of the future Hong Kong government depends on three sets of concerns stipulated in both the 1984 Sino-British agreement and the 1990 Basic Law: (1) the autonomy of the post-1997 government, (2) the development of representative institutions, and (3) the maintenance of civil liberties. But the Chinese, the British, and the Hong Kong governments have been long on rhetoric and short on substance on the above concerns. Scott contends that it is this erosion of the provision of the Joint Declaration that explains the substantial emigration of the new middle class, aspects of civil service unrest, and the general sense of malaise over the future (Kwok and So, 1995).

Along similar lines, Ming-kwan Lee's surveys report that anticipation of 1997 has transformed the political culture of Hong Kong. There was distrust of the Chinese government, a strong sense of political helplessness, a carefree attitude toward public affairs, and a shift to such values as "it is of utmost importance to make as much money as possible" and "enjoy life and forget about the future." As a result of this political alienation, sixty thousand persons emigrated from Hong Kong in 1990 alone, because they foresaw deterioration on every front after

1997, including the curtailment of civil rights and the lowering of living standards. Furthermore, there emerged a new political identity among the Hong Kong residents. Lee's surveys show that only 29 percent regarded themselves as "Chinese," with the majority identifying themselves as "Hong Kong persons" (Kwok and So, 1995).

In addition, there is the development of a nascent democracy movement to resist the political peripheralization of Hong Kong (So and Kwitko, 1990; So and Kwitko, 1992). The democrats want direct elections, a fully representative legislature, a highly autonomous government, and an independent judiciary so as to protect Hong Kong from Beijing interference. The democrats began to campaign on an anti-Beijing line in the early 1990s, and many of them have been elected to the legislature council. With Chris Patten, the current Hong Kong governor, echoing the democrats' demand for representative government, the political conflict between Hong Kong and Beijing has become more acute since the early 1990s.

In sum, there is an imbalance between socioeconomic and political integration. On the one hand, Hong Kong has become the socioeconomic center of Guangdong, and the Pearl River Delta economy and culture are flourishing. On the other hand, Hong Kong has become the political periphery of Beijing, and Hong Kong's resistance to political peripheralization is on the rise.

How, then, can this imbalanced integration process between Hong Kong and Guangdong/Beijing be resolved in the near future? What will happen to Hong Kong in 1997?

## Hong Kong's Uncertain Transitions

The imbalanced integration helps to explain not just the disagreement between the economists and the political scientists in this volume, but also Hong Kong's uncertain transition toward the twenty-first century. It is possible that Hong Kong will go through one of three scenarios.

### *The Collapse Scenario*

This is the argument of the political pessimists. They predict that if political peripheralization is to be intensified in 1997—that is, if there is prevailing civil alienation, out-migration of professionals, urban riots, political unrest, and the like—then there will be a crisis of confidence among Hong Kong's entrepreneurs, and the economic superiority of Hong Kong will quickly erode. If this happens, there will be large-scale out-migration of capital, depreciation of Hong Kong currency, a downfall of stock and real estate prices, followed by inflation, unemployment, and panic buying at supermarkets. Anticipating that the Hong Kong economy could collapse at any moment, Beijing will then be forced to take over Hong Kong, abolish the capitalist market economy, and impose the Chinese style of socialist economy (Davies, 1991; Hicks, 1987). In this respect, the integration balance is restored when economic peripheralization is followed by political peripheralization.

### *The False-Alarm Scenario*

This is the argument of the economic optimists. They figure that Hong Kong will continue to prosper and play a significant role in China's Four Modernizations. Hong Kong is the single largest foreign investor in China and its investment is expanding from Guangdong to all over the nation. Hong Kong's expanding higher education is producing a higher level of human resource to replace the migrants, and there is a massive return of migrants to Hong Kong after they have fulfilled residence requirements and cannot find a decent living overseas. Thus the Hong Kong economy will continue to prosper in the late 1990s, and Hong Kong people are just having a false alarm on the 1997 issue. On the other hand, China's economic problems are getting more severe. Market socialism not only does not work, it leads to overheating of the economy accompanied by unemployment, inflation, strikes, and political protests. The Pearl River Delta economy is the only bright spot for the Chinese nation. In gaining economic power, however, the delta region will also grow in political power. By becoming China's most advanced economy and most influential political region, the Pearl River Delta may set itself up as a strong rival to Beijing (Chen, 1991; Hicks, 1987). In this respect, the integration balance is restored when the Delta region is turned into a model for mainland development—acquiring status as both economic center and political center.

### *The Cyclical Scenario*

This is what the realists are hoping for as Hong Kong moves toward the twenty-first century. The realists agree that the few years before and after 1997 will definitely cause political chaos and economic nervousness in Hong Kong, and its economy will suffer. By the first decade of the twenty-first century, however, after the transition is over and after the new Hong Kong government is firmly in place, business confidence will be quickly restored. Capital will return to Hong Kong and continue to invest in the Pearl River Delta region. With the Hong Kong economy booming, the professionals too will seek to return to Hong Kong. Subsequently, Hong Kong will regain its economic prosperity and center status over Guangdong in the Pearl River Delta region, although it will still be politically peripheral to Beijing. In this respect, in the future integration process, there will still be an imbalance. But after the 1997 storm is over, political peripheralization will not cause much harm to the Hong Kong center economy.

Which scenario is more likely to happen in 1997? It depends. History never follows a determined path but is always subject to the intervention of human agency. The future of Hong Kong integration depends on socioeconomic and political changes currently under way in Hong Kong, Guangdong, and Beijing. More studies are needed in order to examine the complexity and the undetermined nature of the Hong Kong integration process. Thus it may be appropriate to end our discussion here by calling for the following research agenda.

## Future Research Agenda

First, it is necessary to adopt a multidisciplinary approach that goes beyond the study of either political or economic or sociocultural topics. It is vitally important to examine how politics, economics, and sociocultural values interact and affect one another.

Second, it requires a geopolitical focus that goes beyond the territorial confines of Hong Kong. Instead of studying Hong Kong or Guangdong or Beijing in isolation from one another, it is important to trace the intricate economic and cultural integrations between Hong Kong and Guangdong, to examine the dynamic political connections between Hong Kong and Beijing, and to investigate the profound developmental strategies that bring Hong Kong, mainland China, and Taiwan together (Hsiao and So, 1993).

Third, it is important to take a historical perspective that goes beyond the short-term episodes that make news headlines. It is important to trace and analyze the long-term, complex structural transformations in Hong Kong, Guangdong, and Beijing.

## References


Chen, Edward (1991), "Recent Development in Hong Kong and Its Relationship with China," paper presented at the International Symposium on Pacific Asian Business, Pacific Asian Management Institute, University of Hawaii at Manoa, Honolulu, January 6–9, 1991.

Davies, Derek (1991), "Comments on Recent Development in Hong Kong," paper presented at the International Symposium on Pacific Asian Business, Pacific Asian Management Institute, University of Hawaii at Manoa, Honolulu, January 6–9, 1991.

Hicks, George (1987), "Hong Kong on the Eve of Communist Rule," in *The Future of Hong Kong: Toward 1997 and Beyond,* ed. Hungdah Chiu et al., New York: Quorum Books.

Hsiao, Hsin-Huang Michael, and Alvin Y. So (1993), "Ascent Through National Integration: The Chinese Triangle of Mainland–Taiwan–Hong Kong," in *Asia-Pacific and the Future of the World Economy,* ed. Ravi Palat, Westport, CT: Greenwood Press.

Kwok, Reginald Y. (1992), "An Overseas Assessment of the Pearl River Delta Development," paper presented at the Conference on Pearl River Delta Economic Development: Review and Prospect, Research Center of Pearl River Delta Economic Development and Management, Zhongshan University, Zhongshan, May 7–11, 1992.

Kwok, Reginald Y. and Alvin Y. So (1995), *The Hong Kong–Guangdong Link: Partnership in Flux*, Armonk: M.E. Sharpe.

So, Alvin Y. (1990), *Social Change and Development: Modernization, Dependency, and World-System Theories,* Newbury Park, CA: Sage Publications.

——— (1993), "Hong Kong People Ruling Hong Kong! The Rise of the New Middle Class in Negotiation Politics, 1982–1984," *Asian Affairs: An American Review,* Vol. 20, pp. 67–87.

So, Alvin Y., and Ludmilla Kwitko (1990), "New Middle Class and the Democratic Movement in Hong Kong," *Journal of Contemporary Asia,* Vol. 20, pp. 384–98.

——— (1992), "The Transformation of Urban Movements in Hong Kong, 1970–1990," *Bulletin of Concerned Asian Scholars,* Vol. 24, No. 4, pp. 31–42.

*South China Morning Post,* December 23, 1992.

# Index

## C



## D



## E